The True Identity of the People of the Way

The True Identity of the People of the Way

The Referent and Function of "The Way" in Acts

ROSS D. HARMON

Foreword by Patrick Schreiner

WIPF & STOCK · Eugene, Oregon

THE TRUE IDENTITY OF THE PEOPLE OF THE WAY
The Referent and Function of "The Way" in Acts

Copyright © 2024 Ross D. Harmon. All rights reserved. Except for brief quotations in critical publications or reviews, no part of this book may be reproduced in any manner without prior written permission from the publisher. Write: Permissions, Wipf and Stock Publishers, 199 W. 8th Ave., Suite 3, Eugene, OR 97401.

Wipf & Stock
An Imprint of Wipf and Stock Publishers
199 W. 8th Ave., Suite 3
Eugene, OR 97401

www.wipfandstock.com

PAPERBACK ISBN: 978-1-4982-1789-7
HARDCOVER ISBN: 978-1-4982-1791-0
EBOOK ISBN: 978-1-4982-1790-3

10/04/24

To my children,
Thomas, Alexandria, Sophia, Luke Ellis, Abe, and Micah
Born weird; Die weird.

To my wife Nichole,
I love you.

Contents

Foreword by Patrick Schreiner | ix

1 Introduction | 1

2 Review of Literature | 27

3 An Analysis of "the Way" in the Book of Proverbs | 39

4 The Cognitive Environment of Luke-Acts | 73

5 An Analysis of "the Way" in the Book of Acts | 99

6 Conclusion | 143

Appendix | 163

Bibliography | 175

Scripture Index | 187

Foreword

FOR TOO LONG PEOPLE have been doing biblical theology and overlooked a vital portion of the Scripture—the wisdom writings. Biblical theology traces themes, figures, and patterns through the Scriptures. Because of this linear development, the narrative portions of the Scriptures are usually highlighted in biblical theology. However, the more meditative books in the Hebrew Bible hold untold riches that can enhance our biblical and theological projects.

Harmon recognizes this and applies a biblical theological look at an underdeveloped theme in the book of Acts—the Way. Christians are not first called "Christians" but "the Way" (Acts 9:2; 19:9, 23; 22:4; 24:14, 22). Not enough work has been done diving into the source and implications of this designation.

Harmon turns to Proverbs showing that this theme of "the way" is a major refrain. In Proverbs God creates the path, draws people toward his path, directs and sustains his people on this path, and choosing your path has life or death consequences. Acts picks up on this designation showing that Christians are a distinct people.

To prove this Harmon performs careful exegesis in intertextuality, metaphor studies, and even thematic classifications. Too often people dive straight into the biblical text without first asking more metaphysical, ontological, and methodological questions that undergird the study.

My hope is that after reading this Christians will more quickly claim their distinct status as Jesus followers who are seeking God's face in a world where there are two paths to choose from.

PATRICK SCHREINER
Associate Professor of New Testament and Biblical Theology
Midwestern Baptist Theological Seminary

1

Introduction

LUKE'S USE OF "THE WAY"[1] in the book of Acts is reminiscent of "the path" in Proverbs. In fact, there appear to be similarities between how the Way and the path function within the two books. With these similarities in mind, does Luke intentionally refer to the book of Proverbs? Prior to the discovery of the Dead Sea Scrolls (DSS), scholars glossed "the Way" as a designation for the early church, with little to no research to determine the source, the background of the term, or the exact referent. Some scholars perpetuated the traditional understanding of Luke's use of the Way into modernity. Since the discovery of the DSS, scholars either suggest the term is an allusion to Isaiah or note how the Qumran community similarly used the Way as a descriptor for a community. This book will re-examine Luke's use of "the Way" to suggest a fresh approach of reading Acts alongside Proverbs, in order to better understand Luke's use of the term to describe early Christians.[2]

1. As a general rule, the Way is reserved for ὁδός as a name for Christians. However, at times the Way denotes the possibility of a proper name or several uses of "the way," that include using ὁδός as a proper name. Therefore, the introduction uses the Way almost exclusively unless otherwise denoted as referring to a metaphor.

2. *Reading alongside* refers to both inner-biblical exegesis and inner-biblical allusion. Russell Meek writes, "The primary difference in these two methodologies is that inner-biblical exegesis argues that the receptor text has in some way modified the source text, whereas inner-biblical allusion argues that the receptor text alludes to the source text with no attempt at modification." Meek, "Intertextuality, Inner-Biblical Exegesis, and Inner-Biblical Allusion: The Ethics of a Methodology," 280–91. See also Weyde, "Inner-Biblical Interpretation: Methodological Reflections on the Relationship between Texts in the Hebrew Bible," 287–30.

THE NEED FOR A REEVALUATION OF "THE WAY"

There is a lack of scholarly consensus over Luke's use of "the Way" in Acts to describe early Christians (Acts 9:2; 19:9, 23; 22:4; 24:14, 22). In the late 1950s, Vernon McCasland's detailed research brought to an end the unexamined glosses.[3] McCasland noted the similarities between Luke's use of the Way and that of both Isaiah 40:3, which refers to preparing a way for the Lord, and the Qumran community.[4] This solution does not satisfy those who see a disconnect between Luke's use of the Way in the text and a narrow definition of the term "the way" with "teaching."[5] Scholars intuitively understand Luke's reference to a way of life or postulate "the Way" in Acts as a reference to Isaiah.[6] However, does the traditional proposal offer the best fit, or does Isaiah? Or might Luke be referencing a further use of the term found elsewhere in Scripture?

THE PREMISE FOR POTENTIAL USE OF PROVERBS

While it is clear that Luke references other Scripture found in the OT, the question concerns which passages he references. In Joseph Fitzmyer's 1992 article on Luke's use of the OT in Luke-Acts, relying on the Nestle-Aland 20, he writes, "Though he [Luke] quotes from the prophets Isaiah, Jeremiah, Joel, Amos, Habakkuk, and Malachi, there are no quotations from Ezekiel or Daniel, and none from the so called Writings, apart from the Psalter."[7] Thus, in 1992, Fitzmyer did not identify any reference to Proverbs in Luke-Acts. However, since his publication, the NA28 has been released, which identified more OT references in Luke-Acts. The NA28 recognizes four references to the Wisdom literature in Luke-Acts, plus numerous references to other OT Scripture.[8] The *NA28 Apparatus* identifies eleven

---

3. McCasland published in 1958, six years prior to Eero Repo, who published a more detailed work on the Way later. F. F. Bruce appears to restate the pre-critical thought of Chrysostom, even in the 1970 edition of his commentary on Acts (194). McCasland, "The Way." Calvin refers to the early Christians as a sect and holds that Luke uses "the Way" to describe all Christians. Calvin and King, *Calvin's Commentaries (Complete)*, Acts 9:2.

4. McCasland, "The Way," 230.

5. Haenchen, *The Acts of the Apostles*, 320.

6. Haenchen, *The Acts of the Apostles*, 320; Bock, *Acts*, 356; Keener, *Acts: 3:1—14:28*, 1626.

7. Fitzmyer, "The Use of the Old Testament in Luke-Acts," 532.

8. Eberhard Nestle, Erwin Nestle, B. Aland, K. Aland, Karavidopoulos, Martini, and

Introduction

possible allusions to Proverbs in Luke and five in Acts.[9] Also, scholars similarly identify the influence of Proverbs in Luke-Acts, e.g., Lady Wisdom or a wisdom tradition influence in Luke 7:31–5[10] or the similarities in teachings on casting lots between Proverbs 16:33 and Acts 1:26.[11] Douglas Huffman, with the greatest survey to date concerning Luke-Acts use of the OT, identifies 57 citations and 889 alluions and recollections.[12] Craig Keener writes about Luke's use of the Greek OT as follows: "His immersion in the LXX, however, is considerable; if he did not grow up with it, he must have acquired it long before and thoroughly, for he knows how to write Greek with a 'biblical' or 'Jewish accent,' so to speak."[13] Concerning Luke's diverse use of the OT, James Meek writes, "While Darrell Bock has correctly observed that Christology is 'the key area of Luke's OT usage as acknowledged by all,' it is not the only area in which Luke employs the OT."[14] Since Luke uses the OT to develop his Christology, it is plausible that Luke uses "the Way" in connection with themes of salvation, the rejection of the Gospel by the Jews, and the acceptance of the Gospel by the Gentiles.[15] The last scholarly piece to note is Andrew Litke's entry titled "Journey" in the *Lexham Theological Wordbook*. Within his entry, Litke places a summary of the NT's use of "the way" directly aside the book of Proverb's use of "the way."

> Both Jesus' regular call to "follow (ἀκολουθέω, akoloutheō) me" (e.g., Matt 9:9) and the early Christian sect being called "the Way" (ὁδός, hodos; e.g., Acts 9:2) invoke the idea of movement. Along with this language of journeying, the biblical writers use the same terminology to refer to a person's actions and their general way of conducting themselves. The book of Proverbs often contrasts the ways (דֶּרֶךְ, derek) of the righteous with the ways of the wicked

---

Metzger, eds., *Novum Testamentum Graece*, 28th rev ed. Wisdom: Luke 1:51–52; 19:44; Acts 2:15; 17:31; Examples of other OT passages: Luke 1:5 (1 Chr 24:10; 2 Chr 8, 14); Luke 1:6 (Dt 4:40; Ex 36:27); Lk 1:7 (Gn 18:11); Lk 1:10 (Dn 9:21); Acts 1:6 (Is 49:6 LXX); Acts 1:8 (Is 49:6); Acts 1:9 (2 Kgs 2:11).

9. K. Aland, B. Aland, Karavidopoulos, Martini, and Metzger, eds., *Novum Testamentum Graece (Greek New Testament) Apparatus (Na28 Apparatus)*, 5th Corrected ed., Accordance ed.

10. Bovon and Koester, *Luke 1*, 287–88.

11. Peterson, *The Acts of the Apostles*, Accordance electronic ed., 127.

12. Huffman, *Understanding the New Testament Use of the Old Testament: Forms, Features, Framings, and Functions*, 135.

13. Keener, *Acts: 1:1—2:47*, 405.

14. Meek, *The Gentile Mission*, 1.

15. Meek, *The Gentile Mission*, 1.

(e.g., Prov 13:6), and the nt writers point out that Christianity introduces people to a new ethic—a walking (περιπατέω, *peripateō*) in faith, new life, and wisdom (e.g., Rom 6:4; 2 Cor 5:7).[16]

In spite of recognition of a theologic relation, Litke does not make the explicit claim that the NT references Proverbs. The above examples and statements on Luke's use of the OT challenge older literature that does not find Proverbs as a possible referent in Luke-Acts and supports the possibility that Proverbs may be the referent of "the Way" in Acts.

RESEARCH QUESTIONS AND HYPOTHESES

Knowing that Luke references the OT raises two research questions: (1) Does previous scholarship provide an adequate understanding of Luke's use of the Way? and (2) Is it plausible that Proverbs might function as an interpretive guide for understanding Luke's use of the Way in Acts? In answering these questions, three concerns arise. First, Wisdom literature's role in the writings of the NT needs to be clarified. Second, scholars have yet to propose the book of Proverbs as a source for Luke's use of the Way. Third, the limited references to a people group as the Way within Scripture and, similarly, the absence of extra-biblical texts and artifacts that can be used as evidence to support Christians as the Way prevent definitive conclusions.

Scholars continue to debate the theological or literary influence of the Wisdom literature on the writings of the NT. James Meade notes that modern biblical theology has struggled to integrate the Wisdom literature within the Bible's message.[17] The struggle comes from Wisdom's focus on the "human experience of life within creation and society" or day-to-day life as compared to "the material in the Torah and Former Prophets."[18] Recent scholarship questions whether Wisdom literature as a genre has limited scholars' abilities to identify how Israelite wisdom integrates into the Canon.[19] This question has led scholars to re-examine how concepts of Wisdom literature might be integrated with the rest of the Bible, and as a result they have found correlations between the Wisdom literature

---

16. Litke, "Journey."
17. Meade, *Biblical Theology*, 213.
18. Meade, *Biblical Theology*, 213.
19. Kynes, "'Wisdom' as Mask and Mirror: Methodological Questions for 'Wisdom's' Dialogue with the Canon," 19–29.

INTRODUCTION

and prophecy, along with connections between wisdom, law, and the covenant.[20] This recognition of the broader impact of Israelite wisdom on the biblical Canon justifies a re-examination of the relationship of the book of Proverbs to the book of Acts. However, scholars also propose that Israel saw wisdom as part of salvation history and that the Hellenistic writers then clarified the unity of wisdom and Israel's salvation history.[21]

Of the second concern (i.e., whether or not the book of Proverbs can be considered a source for Acts), while scholars like Bruce Waltke find Proverbs at home within OT biblical theology, can the book likewise be found at home within the NT?[22] Modern scholarship has yet to harmonize the theology of Proverbs with the New Testament effectively. The NA28 and UBS5 do not find any allusion to the Wisdom literature in "the way" passages of Acts 9:2; 19:9, 23; 22:4; or 24:14, 22.[23] Amongst Huffman's list of 889 allusions and recollections, he includes eight additional references to Proverbs in Luke-Acts to those found in the NA28 and UBS5, but unfortunately, he does not find any for "the way" passages.[24] In possibly the most influential commentary on this topic, *Commentary on the New Testament Use of the Old Testament*, Howard Marshall does not find any parallels in Proverbs for Acts 9:2; 19:9; 22:4; 24:14, 22, either.[25] Marshall does mention Proverbs 10:29 as another passage that speaks of the way of the Lord, but he falls short of declaring it an allusion.[26] Thus, the presuppositions of NT scholars concerning the book of Proverbs lead them to view the book as ethical guidance, lacking in references to Israel's salvation history, and tied to the myth of personified wisdom.[27] Perhaps this perception causes

20. Longman III, "Prophecy and Wisdom: Connections, Influences, Relationships," 259–68.

21. Scott, *The Way of Wisdom in the Old Testament*, 17–18. Bartholomew and O'Dowd note: "It needs to be remembered that the strong distinction between law and wisdom is a modern construct." They also understand that the relationship between the Law and Wisdom literature was formed as early as Proverbs and Job. Bartholomew and O'Dowd, *Old Testament Wisdom Literature*, 286.

22. Waltke, *The Book of Proverbs: Chapters 1–15*, 64.

23. Eberhard Nestle, Erwin Nestle, B. Aland, K. Aland, Karavidopoulos, Martini, and Metzger, eds., *Novum Testamentum Graece*, 28th rev ed.; K. Aland, B. Aland, J. Karavidopoulos, C. M. Martini, and Bruce M. Metzger, eds., *The Greek New Testament*, 5th rev. ed.

24. The verses include Lk 22:49; Acts 1:24; 2:34; 4:31b; 7:49; 10:22a; 13:16, 26; 21:13. Huffman, *Understanding the New Testament Use of the Old Testament*, 219–33.

25. Marshall, "Acts."

26. Marshall, "Acts," 513–606.

27. Strecker, *Theology of the New Testament*, 37–45.

scholars to overlook allusions to Proverbs, and why the book appears to be absent from commentaries on Acts.

Third, the limited textual evidence of "the Way" being used to describe a manner of living or a people group creates difficulty in reaching certain conclusions. While a reduced ability to corroborate one's findings should not dissuade the researcher from continuing, the limited occurrences of "the Way" in Acts and the absence of similar uses in extra-biblical texts or artifacts necessitates a conclusion of plausibility or probability. Such a conclusion need not hinder the research, however. Determining the plausibility or probability of Proverbs serving as Luke's referent for the Way advances the understanding of the term in two respects: It demonstrates the need to improve on previous claims (i.e., Isaiah 40:3 as the referent or the Qumran community establishing a precedent), and it provides a foundation for a way forward in future studies.

In sum, concerns over the compatibility of Wisdom with the message of the book of Acts and the limited textual occurrences of "the Way" within the book of Acts should not dissuade further research. As attested by numerous books on biblical theology, and of the use of the OT in the NT, scholars recognize that the OT influences NT authors.[28] Nevertheless, there are gaps. Thus, Meek writes, for example, "Luke's use of the OT with reference to the Gentiles has been largely omitted from studies of the OT in Luke-Acts."[29] This omission occurs despite Scripture prophesying the Gentiles' acceptance of the Gospel and the acceptance of the importance of the OT in Luke-Acts.[30] Similarly, an examination of Proverbs and Acts is needed to determine whether Luke is referencing Proverbs in invoking the terminology of "the Way."

LITERARY METHOD

The success of the inquiry will depend on whether it is possible to establish that Luke has multiple uses for the way metaphor: as a motif beyond the journey or travel narratives and as an allusion to Proverbs, not Isaiah. A review of the literature prior to this present study shows that scholars

---

28. Meek, *The Gentile Mission*, 1; Klink III and Lockett, *Understanding Biblical Theology*, 17; Goldingay, *Biblical Theology*, 16–17.

29. Meek, *The Gentile Mission*, 2.

30. Meek, *The Gentile Mission*, 1–2.

Introduction

consider "the way" a motif used in the journey or travel narratives,[31] and that they also tend to associate Luke's use of the term with Isaiah theologically.[32] If this investigation cannot demonstrate that the motif is present outside of the travel narratives, Beale's method may prove a helpful tool in arguing for Luke's use of "the way" as an allusion to Proverbs.

Method

The methods used to identify Luke's use of Proverbs in Acts entail two approaches. One literary analysis is a technique based on William Freedman's method for identifying motifs, and another literary method developed by G. K. Beale for identifying allusions. The two methods will work in concert to refine one another. The two techniques overlap, as both rely on the themes identified in the literature to identify either a motif or allusion. For readers familiar with *The Dictionary of the New Testament Use of the Old Testament*, Christopher Beetham places quotation, allusion, and echo under the literary concept called intertextuality and, more broadly, literary criticism.[33] However, the use of multiple literary analyses helps refine the work. In reference to combining two literary analyses, Michal Beth Dinkler's work *Literary Theory and the New Testament* is a helpful resource.[34] She presents four approaches to literary theories, and two are of particular relevance: "expressive, author-oriented approaches" and "work-oriented, objective approaches."[35] Beginning with the latter, work-oriented approaches view a written work as objective; specifically the literature is viewed independently from authorial intent or the audiences' reaction.[36] Dinkler highlights the work of David Rhoads and his narrative analysis of Mark as an example.[37] "Expressive, author-oriented approaches" desire to uncover the author's

---

31. Osborne, *Acts*, 459; Baban, *On the Road Encounters*, 33, 56.

32. Pathrapankal, "Christianity as a 'Way' According to the Acts of the Apostles," 533–39; Pathrapankal, "Way, The," 793–94.

33. Beetham, "Quotation, Allusion, and Echo," 684.

34. Dinkler, *Literary Theory and the New Testament*.

35. Dinkler notes that narrative approaches do not assume a reader-response interpretation (28), and quality narrative approaches learn about the historical context and original audience (29). Dinkler, *Literary Theory and the New Testament*, 24–25, 28–29.

36. Dinkler, *Literary Theory and the New Testament*, 25.

37. Dinkler, *Literary Theory and the New Testament*, 28.

internal views, i.e., "perceptions, thoughts, and feelings."[38] Dinkler identifies the works of Richard Hays' *Reading Backwards* as an example of an expressive, author-oriented approach.[39] Concerning this study, Freedman's analysis is a work-oriented approach covering themes and motifs, and Beale's analysis is an expressive, author-oriented approach that examines themes and allusions. Regardless of titles, the introduction of Freedman's method for determining motifs provides an additional tool to assist in eliminating subjective judgments in identifying allusions and echoes, which is a concern for Beale.[40] The next section presents the necessary definitions and clarification of terms. Second, the literary section discusses the metaphor. Third, the section considers terminology and the method used for identifying a motif. Fourth, the section titled theological analysis (expressive, author-oriented approach) outlines the method for identifying allusions.

Definitions

Allusion

"An 'allusion' may simply be defined as a brief expression consciously intended by an author to be dependent on an OT passage," "of which one or more components must be remembered and brought forward into the new context in order for the alluding text to be fully understood."[41] Allusions are indirect references supposed to the direct reference made by quotations.[42]

---

38. Dinkler, *Literary Theory and the New Testament*, 24. The direct quote is derived from Abrams, *The Mirror and the Lamp*, 22. "A work of art is essentially the internal made external, resulting from a creative process operating under the impulse of feeling, and embodying the combined product of the poet's perceptions, thoughts, and feelings."

39. Dinkler, *Literary Theory and the New Testament*, 28.

40. Beale, *Handbook*, 34–35. Dinkler is concerned that scholars use an approach that suits them while ignoring other scholars' concerns: Dinkler, *Literary Theory and the New Testament*, 23.

41. Beetham, *Echoes of Scripture in the Letter of Paul to the Colossians*, 17. See Beetham, "Quotation, Allusion, and Echo," 687.

42. Huffman has thoughtfully classified citations (what he labels as a broad category for the NT's use of the OT) as either "introduced quotations," "introduced paraphrases," "unintroduced quotions," and "unintroduced paraphrases" (30–31). Huffman has also classified a second broad category as "allusions and recollections," which contains "Scripture summaries," "historical reminiscences," "specific allusions," and "thematic echoes" (32–33). His work has great potential for bringing clarity, but this study does not adopt his proposed classifications. Huffman, *Understanding the New Testament Use of the Old Testament*, 30–33.

Introduction

"The tell tale key to discerning an allusion is that of recognizing an *incomparable or unique parallel in wording, syntax, concept, or cluster of motifs in the same order or structure.*"[43]

Motif

A motif is a recurrent thematic element, idea, symbol, or image, used at selected moments to support a theme of the work.[44] A motif has no meaning without the context of its controlling theme.[45]

Quotation

"A quotation is a direct citation of an OT passage that is easily recognizable by its clear and unique verbal parallelism."[46] A quotation is recognizable by the original audience and causes that audience to recall a previous text for an exegetical purpose or where "an understanding of an earlier text" is essential for proper interpretation of the text.[47] In comparison to an allusion (or echo not used here), a quotation is the most explicit literary mode.[48]

Theme

A theme is an idea or point of view used by an author throughout their work to highlight the topic or central idea of the work.[49]

---

43. Beale, *Handbook*, 31.

44. This definition comes from *A Dictionary of Literary Terms and Literary Theory*, rev ed., s.v. "Motif"; American Heritage Dictionary, 2nd ed., s.v. "Motif"; Urban, "Imagery," 319–21. Fullmer, *Resurrection in Mark's Literary-Historical Perspective*, 34; Daemmrich, *Themes & Motifs in Western Literature*.

45. This addition takes into consideration part of Alter's definition of motif. Alter writes, "it has no meaning in itself without the defining context of the narrative." Alter, *The Art of Biblical Narrative*, 120.

46. Beale, *Handbook*, 29.

47. Schultz, *The Search for Quotation Verbal Parallels in the Prophets*, 120, 221.

48. Beetham places quotation, allusion, and echo under the literary concept called intertextuality and, more broadly, literary criticism. Beetham, "Quotation, Allusion, and Echo," 684–85. See 687; Beetham, *Echoes of Scripture in the Letter of Paul to the Colossians*, 17.

49. Harmon, *A Handbook to Literature*, 12th ed.; *A Dictionary of Literary Terms and Literary Theory*, rev. ed., s.v. "Theme"; Webster's Basic Dictionary, s.v. "Theme"; and *American*

Metaphor

The metaphor is a linguistic tool that creatively describes an object or concept with another object or concept.[50]

The Metaphor: How to Define, Identify, and Interpret It

It is vital to define the term metaphor and establish how the reader may identify and understand metaphors for a study on metaphors. First, the definition of the word metaphor is given for later study of *the way* metaphor. Second, two sets of metaphor theories are discussed: traditional linguistic theories and modern metaphor theories. With both the definition and methods for identifying metaphor clarified, the reader will know: (1) How to identify a non-metaphorical use of a word like *the way*, (2) how to identify *the way* as a metaphor, and (3) how to distinguish similar metaphors from one another (i.e., how *the way* can mean in one verse Christians and another Christianity).

The metaphor is a linguistic tool that creatively describes an object or concept with another object or concept.[51] Similarly, Rotasperti writes, "A metaphor is an image that plays both a cognitive and an aesthetic role."[52] Because of the creative function of a metaphor and the presumption of knowledge necessary to understand them, metaphors may be difficult to identify or understand. Further, Stöckl writes, "metaphors confront us with the conundrum of saying one thing and meaning another, associated with a more or less distant idea—this concerns the notion of non-literal or figurative language use."[53] The metaphor is more than a linguistic exchange of

---

Heritage Dictionary, 2nd ed., s.v. "Theme." Alter, *The Art of Biblical Narrative*, 120.

50. This definition arises from a synthesis of several works. Rotasperti, *Metaphors in Proverbs*; Stöckl, "Metaphor Revisited Cognitive-Conceptual Versus Traditional Linguistic Perspectives"; Eubanks, *Metaphor and Writing*; Black, "Metaphor"; Wassell and Llewelyn, "'Fishers of Humans,' the Contemporary Theory of Metaphor, and Conceptual Blending Theory," 628.

51. This definition arises from the synthesis of the definitions within this paragraph. Rotasperti, *Metaphors in Proverbs*; Stöckl, "Metaphor Revisited Cognitive-Conceptual Versus Traditional Linguistic Perspectives."; Eubanks, *Metaphor and Writing*.; Black, "Metaphor." Also not listed, Wassell and Llewelyn write, "Metaphors seek to understand one thing in terms of another." Wassell, and Llewelyn, "'Fishers of Humans,' the Contemporary Theory of Metaphor, and Conceptual Blending Theory," 628.

52. Rotasperti, *Metaphors in Proverbs*, 2.

53. Stöckl, "Metaphor Revisited Cognitive-Conceptual Versus Traditional Linguistic

words in many ways. Metaphors evoke a vast number of conceptual images. Philip Eubanks writes, "Metaphors are enmeshed in a constellation of relationships that complicate what people mean by them and how they are likely to influence people's writing."[54] Similarly, Max Black suggests metaphors "enrich the vocabulary" (i.e., "there is no literal equivalent") or are a stylistic choice by the author.[55]

Knowing the theories about metaphors assists in understanding how to identify and interpret metaphors. The models discussed here are the traditional linguistic theories (i.e., the substitution theory and the interaction theory) and the modern metaphor theories: Conceptual Metaphor Theory and Blending Metaphor Theory. Lanier presents a history of metaphor theory that shows a linear progression: substitution theory, interaction theory, conceptual Metaphor theory, and Conceptual Blending Theory.[56] Each theory is presented below to establish how this study understands and identifies metaphors.

First, from the traditional metaphor theories, the substitutionary metaphor theory is summarized. This theory essentially understands a metaphor as substituting one word for another.[57] Moreover, the connection between the two terms is linguistic (i.e., the association of the original word's meaning with the substitutionary word of a similar or identical meaning).[58] It is typical to use one word literally and one metaphorically.[59] Black uses the term *frame* (i.e., the sentence containing the metaphor) to help understand when a metaphor occurs.[60] In fact, the frame or context of the sentence dictates when a word is used literally or metaphorically.[61] Therefore, a term like *the way* may sometimes literally describe a road, and in another frame, it may represent a lifestyle (e.g., Christianity). Further, the frame can distinguish between two metaphorical uses of a word[62] (e.g., *the way* meaning

---

Perspectives," 189.

54. Eubanks, *Metaphor and Writing*, 2.

55. Black, "Metaphor," 281.

56. Lanier, *Old Testament Conceptual Metaphors and the Christology of Luke's Gospel*, 17–27.

57. Rotasperti, *Metaphors in Proverbs*, 2.

58. Rotasperti, *Metaphors in Proverbs*, 3.

59. Black, "Metaphor," 275.

60. Black, "Metaphor," 276.

61. Black, "Metaphor," 276.

62. Black, "Metaphor," 276.

either Christian or Christianity). Black states that "the rules of our language determine that some expressions must count as metaphors," but the author's nuance on a metaphor may be conveyed through different contexts.[63] Alongside the substitutionary theory, Black suggests a comparison view of metaphor. He notes the comparison view "is a special case of a 'substitution view,'" and may be summarized as a simile where "the metaphorical statement might be replaced by an equivalent literal *comparison*."[64]

Second, Black considers the *interaction view* (the Interaction Theory) to be occurrences of a metaphor where the "ground" metaphor brings in associated characteristics (e.g., a wolf may be associated with a "wolf-system" that includes hunting prey, eating other animals, and being fierce).[65] For a method to identify metaphors, Black provides diagnostic criteria (i.e., "a reliable sign . . . not necessarily qualifying as a defining condition.").[66] He finds no defining characteristics because "recognition of a metaphorical statement depends essentially upon two things: knowledge of what it is to be a metaphorical statement, and our judgment that a metaphorical reading of a given statement is here preferable to a literal one."[67] Signs of a metaphor include an incoherent understanding of the text or a blatantly false statement when read literally.[68] He resists using defining criteria for identifying metaphors because such measures inevitably fail.[69]

Third, the Conceptual Metaphor Theory (CMT) seeks to explain metaphors with human experience. Gregory Lanier uses the Conceptual Metaphor Theory (CMT), which defines metaphor as "the mapping of a 'source domain' onto a 'target domain.'"[70] In comparison with the traditional method of interpretation metaphor, Stöckl writes, "Contrary to a semantic explanation, cognitive theory locates metaphor in conceptual structure, not in linguistic knowledge."[71] Edward Slingerland writes the "[c]onceptual metaphor theory argues that our primary and most highly structured experience is with

---

63. Black, "Metaphor," 277.
64. Black, "Metaphor," 283.
65. Black, "Metaphor," 288.
66. Black, "More About Metaphor," 49.
67. Black, "More About Metaphor," 450.
68. Black, "More About Metaphor," 450.
69. Black, "More About Metaphor," 450.
70. Lanier, *Old Testament Conceptual Metaphors and the Christology of Luke's Gospel*, 16.
71. Stöckl, "Metaphor Revisited Cognitive-Conceptual Versus Traditional Linguistic Perspectives," 194.

the physical realm, and the patterns that we encounter and develop through the interaction of our bodies with the physical environment therefore serve as our most basic source domains."[72] George Lakoff and Mark Johnson explain some connections between physical encounters and concepts. They determine that metaphors contain metaphorical and non-metaphorical concepts.[73] They write, "These include at least (1) *spatial orientations* (e.g., UP-DOWN, IN-OUT, NEAR-FAR, FRONT-BACK), (2) *ontological concepts* arising in physical experience (e.g., ENTITY, SUBSTANCE, CONTAINER, PERSON), and (3) *structured experiences and activities* (e.g., EATING, MOVING, TRANSFERRING OBJECTS FROM PLACE TO PLACE, etc.)."[74] Slingerland gives an example of the conceptual metaphor theory with purposes and destinations: "Subjective Judgment: achieving a purpose Sensorimotor Experience: reaching a destination Example: 'He'll ultimately be successful, but he isn't there yet.'"[75] Slingerland states that individuals use "conceptual topology—that is, inference patterns, imagistic reasoning patterns, salient entities, and so on—are preserved, thereby importing a high degree of structure into the target domain [i.e., the non-metaphorical represented idea]."[76] Further, Slingerland cites a relevant example to this study: the use of the journey concept to comprehend life better.[77]

Fourth, Rotasperti identifies *conceptual blending theory* as an "offshoot" of CMT.[78] Rotasperti aptly summarizes Gilles Fauconnier's and Max Turner's Conceptual Blending Theory (CBT):

> Fauconnier and Turner define a metaphor as a space where various mental fields are integrated, one that contains *input* from the *source* and from the *target* of a given thought. Their study is based on the grammatical analysis of text and is founded on the

---

72. Slingerland, "Conceptual Metaphor Theory as Methodology for Comparative Religion," 10.

73. Lakoff and Johnson, "The Metaphorical Structure of the Human Conceptual System," 193.

74. Lakoff and Johnson, "The Metaphorical Structure of the Human Conceptual System," 193; italics in the original.

75. Slingerland, "Conceptual Metaphor Theory as Methodology for Comparative Religion," 10.

76. Slingerland, "Conceptual Metaphor Theory as Methodology for Comparative Religion," 11.

77. Slingerland, "Conceptual Metaphor Theory as Methodology for Comparative Religion," 11.

78. Rotasperti, *Metaphors in Proverbs*, 4.

assumption that metaphors already contain conceptual structures in and of themselves (*structured conceptual framework*). The text is 'evoked' by the experience of the reader, and it is at this level that the semantic phenomenon is introduced. According to this framework, there is no clean demarcation or rupture between the grammatical aspect and the semantic phenomenon.[79]

The Conceptual Blending Theory shows promise in understanding metaphors. However, Lanier finds that the CBT may still be too burdensome to introduce into NT studies.[80] He cites the extensive vocabulary and elaborate diagramming as the heavy burden when analyzing more than a single instance of a metaphor.[81] Because of the burden described by Lanier, this study does not use the CBT.

This study finds value in both the traditional and modern metaphor theories. Stöckl suggests the two metaphor models (traditional vs. modern) do not make one another obsolete.[82] He also recognizes that each model contains weaknesses.[83] Consequently, the two models may be used in conjunction with one another.[84] Rotasperti employs a co-operative metaphor theories approach. He writes, "I do not apply any specific theory of metaphor, but nonetheless use—on a case-by-case basis—contemporary rereadings of Aristotle's thought on metaphor, setting myself up to decipher the fields (or the conceptual ideas) from which the dynamism of the expression originates."[85] This study takes a similar approach.

First, to differentiate between metaphor and non-metaphor, Black's "diagnostic" approach helps. Hence, in Acts, when ὁδός describes something other than a physical road or path, the word's literal meaning makes the passage not understandable, so a metaphor is present. Second, CMT is helpful in understanding the relationship between the concepts within a metaphor. When considering CMT, the "source domain" would be

---

79. Rotasperti, *Metaphors in Proverbs*, 4; italics in the original. See Fauconnier and Turner, *The Way We Think*, 39–50.

80. Lanier, *Old Testament Conceptual Metaphors and the Christology of Luke's Gospel*, 27.

81. Lanier, *Old Testament Conceptual Metaphors and the Christology of Luke's Gospel*, 26.

82. Stöckl, "Metaphor Revisited Cognitive-Conceptual Versus Traditional Linguistic Perspectives," 196.

83. Stöckl, "Metaphor Revisited Cognitive-Conceptual Versus Traditional Linguistic Perspectives," 196.

84. Stöckl, "Metaphor Revisited Cognitive-Conceptual Versus Traditional Linguistic Perspectives," 196.

85. Rotasperti, *Metaphors in Proverbs*, 8–9.

"the way," and the "target domain" is the Christian community or faith in God (i.e., Judaism in Proverbs and Christianity in the NT).[86] Because the "source" and "target" domains remain the same when ὁδός is used as a metaphor for the Church or to describe Christianity, there must be a means to differentiate the two options. Third, to distinguish between two similar metaphors, this study favors a semantic approach where the greater context of the passage assists in limiting the availability of interpretation (e.g., Acts 9:2 depicts Paul seeking a particular people group and ὁδός is supplemented in as a name or description). In contrast, Luke uses ὁδός in the accusative case to describe a means to salvation in Acts 16:17. However, the study recognizes that CMT assists in Acts 16:17, where the directional movement may be associated with salvation. In short, this study uses both the traditional and modern metaphor theories when determining and analyzing metaphors to ultimately show that Acts uses *the way* metaphor as Proverbs uses *the way* metaphor.

Differentiating Between Literary References: "work-oriented, objective approaches" and "expressive, author-oriented approaches"

It is essential to recognize that motifs are not the same as allusions. The literary themes of a book and the book's theology are often the same or similar. However, the two references, motifs and allusions, differentiate themselves based on their respective field of study (i.e., "work-oriented, objective approaches" and "expressive, author-oriented approaches"). Motifs reside within a single piece of writing, relate to the theme of the same writing, and are associated with "work-oriented, objective approaches." Motifs are not to be compared across different texts. Allusions are indirect references that require a host of linguistic and thematic elements to associate one text with another and are associated with "expressive, author-oriented approaches." Moving forward, Beale's literary approach, an author-oriented approach, will be referenced as a *theological analysis*. This change, in part, is to differentiate between the literary analyses and, in part, due to the divine authorship of Scripture.

---

86. When considering the Gospel of Luke, Lanier finds that the "OT should be treated as the chief influence on these [the Gospel of Luke's] metaphors." This study seeks to show that the way metaphor from Proverbs is the chief influence of the way metaphor in Acts. Lanier, *Old Testament Conceptual Metaphors and the Christology of Luke's Gospel*, 29.

Literary Analysis

Defining Theme and Motif

Standard literary definitions of "theme" do not suffice for an accurate and precise study: A theme is the subject of a piece of writing;[87] or, according to the *American Heritage Dictionary*, a theme is "a topic of discourse or discussion. . .An idea, point of view, or perception embodied and expanded upon in a work of art; an underlying or essential subject of artistic representation."[88] Varying definitions of theme in the field of literary criticism also create confusion. Contributing to the confusion, Randall Buth notes that from the Praguian Functional Sentence Perspective, each topic of the sentence is a theme.[89] Thus, the definition of theme is unclear based on the scope of the literature (e.g., the entire book or a sentence). In addition to the inadequacy of elementary definitions and confusion from differing definitions of "theme" in the field of literature, biblical scholars also expound in different ways on the meaning of a theme.[90] For example, Paul Fullmer proposes that a theme or themes are an image(s) or an idea(s) that are presented throughout the work.[91] This work uses a hybrid definition based on the above definitions: A theme is an idea or point of view used by an author throughout their work to highlight the topic or central idea of the work.[92]

Along with a definition, this research requires a method for identifying themes in literature. When identifying themes, the main point of the text must be determined first. Also, this theme must be present throughout, because a theme supports a main point found throughout the entire work.

What may create difficulty in identifying themes in Scripture is the uniqueness of some NT books, such as the Gospels and Acts, which have unique genres. A book's genre assists the reader in identifying its themes. The narrative genre and books with clear structures enable the reader to identify themes better. Therefore, books belonging to no conclusive genre,

---

87. *Webster's Basic Dictionary*, s.v. "Theme."

88. *American Heritage Dictionary*, 2 ed., s.v. "Theme."

89. Buth, "Language, Linguistics," 431–35.

90. Zevit, "Echoes of Texts Past," 12–13.

91. Fullmer, *Resurrection in Mark's Literary-Historical Perspective*, 34.

92. *A Dictionary of Literary Terms and Literary Theory*, rev ed., s.v. "Theme"; *Webster's Basic Dictionary*, s.v. "Theme"; and *American Heritage Dictionary*, 2nd ed., s.v. "Theme." Alter, *The Art of Biblical Narrative*, 120.

such as the narratives of the Gospels or Acts, can create uncertainty when determining the theme.[93] The uncertainty surrounding genre is mentioned here because the perceived genre impacted how scholars have identified themes in the past and seem to influence the number of themes identified.

Modern scholarship is actively debating the genre of Luke-Acts. Hubert Cancik suggests the writings are one to the degree that Luke-Acts needs an appropriate title for the "whole work, not 'gospel.'"[94] He indicates that Luke-Acts is best captured by Ancient Western Historiography, giving particular attention to the establishment of institutions.[95] Gregory Sterling identifies Luke-Acts "most closely with Hellenistic Jewish historians,"[96] and Luke-Acts participates in apologetic historiography.[97] Daniel Marguerat proposes that Luke provides a "biblical historiography," i.e., a "confessional history."[98] He suggests that Acts functions as a sequel to the Gospel of Luke and as an origins story for Christians.[99] Similarly, Keener understands Luke and Acts as histories with "one biographic segment [Luke] belonging to a longer history."[100] Keener finds support from ancient authors who, at times, "mixed genres."[101]

The genre of Acts can not be fully covered without a discussion of the unity between the Gospel of Luke and Acts, which scholars still discuss.[102] First, there exists the discussion of whether these two biblical books are separate works by differing authors. Second, supposing Luke-Acts has a single author, what is the relationship between the two documents, e.g., did the author create the gospel without knowledge of Acts, write Luke with Acts in view, or write Luke and Acts as a single literary unit? In response to the first question, it appears that as-far-as scholarly consensus exists, scholars accept that a single author created both the Gospel of Luke and Acts.[103]

---

93. The author recognizes that the Gospels and the book of Acts do not fit modern genre types and that scholars still debate these genres. See Keener, *Christobiography*.

94. Cancik, "The History of Culture, Religion, and Institutions in Ancient Historiography," 673.

95. Cancik, "The History of Culture, Religion, and Institutions in Ancient Historiography."

96. Sterling, *Shaping the Past to Define the Present*, 229.

97. Sterling, *Shaping the Past to Define the Present*, 4.

98. Marguerat, *The First Christian Historian*, 25.

99. Marguerat, *The First Christian Historian*, 40.

100. Craig S. Keener, *Acts: 1:1—2:47*, 553.

101. Keener, *Acts: 1:1—2:47*, 553–54.

102. Schreiner, *Acts*, 64.

103. Bird, Rowe, and Gregory, eds., *Rethinking the Unity and Reception of Luke and*

With regard to the second question(s), Mikeal C. Parsons and Richard I. Pervo questioned the somewhat blind acceptance of a complete literary unity between Luke and Acts.[104] Keener finds that "the recapitulation of the Gospel's conclusion in Acts' introduction and the second preface's mention of the first volume have sufficient ancient analogies . . . to leave no room for doubt that we should view Luke's Gospel and Acts as two volumes of a single work."[105] He further finds the narrative is unified.[106] Still seeing literary unity, Marguerat describes the relationship between the books as a "diptych."[107] Understanding the relationship of Luke-Acts by a diptych, or hinge, Marguerat finds the best description of Acts as a sequel.[108] Beverly Gaventa finds that the shared authorship between Luke-Acts is a reason to read the two works together.[109] Revisiting the pursuit of Parsons and Pervo in a volume edited by Gregory and Rowe, scholars look again at the literary unity of Luke and Acts and the reception history of Luke and Acts.[110] Rowe references second-century evidence for removing the close unity of Luke-Acts, citing that "as far as we know, though Luke was on occasion in the fourth position among the four Gospels—thus giving the opportunity for Acts to follow—Luke and Acts were never placed beside each other in any ancient manuscript."[111] Some literary evidence may support Rowe's conclusion. For example, Alexander Loveday proposes that the prefaces of Luke and Acts share similarities to scientific treatises, which indicates that Luke and Acts' unity is not certainly so strongly linked.[112] However, Luke Timothy Johnson exposes some of the difficulties with using reception history to understand the unity of Luke-Acts, e.g., the lack of "evidence that any New Testament writings were read in the late second century—or for much of the patristic period—as 'literary compositions.'"[113] Without wading further into the weeds, this author agrees with most scholars that Luke-Acts is

---

Acts, xi. Keener, *Acts: 1:1—2:47*, 551.

104. Parsons and Pervo, *Rethinking the Unity of Luke and Acts*.
105. Keener, *Acts: 1:1—2:47*, 551.
106. Keener, *Acts: 1:1—2:47*, 553, 33n28. In note 28 Keener cites Tannehill, *Luke*, xiii.
107. Marguerat, *The First Christian Historian*, 63–64.
108. Marguerat, *The First Christian Historian*, 63.
109. Gaventa, *The Acts of the Apostles*, 52.
110. Bird, Rowe, and Gregory, eds., *Rethinking the Unity and Reception of Luke and Acts*.
111. Rowe, "History, Hermeneutics, Adn the Unity of Luke-Acts," 47.
112. Alexander, *The Preface to Luke's Gospel*, 145–46, 211.
113. Johnson, "Literary Criticism of Luke-Acts: Is Reception History Pertinent?," 66.

authored by the same individual. Moreover, the author finds that Luke-Acts is most likely a single literary unit, as suggested by Tannehill.[114] However, like Patrick Schreiner, this author finds there is value in giving an independent analysis of Luke and Acts in addition to an analysis of Luke-Acts.[115]

The motif concept manifests the same difficulties that occur with a theme: i.e., inadequate broad definitions, differing literary definitions, and definitions again modified by biblical scholars. One example of such an insufficient and broad definition comes from the *American Heritage Dictionary*, which defines a motif as "a recurrent thematic element used in an artistic or literary work."[116] Dennis Horton expresses his frustrations about general definitions: "Proliferation of the generic view of motif necessarily entails a loss of specificity, consequently diminishing the value of motif as an analytical tool. Without clarity of definition, motif is as helpful to the biblical scholar as bifocals are to a surgeon performing microscopic surgery."[117] Fullmer defines a motif slightly differently,[118] as "ideas or images that recur at select points in a literary work.[119] David Urban defines a motif as an image or symbol present "in a pattern that recurs throughout a piece of literature."[120] A composite definition of motif can thus assist the reader in moving forward: A motif is a recurrent thematic element, idea, symbol, or image, used at selected moments to support a theme of the work.[121] A motif has no meaning without the context of its controlling theme.[122]

Method for Identifying a Motif

Now that the terms have been defined, with a clear demarcation between theological and literary analysis noted, it is time to discuss the method used

---

114. Tannehill, *Luke*, 28. Talbert, *Reading Acts*, 3. Talbert finds Tannehill's argument for literary unity between Luke-Acts convincing.

115. Schreiner, *Acts*, 66.

116. *American Heritage Dictionary*, 2nd ed., s.v. "Motif."

117. Horton, *Death and Resurrection*, 1.

118. Fullmer, *Resurrection in Mark's Literary-Historical Perspective*, 34.

119. Fullmer, *Resurrection in Mark's Literary-Historical Perspective*, 34.

120. Urban, "Imagery," 319.

121. This definition comes from *A Dictionary of Literary Terms and Literary Theory*, rev ed., s.v. "Motif"; American Heritage Dictionary, 2nd ed., s.l. "Motif"; Urban, "Imagery," 319–21; Fullmer, *Resurrection in Mark's Literary-Historical Perspective*, 34; Daemmrich, *Themes & Motifs in Western Literature*.

122. Alter, *The Art of Biblical Narrative*, 120.

for literary analysis of motifs. Freedman, professor of English literature emeritus at the University of Haifa, identifies five components of a motif: (1) frequency, (2) avoidability, (3) occurrence in significant contexts, (4) coherence, and (5) symbolic appropriateness.[123] Freedman states that the first two components must be present for a motif to exist, and the final three components help determine the strength of the motif.[124] The following paragraphs review each of Freedman's components, show their application, and summarize how this method of analysis will function in this study.

The two necessary components for identifying a motif are frequency and avoidability. Frequency may be the single most important factor, as mentioned above concerning the identification of allusions. Frequency is both the number of occurrences and the concentration of occurrences,[125] although the criterion of frequency is subjective. Freedman writes, "But members of the family of references should occur often enough to indicate that purposiveness rather than merely coincidence or necessity is at least occasionally responsible for their presence. They should pervade the atmosphere sufficiently to assure that they will be at least subliminally felt."[126]

This study will take into account several factors when determining frequency: occurrence of a word within the context of all of Scripture, individual books, and segments of books; the uses of a word and its available cognates, and the concentration of words based on percentage use in a given set of passages in comparison with the entirety of the book. In addition to frequency, the method involves an assessment of avoidability. Avoidability refers to the likelihood that the author used the motif intentionally.[127] A good example of a motif with issues around avoidability is John's use of darkness. Is John referring to evil, nighttime, or both? John may use darkness as necessary in describing nighttime but not deliberately suggesting evil. In the matter of avoidability, Freedman concerns himself with the use of words or phrases that have a pattern of frequency in common with a motif but that do not serve as a motif.[128] Identifying multiple markers can

---

123. William Freedman, "The Literary Motif," *Novel: A Forum on Fiction* 4, no. 2 (1971): 126–27.

124. Freedman, "The Literary Motif," 126.

125. Freedman, "The Literary Motif," 126.

126. Freedman, "The Literary Motif," 126.

127. Freedman, "The Literary Motif," 126.

128. Freedman, "The Literary Motif," 126.

Introduction

assist in determining whether a term is avoidable (i.e., does the author use a word to convey a motif). A helpful example about decerning the presence of the Holy Spirit (רוּחַ) brings clarity. The word "spirit" may be used to capture the weather (wind) and may not refer to the Holy Spirit (e.g., "the wind from the Lord" Num 11:31). However, if the spirit is in construct with holy like in Psalm 51 (וְרוּחַ קָדְשְׁךָ) the translation renders Holy Spirit. Similarly, if a motif is present, the context of the passage should suggest an intentional use of one word over another.

Freedman's remaining three criteria are not necessary for identifying a motif, but the presence of one or more of these enforces the strength of a motif. Freedman also states that these three criteria may only be met if a motif is present because they discuss a motif's effectiveness.[129] Therefore, the absence of any of the following criteria does not negate the presence of a motif. Thus, "occurrence in significant contexts" is concerned with determining the potency of a motif, due to its appearance in significant contexts which appear at climactic points in the text.[130] This does not mean that some verses in Scripture are of greater or lesser significance, but rather that specific texts are more suitable for including a motif. In biblical literature, the significance of the context depends on the literary features (e.g., opening statements, transitions, summary statements). In Acts, significant points may include climaxes in the narrative, such as those found in literature, but may also include introductions, transitions, and conclusions. One example of a significant context in Scripture is the purpose statement in the Gospel of John (21:24). Also, the techniques used in discourse analysis can assist in identifying significance, i.e., the identification of points, and boundary markers. By identifying features such as transition points or introductions, the motif is strengthened because of its "occurrence in significant contexts" where it is used to establish the main point of a passage.

Coherency is the degree to which "the motif is relevant to the principal end of the motif as a whole and to which they fit together into a recognizable and coherent unit."[131] Scripture manifests such coherence through the unity of multiple uses of a motif and how well that motif supports the themes of books or passages. An example of such cohesion would be the motifs of death and resurrection in support of a theme of salvation.[132]

---

129. Freedman, "The Literary Motif," 126.
130. Freedman, "The Literary Motif," 126.
131. Freedman, "The Literary Motif," 127.
132. Horton does not say death and resurrection are examples of cohesion, but rather

The final criterion is symbolic appropriateness, or "the appropriateness of the motif to what it symbolizes."[133] Freedman gives the example of a writer using doors, fences, and gates to represent physical or spiritual isolation.[134] He provides another example, writing, "Obviously a motif of circularity is more appropriate to a book about the circular repetitiveness of human fortune and behavior and the circular, futile strivings of the ill-equipped dreamer, as in Sister Carrie, than to one about, say, a love triangle."[135] Therefore, a motif is stronger if the symbolic image suggests authorial intent. Along with a symbol being either appropriate or inappropriate, there are different levels of symbolic appropriateness.

This study places more emphasis on the final three criteria than Freedman does. Where Freedman considers these criteria dispensable in determining a motif, this study finds them important because the motif must be both present and effective. Therefore, in this study, the presence of one or all of the additional three criteria is sought. Moreover, the more criteria that are met, the greater the likelihood the motif is present. By requiring more criteria, the analysis mitigates the subjectivity of the identification of the motif with a stronger case. The additional criteria act as elements of gradation on a scale of one to three, with all three elements indicating the presence of a very strong motif.

Although Freedman was writing about fiction, his method is transferable to the Bible. Thus, Dennis Horton uses his method to identify motifs in the book of Acts. Horton is able to identify the possible presence of a motif using these modern criteria and also determines the function of that motif within Acts.[136] Horton follows a threefold procedure:

> (1) an examination of the diegetic references to death and resurrection; (2) an analysis of mimetic examples of this messianic pattern among the experiences of major and minor characters; and (3) a demonstration of the way the motif becomes intensified through contrast with a secondary motif, that of death and decay.[137]

---

that both are tied to salvation. Horton, *Death and Resurrection*, 33–34.

133. Freedman, "The Literary Motif," 127.

134. Freedman, "The Literary Motif," 127.

135. Freedman, "The Literary Motif," 127.

136. Horton, *Death and Resurrection*, 2.

137. Horton, *Death and Resurrection*, xiii, 7. Horton provides his definition of diegesis on page seven, where he writes, "'Diegesis,' as Robert W. Funk defines, is the classical term that refers to the 'recounting' or 'telling' of events in the 'unfocused or mediated narrative segment'" (7). See, Funk, *Poetics of Biblical Narrative*, 134. Funk also refers to

Restated, Horton uses Freedman's method to (1) examine the telling of a narrative; (2) examine the references in the narrative to historical texts; and (3) show how cohesion with other motifs strengthens the motif of death and resurrection.[138] Freedman's method proves helpful because Horton treats the book of Acts as a narrative.[139]

In a similar manner, this present study applies this method because here too Acts is viewed as a narrative. Freedman's method will allow (1) an examination of Acts' narrative references to "the Way," and (2) provide a means to examine the historical references (Proverbs).[140] In this study, Freedman's method will be used to first identify the use of the Way as a motif in Proverbs and then examine the Way as a motif in Acts. By examining both Acts and Proverbs independently via Freedman's method, a proper comparison of ways Acts and Proverbs use the motif will reveal any similarities that might allow for preliminary conclusions as to whether or not Proverbs is a fitting referent for Luke.

Theological Analysis (Literary analysis: expressive, author-oriented approach)

Beale's work is the foundation for the theological method. Beale bases his method upon the work of Richard Hays, who uses the criteria of *availability, volume, recurrence, thematic coherence, historical plausibility, history of interpretation,* and *satisfaction* as indications of an allusion.[141] However, Beale finds that only Hay's first four criteria are valid for identifying allusions: *availability, volume, recurrence,* and *thematic coherence*.[142] He recog-

---

diegesis as "summary" (134).

138. This restatement considers the definitions of "diegetic" and "mimesis" used by Horton. Horton uses the definitions provided by Funk. Funk, *Poetics of Biblical Narrative*, 134–35. Mimesis is the showing of the events of a narrative by transporting a reader to a specific time and place, and in Horton's research this would include the Old Testament, which I call historical texts.

139. Rowe also notes that the method works well but is monotonous in its presentation. C. Kavin Rowe, *Death and Resurrection: The Shape and Function of a Literary Motif in the Book of Acts*, by Dennis J. Horton, *The Catholic Biblical Quarterly* 72 (2010): 829–30.

140. Horton's third procedure is specific to his study. However, Freedman's method brings cohesion of motif to bear so that some overlap may exist between the studies.

141. Beale, *Handbook*, 35.

142. Beale, *Handbook*, 35. Porter finds only the first three criteria valid for interpreting

nizes the difficulty in distinguishing between allusions and echoes. Echoes are more subtle references to the OT and possess less clarity than allusions. Therefore, Beale uses the same criteria for identifying allusions to identify echoes.[143] Similarly, this research will not seek to distinguish between an allusion and an echo and only use the term allusion.

Hays and Beale represent the leading voices in biblical scholarship for identifying NT allusions to the OT. However, many other scholars are attempting to refine the process in order to make the identification of allusions less subjective. Scholars are similarly working on improving the process of identifying the OT use of other OT texts and the dependence of Scripture on extra-biblical texts. In *Subtle Citation, Allusion, and Translation in the Hebrew Bible*, Joseph Kelly notes that scholars generally recognize, and with elevated importance, three attributes of literary allusion: an identifiable form, a hermeneutically active and intentional author, and a hermeneutically passive and receptive reader.[144] In his analysis, Kelly synthesizes the work of Michael Fishbane, Jeffery Leonard, and Hays, arguing that shared language may function as the initial indicator of allusion, and that it is "the most objective and verifiable criteria when identifying allusion."[145] Yet, shared language and greater amounts of shared language, *volume*, cannot alone demonstrate literary allusion.[146]

In the same book, Marc Brettler expounds on the clarity which shared language brings:

> 1. Shared language is the single most important factor in establishing a textual connection; 2. Shared language is more important than non-shared language; 3. The shared language that is rare or distinctive suggests a stronger connection than does the language that is widely used; 4. Shared phrases suggest a stronger connection than do individual shared terms; 5. The accumulation of shared language suggests a stronger connection than does a single shared term or phrase; 6. Shared language in similar contexts suggests a stronger connection than does shared language alone;

---

allusions, although needing refinement (38–9). Stanley E., "Allusions and Echoes," 29–40.

143. Beale, *Handbook*, 32.

144. Kelly, "Identifying Literary Allusions," 25.

145. Kelly, "Identifying Literary Allusions," 31. Kelly cites Leonard 2008: 247. See Fishbane, *Biblical Interpretation in Ancient Israel*, 285. However, Kelly cites the 1988 publication of *Biblical Interpretation in Ancient Israel*. Leonard, "Identifying Inner-Biblical Allusions," 246–48.

146. Kelly, "Identifying Literary Allusions," 32.

7. Shared language need not be accompanied by shared ideology to establish a connection; and 8. Shared language need not be accompanied by a shared form to establish a connection (Leonard 2008). Carr's method determines that a text is dependent on another text if it 1. verbally parallels that text and yet includes substantial pluses vis-á-vis that text, 2. appears to enrich its parallel (fairly fully preserved) with fragments from various locations in the Bible (less completely preserved), 3. includes a plus that fills what could have been perceived as an apparent gap in its parallel, 4. includes expansive material in character speeches, particularly theophanic speech, 5. has an element that appears to be an adaptation of an element in the other text to shifting circumstances/ideas, and 6. combines linguistic phenomena from disparate strata of the Pentateuch (Carr 2001:110–11).[147]

Brettler's method expands upon Leonard's notion of shared language with Carr's method.[148] Greenstein similarly writes that allusions should share "(1) similar themes, preferably in similar contexts; (2) similar motifs; (3) a similar sequence in the parallels that are adduced; and, wherever possible, (4) similar wording."[149] The similarity between all these scholars is the use of shared language to identify an allusion. After identifying the shared language, the scholars examine the context of the passage. Marc Brettler requires that an allusion enrich the parallel, while Greenspan requires that the passage alluded to shares similar themes, motifs, and context. Beale's method for interpreting an allusion takes into consideration the criteria of Brettler and others.

Beale incorporates these four criteria for identifying allusions into a nine-fold approach to interpreting the use of the OT in the NT (see chapter 6 for nine-fold approach).[150] Beale's nine-fold approach begins after an allusion has been identified using his four criteria of *availability*, *volume*, *recurrence*, and *thematic coherence*.[151] Steps two through nine are used to interpret the use of the allusion. These steps reflect a similarity with Brettler's wish that the paralleled content share similar themes and enrich the

---

147. Brettler, "Identifying Torah Sources in the Historical Psalms," 73–90.

148. See Leonard, "Identifying Inner-Biblical Allusions"; Carr, "Method in Determination of Direction of Dependence."

149. Greenstein, "Method in the Study of Textual Source Dependence," 145.

150. Beale, *Handbook*, 42–43.

151. Beale uses these to validate the presence of an allusion. Here, the four criteria are to determine the initial presence of an allusion, as Kelly suggests for similar language.

understanding of the text containing the allusion.[152] In fact, Beale's criteria for identifying allusions and his approach to interpreting allusions addresses several scholars' efforts to refine the use of allusions in biblical studies. Therefore, this present study will employ Beale's method for a theological analysis of Acts.

This study will attempt to eliminate some subjectivity through the literary technique developed by Freedman to help identify motifs in literature. Thus, in addition to using Beale's four criteria, this study will employ the literary analysis that identified motifs in Acts. The OT allusions of passages in Acts that contain a motif of "the Way" and exhibit the four criteria for allusions will be interpreted.

CONCLUSION

This chapter has introduced the method used to identify OT references in the NT, which includes a theological and literary analysis, based on the work of Beale and Freedman respectively. The combination of theological and literary methods can reduce subjectivity when identifying textual references within the book of Acts.

To determine if Luke is referencing Proverbs when using "the Way," the study will follow four steps. Chapter two, a review of the literature, will examine scholarship on both Proverbs and Acts to demonstrate past and current understandings of the term in both books. Freedman's literary analysis will be used to examine the books of Proverbs and Acts in chapter three. Chapter four provides an analysis of the book of Acts using Beale's theological analysis. A synthesis of both analyses will then be offered in chapter five. Last, the final chapter provides a summary of the research and a proposal for future studies.

---

152. This contextual analysis also takes into consideration Brettler and Greenspan's methods.

2

Review of Literature

THE WAY AS THE PEOPLE

A REVIEW OF THE literature on "the Way" in Acts can be divided into two categories. The first discusses scholars' understanding of "the Way" as a name for Christians, while the second class examines the theology of the Way as a literary or theological device.

Luke presents the Way as a people group in Acts 9:2, 31; 19:23; 24:14, 22.[1] Scholars predominantly understand the Way as a reference to following Jesus and being a Christian. The Dead Sea Scrolls have had significant influence on how scholars understand "the Way," with the Qumran community a potential source for use of the term to describe a people group. Therefore, the history of interpretation is divided into two time periods: a traditional period of interpretation pre-1949 and a modern understanding beginning with the discovery of the DSS and continuing to the present day.

The traditional interpretation includes conjectures about the meaning of "the Way" from simple observation of Acts 9:2, "and asked him for letters to the synagogues at Damascus, so that if he found any belonging to the Way, men or women, he might bring them bound to Jerusalem." For

---

1. Acts 16:17, 18:25, 26 also comes into the conversation when discussing the Way as a people group, but the verses reflect its use more as a concept or referent, and are not as frequently reflected in the discussion. Lake and Cadbury, *The Beginnings of Christianity*, 100.

The True Identity of the People of the Way

example, John Calvin translated the Way as a sect.[2] For Calvin, this was a common metaphor in Scripture, with Luke using it to declare Saul's purpose to destroy the name of Christ.[3] Moving to the 1800s, scholars continued to understand the Way as a metaphor for Christians, as in Horatio Hackett's commentary of 1882.[4] The metaphor was then expanded slightly to include living and faith in Jesus, and salvation, but these interpretations still relate closely to the concept of being a Christian. In the late 1880s, however, the Reverend W. Denton sought to connect the Way to the Old Testament, writing that the term is "used similarly to the Hebrew usage, 'The way of the Lord,' and as a way of living in Christ."[5] Denton makes no further elaboration about the OT connection, however.[6] This trend continued into the early 1900s, with few attempts made at novel forms of literary criticism (See Table 2). Breaking from the scholarly consensus, in 1916 Charles Torrey proposed the Way was a Semitic locution, as evidenced by the Talmud and Arabic sources, but in 1933 scholars dismissed the idea.[7] An edited work by F. J. Foakes Jackson, Kirsopp Lake, and Henry Cadbury, *The Beginnings of Christianity*, represents the most significant work before the discovery of the Dead Sea Scrolls. The authors argue the term "the Way" is not Aramaic, but likely connects to the OT, and that the OT use of the Way is similar to the Tao and also to Methodist usage.[8] They suggest the term may have been be used in Greek-speaking Jewish circles in a derogatory sense, much like the word "Christian," but Lake and Cadbury suggest this without evidence.[9] They add that the saying is in keeping with the Jewish idiom.[10] However, most scholars from this period consider Luke's use of the Way a metaphor derived from the OT with few details, if any. The DSS discovery marks the transition to literary and source criticism in uncovering the meaning of the Way.

2. Calvin and Beveridge, *Commentary upon the Acts of the Apostles*, 368.
3. Calvin and Beveridge, *Commentary upon the Acts of the Apostles*, 368.
4. Hackett, *A Commentary on the Acts of the Apostles*.
5. Denton, *A Commentary on the Acts of the Apostles*, 301.
6. Denton, *A Commentary on the Acts of the Apostles*, 301.
7. Torrey, *The Composition and Date of Acts*, 391–92.
8. Lake and Cadbury, *The Beginnings of Christianity*, 100.
9. Lake and Cadbury, *The Beginnings of Christianity*, 100.
10. Lake and Cadbury, *The Beginnings of Christianity*, 391–92.

Review of Literature

Following the DSS discovery, the 1950s was a time when the historicity of Acts came under attack.[11] A major shift in scholarly research began, although some scholars were still cursory in their examination of the Way.[12] Then McCasland began a scholarly search into understanding the Way after reading a lexicon entry, which prompted him to write, "The word refers to the whole way of life from a moral and religious viewpoint, the Way, teaching in its most comprehensive sense."[13] He found the lexical entry lacked any corroborating research-based evidence.[14] The entry McCasland referenced resonates with pre-critical interpretations of the Way, such as that of John Chrysostom, who wrote of Acts 19:8–10 as follows:

Fittingly do they call this "the way," as it truly was the way that leads to the kingdom of heaven. Or the Scripture is saying that Christ is the way, as he is called the way, or it is speaking of the true faith, that which is proclaimed through Paul, by which any wayfarer arrives at the kingdom of heaven.[15]

Before McCasland, scholars relied on Rabbinic literature, connections to the Pauline literature, and unsubstantiated commentaries.[16] McCasland used the recently discovered Qumran *Manual of Discipline* (1QS) to argue that the Way is a designation for Christianity,[17] adding that the Qumran community derived their understanding of the Way from Isaiah 40:3 and that it is short for "the way of the Lord."[18] Later, Eero Repo provided more detailed analysis and similarly concluded that the ὁδός used for the motif of the Way has many facets: directional, geographical, legal, Christological, eschatological, and ethical.[19] Repo also suggests a New Exodus theme linking

---

11. Wingren, "'Weg,' 'Wanderung,' Und Verwandte Begriffe," 122. In his article discussing the relation between the terms path and travel, Wingren discusses the need to maintain Jesus' historical existence.

12. The discovery of the DSS did not lead to a clear shift in understanding. For instance, Bruce, writing in 1954, restates previous uncritical thinking concerning the Way: "It was evidently a term used by the early Christians to denote their own movement, considered as the way of life or the way of salvation." Bruce, *The Book of Acts*, 1970. Recent additions to Bruce's commentary suggest the DSS as a possible referent for the Way.

13. McCasland, "The Way," 222.

14. McCasland, "The Way," 222.

15. Oden and Martin, *Acts*, 236.

16. McCasland, "The Way," 223.

17. McCasland, "The Way," 230.

18. McCasland, "The Way," 230.

19. Baban, *On the Road Encounters*, 32. See Repo, *Der "Weg" als Selbstbezeichnung des*

the people of the Way to the Exodus.[20] In comparing the Way to the Exodus, the Way motif carries an ethical dimension.[21] William Robinson and Hans Conzelmann find the process of idealization, or an ethical metaphor of the Way, continues into the New Testament, such that the Way "transformed the geographical space into a faith symbol, the symbol of humanity's link with the spiritual world."[22] Reflecting on thirty-three years of scholarship on the Way (1950–1983), François Bovon found the metaphor has three connotations: Christological or soteriological, eschatological, and ethical.[23] He considered that theologically "the Way" reflects each category, but not necessarily philologically.[24] Octavian Baban appears to credit Repo with the first proposal for a complete *Hodos* Christology, despite its poor reception amongst scholars.[25] One of those in opposition was Ernst Haenchen, who found Repo's work inconclusive in determining an absolute use of ὁδός, and proposing instead that the Way functions as a proper name for a Christian community and teaching.[26] Paul S. Minear understands that members of the Way are Jesus' followers, but he finds that the use of the word "the Way" "was restricted within certain limits."[27] Minear recognizes that Paul functionally uses the Way to differentiate disciples of Christ from the Jewish community.[28] Further, Minear finds that Paul avoids the term "sect" for Jesus' followers because they were not a segment of the Jewish community but a group claiming to be the true people of God, similar to the Qumran community.[29] Minear falls short of identifying a referent for the word "the Way." Moving closer to the present, scholars have continued to seek more satisfactory interpretations of the Way.

Urchristentums, 322.

20. Baban, *On the Road Encounters*, 33.

21. Baban, *On the Road Encounters*, 33.

22. Robinson, *Der Weg des Herrn*, 22.

23. Bovon, *Luke the Theologian: Thirty-Three Years*, 322. Bovon's revised edition provides no additional information concerning the Way, so the first edition remains cited below. Bovon, *Luke the Theologian Fifty-Five Years of Research (1950–2005)*.

24. Bovon, *Luke the Theologian: Thirty-Three Years*, 322.

25. Baban, *On the Road Encounters*, 49.

26. Haenchen, *The Acts of the Apostles*, 320.

27. Minear, *Images of the Church*, 148–49.

28. Minear, *Images of the Church*, 149.

29. Minear, *Images of the Church*, 149.

Review of Literature

Scholars today still understand the Way as a designation for early Christians. The term evidently has multiple meanings. Scott Shauf captures this by saying the Way "can embody many aspects of a community at once—including, no doubt, its teaching."[30] The Way is thus the disciples who identify themselves with Jesus the Messiah, and through this identification, place themselves on the Way.[31]

The Way may have been a self-designation of Christians, while "sect" may have been the name the Jewish people preferred to give to Christians.[32] The usage of the Way would need to be metaphorical in these instances. Examples of the way metaphor exist in Luke's gospel. For example, Alan Thompson recognizes that Luke 20:21 uses "the way" metaphorically, like that of Acts 18:25–26; 19:9; 22:4; 24:14.[33] David Peterson suggests that Luke first identified the church as the Way so as to properly establish the church's significance before it received a title the world could misconstrue.[34] In his analysis of Acts 24:14, Eckhard Schnabel observes that the Jews understood those of the Way as a sect.[35] Not only was early Christianity at risk of being confused with Judaism, but it was also at risk of being confused with magic and other forms of popular religions.[36] The Way was at risk because of Christianity's new and radical claims alongside the disciples performing miracles.[37] Thus, by using "the Way" to refer to early believers, Luke establishes the early church as God's people, distinct from Judaism, and hence suggests that being ethnically Jewish no longer suffices. Shauf recognizes that Luke uses the designation from a historiographical perspective in Acts 19:23.[38] That is, Luke is intentional in portraying Jesus' followers and the attitudes toward them, e.g., "agitation."

---

30. Shauf, *Theology as History*, 167.

31. Peterson, *The Acts of the Apostles*, 94. The Way is both a description of the disciples and a description for following Jesus. This concept is discussed further in relation to Acts 18:5.

32. Peterson, *The Acts of the Apostles*, 635.

33. Thompson, *Luke*, 318.

34. Peterson, *The Acts of the Apostles*, 93.

35. Schnabel, *Acts*, 958.

36. Witherington III, *The Acts of the Apostles*, 397.

37. Witherington III, *The Acts of the Apostles*, 397.

38. Shauf recognizes that in Acts 9:2, Paul is against the Way, but in Acts 19:9 the response of animosity that ensues is directed at the Way, not at Paul. Also, in Acts 19:23, the riot is against the Way, despite Demetrius' specific attack on Paul, where the Way is mentioned in the introduction but left out of the body of the passage. "Hence the remark

Eckhard Schnabel attempts to capture the early church's self-understanding,[39] listing seven self-designations of the church that Luke uses besides the Way: brothers and sisters, believers, congregation, the Church of God, disciples, saints, and Nazarenes.[40] Schnabel notes that the terms congregation and Nazarenes serve a practical purpose: meaning a gathering of Jesus' followers with the origin specified to identify the correct Jesus.[41] However, Schnabel also finds that Nazarenes is the only name used by non-Christian Jews to describe Christians.[42] Therefore, the term the Way was a self-designation by Christians derived from Isaiah 40:3 and Isaiah more broadly.[43] Schnabel writes, "The followers of Jesus in Jerusalem evidently were convinced that the task of preparing the way of the Lord (Isa 40:3), proclaimed by John the Baptist (Matt 3:3; Mark 1:3; Luke 3:4; John 1:23), is complete, and they are now traveling 'the Way' of God's renewed people."[44]

David Pao makes the most substantial attempt to provide a philological answer to Luke's use of "the Way." As part of his analysis of the New Exodus, Pao examines the use of ὁδός as an identity claim in Acts.[45] He declares there is no parallel in early Christian literature prior to the book of Acts.[46] Pao helpfully outlines two ways to study way-terminology: "(1) the source and background of the term; and (2) the exact referent of and the meaning embedded in the term."[47] Scholars seeking the exact referent seek to connect the Way to Jesus, the Christian life, salvation history, and the church. Pao proposes moving past finding the Way's referent and literary function by studying its terminological function instead. He shows that way-terminology is used in polemical contexts to identify the "true" people of God.[48] Pao finds the occurrences of ὁδός in Acts, which act as identity markers, are

---

that the τάραχος is over 'the Way' is only a matter of Luke's historiographical perspective." Shauf, *Theology as History*, 291.

39. Schnabel, *Acts*, 288.
40. Schnabel, *Acts*, 288–90.
41. Schnabel, *Acts*, 288, 90.
42. Schnabel suggests that the term Nazarene "may imply the rejection of messianic claims concerning Jesus. Or it may be [a] pun on Jesus' designation as the messianic 'shoot' (nēṣer) of David (Isa 11:1; cf., 60:21)." Schnabel, *Acts*, 290.
43. Schnabel, *Acts*, 290.
44. Schnabel, *Acts*, 290.
45. Pao, *Acts and the Isaianic New Exodus*, 59.
46. Pao, *Acts and the Isaianic New Exodus*, 59.
47. Pao, *Acts and the Isaianic New Exodus*, 60.
48. Pao, *Acts and the Isaianic New Exodus*, 60.

in polemical situations between Christians and Jews.[49] He suggests the use of ὁδός in these contexts is also to be understood against the background of the Isaianic New Exodus.[50] Isaiah 40–55, and 40:3 in particular, redefines the people of God.[51] Pao finds Luke is using this redefinition of the people of God in the book of Acts.[52] He notes two supporting arguments for Luke's use of Isaiah 40:3. First, Pao argues that the Qumran literature also uses Way terminology as a referent to Isaiah 40:3 as an identity marker.[53] Second, Pao suggests that Luke's frequent use of Isaiah 40:3–5 throughout his writing confirms that Way terminology is an identity marker referencing Isaiah 40:3.[54]

Beyond Pao, many modern scholars have not committed to identifying an underlying source or function for Luke's use of the Way for early Christianity (See Table 3). Darrell Bock cites the DSS as similar descriptions, and only identifies the Way as an early name for Christians.[55] Keener writes that the Way probably reflects a genuine tradition developed by the early Christians themselves, which probably came from a Semitic context.[56] Also, Keener says, "Whereas the usual Jewish use focused on ethical wisdom and orthopraxy (albeit defined differently by various Jewish sects), the Jesus movement made obedience to Christ part of its orthopraxy."[57] Joseph Fitzmyer finds the Qumran use of the Way a plausible source for an absolute use as an early designation for Christians in Acts.[58] Scholars who note similarities to the Qumran use of the Way include James Dunn and Richard Pervo.[59] Luke Timothy Johnson notes the similarities to "Two Way

49. Pao, *Acts and the Isaianic New Exodus*, 61–65.

50. Pao, *Acts and the Isaianic New Exodus*, 66.

51. Pao, *Acts and the Isaianic New Exodus*, 66.

52. Pao, *Acts and the Isaianic New Exodus*, 66. Fox used Social Identity Theory and wrote, "My [Fox] thesis is that Luke-Acts was written primarily for the purpose of creating identity for a God-fearing audience within the New Christian Movement of the first century CE." Fox, *The Hermeneutics of Social Identity in Luke-Acts*, 232. Fox's thesis about identity may strengthen the literary function of the Way as suggested by Pao.

53. Pao, *Acts and the Isaianic New Exodus*, 66.

54. Pao, *Acts and the Isaianic New Exodus*, 67.

55. Bock, *Acts*, 356.

56. Keener, *Acts: 3:1—14:28*, 1626. Keener maintains this position in his 2020 commentary on Acts. Keener, *Acts*, 276.

57. Keener, *Acts: 3:1—14:28*, 1627.

58. Fitzmyer, *The Acts of the Apostles*, 423–24.

59. Dunn, *The Acts of the Apostles*, 90–91; Pervo, *Acts*, 241.

Theology," such as that found in the *Didache*.[60] Still others, like Parsons in the Paideia series, make no effort to identify the source.[61]

THEOLOGY OF THE WAY

A survey on the theology of the Way can be divided into three types: travel narratives, the new Moses, and the new Exodus.[62] Travel narrative discussions of the Way revolve around Luke 9:51—19:48. The new Moses and new Exodus discussions capture significant trends in understanding the Way in terms of a travel or journey topos.

Travel Narrative

Scholars have interpreted the Way as a destination motif or as the journey itself.[63] The destination may be two places: (1) The way to Jerusalem, and (2) the way to the temple. Hastings supports placing the destination of Luke's travel narrative as Jerusalem.[64] Luke 9:51—19:48 has sometimes been referred to as the "Travel Narrative."[65] Also, the travel to Jerusalem in Luke 9:51—19:48 has been compared with the earlier section of Luke where Jesus travels through the region of Galilee.[66] Both the travel narrative of Luke 9:51—19 and the itinerant ministry in Galilee of Luke 4:14—9:50 inform the reader about Jesus. Second, the temple serves as a destination in Luke's travel narrative, which Conzelmann supports.[67] Along with having a destination point, the section contains the journey motif.[68] Therefore, in his narrative, Luke uses the metaphor of the way to teach about Jesus.

---

60. Johnson, *The Acts of the Apostles*, 162.
61. Parsons, *Acts*, 4, 23, 162–63.
62. Litke notes that the concept of journey, which includes דֶּרֶךְ and ὁδός, in Scripture is used both figuratively and literally. Litke, "Journey."
63. Keener finds it was once proposed that Acts was of the travel story genre (see Knox, *Acts*, 55). This understanding was dismissed for two reasons: travel is only a portion of Acts and the genre of travel stories can be fictitious. Keener, *Acts: 1:1—2:47*, 53.
64. Hastings, *Prophet and Witness in Jerusalem*, 120.
65. Bock, *Luke: Volume 2*, 957.
66. Green, *The Gospel of Luke*, 394.
67. Conzelmann, *The Theology of St. Luke*, 76.
68. du Plessis, "Reading Luke 12:35-48 as Part of the Travel Narrative."

Baban's contribution to understanding the way motif builds upon the journey motif and travel narrative in Luke-Acts through his understanding of Luke's use of mimesis. Because mimesis is ingrained in Hellenistic storytelling, readers should expect it in the NT. In Luke-Acts, two types of mimesis are present: (1) Mimesis of content, such as Luke's use of the LXX, and (2) mimesis of form or composition, such as the representation of events.[69] Of primary interest are the post-Easter events of the Ethiopian's evangelization (Emmaus account) and Paul's conversion (Saul's encounter).

Baban writes:

> Luke's literary paradigm for his post-Easter encounters provides a special place for the hodos symbolism (the "way" as a setting and as major reference in the final lines of the story), includes a journey encounter that plays a special narrative and theological role of transition, and builts [sic] the story plot according to the mimetic requirements presented in Aristotle's *Poetics* and in other literary treaties.[70]

A brief summation of Baban's furthering of the travel narrative and journey motif recognizes the post-Easter events above as narrative and theological markers for the reader. The two events create a fuller journey motif and narrative, which extends beyond the traditional travel narrative set within Luke-Acts. The two post-Easter stories bring narrative coherence, because "their main action is an important encounter set 'on the road,' leading to restoration, to a personalized, positive reversal of destiny."[71] Baban primarily sees a connection between Luke-Acts and Isaiah, and does not consider the possibility of Proverbs. He claims there is an ethical component to Luke's journey stories, since the characters are restored through their interactions with the Lord.[72] However, the travel narrative is only part of the material in Luke-Acts that connects to the Way.

New Moses

Bovon notes that an understanding of Jesus as a *topos* for Moses emerged in the 1950s, when E. L. Allen attempted to identify Christ as the new

---

69. Baban, *On the Road Encounters*, 73–74.
70. Baban, *On the Road Encounters*, 274.
71. Baban, *On the Road Encounters*, 274.
72. Baban, *On the Road Encounters*, 249.

Moses, the Prophet and perhaps the Servant.[73] Though not fully convincing, Allen's work starts to form typological connections that do seem to be present.[74] Jindřich Mánek then developed the connection between Moses and Jesus, as seen through the new Exodus.[75] Bovon writes that Johannes Bihler continued in this field by following the work of Mánek, concluding that although Moses and Jesus have clear typological connections, "the typology is in keeping with the theology of promise."[76] In support of the notion of Jesus as *topos* for Moses, Mark Strauss writes, "When Jesus reaches Jerusalem (the culmination of his 'new exodus' according to Evans, Moessner, et al.), he enters the city not primarily as a Mosaic but as a royal-Davidic figure."[77] Strauss provides a synthesis of Jesus as both Mosaic and Davidic figure: "Empowered by the Spirit, he defeats the forces of sin and Satan and leads God's people in an eschatological new exodus." Strauss bases his conclusion upon Luke's use of the Prophets and the Pentateuch.[78]

New Exodus

Writing after Strauss, Pao seeks to demonstrate that the Isaianic New Exodus is the primary hermeneutical framework for Acts.[79] He finds that Strauss limits the role of Isaiah in Acts because Strauss is preoccupied with Christology.[80] For his part, Pao understands the Isaianic New Exodus as the controlling theme in Acts, which Luke incorporates as "four recurring themes introduced in the Isaianic prologue of Isa 40:1–11: the restoration of Israel, the power of the word of God, the anti-idol polemic, and the concern for the nations."[81] Pao finds evidence for this claim through Isaianic citations, the Isaianic influence on Luke's narrative framework, and broad

---

73. Bovon, *Luke the Theologian*, 91.

74. Bovon, *Luke the Theologian*, 92.

75. Bovon, *Luke the Theologian*, 92. See Jindřich, "The New Exodus in the Books of Luke," 8–23.

76. Bovon, *Luke the Theologian*, 93. Bovon references Bihler, *Die Stephanusgeschichte im Zusammenhang der Apostelgeschichte*, 1963.

77. Strauss, *The Davidic Messiah in Luke-Acts*, 284.

78. Strauss, *The Davidic Messiah in Luke-Acts*, 284.

79. Pao, *Acts and the Isaianic New Exodus*, 10.

80. Pao, *Acts and the Isaianic New Exodus*, 12.

81. Pao, *Acts and the Isaianic New Exodus*, 13.

Isaianic themes that Acts develops.[82] One of Pao's complaints about previous research is that the designation of early Christians as "the Way" is cast aside as unrelated to Luke's use of the travel narrative.[83] Pao reconciles the people of the Way with Luke's use of the Isaianic New Exodus through the early Christian community, as restoring Israel's people.[84] He writes, "The focus on the Gentiles is therefore one of the most significant ways in which the Isaianic New Exodus has been transformed in Acts; and this transformation points to a rather different era in the history of salvation."[85]

In his section of the *Commentary on the New Testament Use of the Old Testament*, Marshall supports the research put forth by Pao by including the Isaianic New Exodus as an overarching biblical pattern in Acts.[86] Marshall cites Pao's research to indicate numerous uses of the Way in Acts, including Acts 9:2.[87] Despite first looking to Isaiah 40:3–4 as a referent for Acts 9:2, Marshall notes that Isaiah is referencing a way of travelling and not a way of life.[88] For other possible OT referents from Acts 9:2, Marshall proposes Proverbs.[89] For his analysis of use of the OT in Acts, Marshall incorporates multiple tools, including Pao's work, inner-biblical references, and intertextual research conducted by Hays and Wall.[90] This allows him to break from the effort to find a single unifying referent, which is what Pao seeks to do.

CONCLUSION

Two categories arise from the review of literature on the Way: (1) the people of the Way and (2) the theology of the Way. Concerning the people of the Way, the literature review reveals that scholars focus on two aspects: the source or background of the Way, and the precise referent or meaning of

---

82. Pao, *Acts and the Isaianic New Exodus*, 18.
83. Pao, *Acts and the Isaianic New Exodus*, 2.
84. Pao, *Acts and the Isaianic New Exodus*, 143.
85. Pao, *Acts and the Isaianic New Exodus*, 245.
86. Marshall, "Acts," 525.
87. Marshall, "Acts," 575.
88. Marshall, "Acts," 575.
89. Marshall, "Acts," 576. Marshall mentions other passages discuss the Way or ways of the Lord (e.g., 2 Sam 22:22; Ps 18:21; 138:5; Prov 10:29; Jer 5:4–5; Hos 14:9.)
90. Marshall, "Acts," 526. See, Wall, "Intertextuality, Biblical," 541–51.

the term.⁹¹ The Qumran texts, which reference Isaiah, are often thought to be the source or background of the Way, along with the "two-way" tradition, such as the *Didache*.⁹² Jesus, the church, and the Christian life are often thought of as referents. Schnabel and Pao provide some variation in the two main categories, however. Schnabel examines the Way alongside other self-designations of the early church but ultimately ends searching for the source or background.⁹³ Pao suggests looking for a literary function of the Way, which he concludes is a polemical term identifying the "true" people of God.⁹⁴

Those exploring the theology of the Way examine Luke's use of the Way beyond its function as a designation for Christians. The three major ways the Way may operate in Acts are as part of a travel narrative, as a topos (new Moses or new Exodus), or as a designation for Christians. This chapter has shown that some scholars incorporate Luke's use of the term as a name for Christians within a theology of the Way. By contrast, others handle the Christian designation separately from a theology of the Way. The following chapter begins to examine a possible alternative referent and function of the Way by outlining use of the term in the book of Proverbs.

---

91. Pao, *Acts and the Isaianic New Exodus*, 60.

92. Pao, *Acts and the Isaianic New Exodus*, 60.

93. Schnabel, *Acts*, 288–90.

94. Pao, *Acts and the Isaianic New Exodus*, 60. A brief note concerning the Jewish-Christian divide (A point where a formal distinction exists near the resurrection) or parting of ways (A division that occurred gradually over tens or hundreds of years). Boyarin discusses a continuum of options that ranges from the Jewish people rejecting Jesus as God and a messiah to Christians rejecting a Jewish heritage, containing many degrees between the two polls. Boyarin, *Dying for God*, 8. Jackson-McCabe writes, "The central question from this [socially constructed identity] perspective is neither the similarities and differences in culture nor even the social interaction among ancient Christians and Jews, but how early Jesus groups imagined themselves and their characteristic cultures in relation to Judeans and theirs" (144). Further Jackson-McCabe suggests that a Christian identity should not be treated "as the functional equivalent of belief in Jesus in practice" (142). Jackson-McCabe, *Jewish Christianity*, 142, 144. The current study does not require identifying functional differences between Jews and first-century Jesus followers, but this writing does find that the first-century cultures (Jewish, Jesus followers, and Pagans) knew their identities and could distinguish themselves from one another.

3

An Analysis of "the Way" in the Book of Proverbs

INTRODUCTION

PREVIOUS CHAPTERS IDENTIFIED A lacuna in research into the use of "the Way" to describe Christians in Acts. This chapter puts forth the book of Proverbs as a possible referent for the theological and literary function of "the way," later to be compared with its use in Acts.[1] As part of this analysis, key terms relating to "the way" are presented (e.g., cognate words and descriptions of "the way").

The analysis has five steps. First, the themes of the book of Proverbs are discussed in order to identify literary motifs. Second, a brief scholarly review reveals how "the way" in Proverbs has been understood. Third, an overview of the theology of "the way" situates its specific usage in Proverbs. Fourth, this theology is traced through selected passages, revealing how the term functions in these passages and how it supports the themes of the book of Proverbs. Step five then combines Freedman's method and the theological analysis of step four to determine if "the way" is a motif within Proverbs.

---

1. In this chapter "the way" is uncapitalized, as it does not refer to a people group. Also, as previously noted, Proverbs uses "the way" and "the path" interchangeably, however this chapter will predominantly use "the way" for uniformity and clarity. Nevertheless, in translations, quotations, and selected areas where differentiation is needed, "the path" will be used instead.

THE THEMES OF PROVERBS

The overall themes of Proverbs must first be determined in order to understand the theological and literary use of "the way" in this book. As stated in chapter 2, literary motifs need a controlling theme. Narrowing Proverbs down to a single theme or a few key themes is difficult, but two stand out:[2] First, God reveals wisdom to His people,[3] and second, the Lord's wisdom builds His relationship with His people.[4] Thus, God reveals His wisdom in Proverbs to teach His people and establish, or reinforce, relationship with them.

First, God is the source of wisdom. Supporting this claim, Ryan O'Dowd writes that Proverbs presents wisdom as something revealed by God to His people.[5] Affirming and restating the claim, Schwab writes that "wisdom is not gained through observation!"[6] Thus, God divulges wisdom to His people.

Second, Proverbs is written to build the inter-personal relationship between God and His people. O'Dowd notes that the entry point to wisdom is "the fear of the Lord."[7] Having the fear of the Lord as the beginning of wisdom suggests a relationship between God and people.[8] Some scholars (e.g., Michael Fox) disagree that Proverbs and its wisdom are specifically aimed at God's people, however, and suggest instead that Proverbs is "clearly a secular work."[9] Yet, as Bruce Waltke rightly notes, Fox's view cannot

---

2. Balentine writes, "Because of its anthological character, scholars generally concede that Proverbs lacks any overarching thematic coherence" (508). He discusses the saying, "the fear of the Lord is the beginning of knowledge" along with the theology of God that is presented in Proverbs. Balentine, "Proverbs," 508–11. Longman points to a theological category of "woman wisdom," suggesting that Lady Wisdom represents God and God's wisdom. Longman, "Book of Proverbs 1," 531–52.

3. Schwab suggests wisdom and creation as two themes in Proverbs. Schwab, "The Book of Proverbs," 463.

4. Longman, "Book of Proverbs 1," 549. Longman suggests "the fear of the Lord" is a theology of wisdom that "characterizes wisdom as a relationship."

5. O'Dowd, *Proverbs*, 33.

6. Schwab, "The Book of Proverbs," 464. Nicholls refers to Proverbs' wisdom as "heavenly wisdom," and adds that "there is no true wisdom without godliness." Nicholls, *The Book of Proverbs*, 5–6.

7. O'Dowd, *Proverbs*, 33.

8. Longman, "Book of Proverbs 1," 549.

9. Fox, *Proverbs 1–9*, 7.

be reconciled with the anchoring of Proverbs in "the fear of the Lord."[10] Allen Ross suggests the teachings "apply to human problems in general, not primarily to the problems of the religious community," and that their purpose is to "inspire faith in the Lord."[11] God may still be the source of knowledge in this view, but the wisdom is not specifically aimed at God's people. However, because wisdom begins with the "fear of the Lord" and living in wisdom bears the fruit of faith in God, it is more likely that Proverbs and God's wisdom was specifically aimed at His people or those soon to be His people.

The message that God is the giver of wisdom who builds a right relationship with His people can be observed in practical wisdom or behavior. R. B. Y. Scott writes that in Hebrew wisdom, religious and ethical elements are more important than intellectual knowledge.[12] God's people observe wisdom by making wise choices and meeting the ethical demands of the covenant with God.[13] Scott adds that in Proverbs wise living is not conducted under one's own power, but is accomplished as the gift of God.[14] Thus, God not only gives wisdom to His people, but sustains or empowers them to obtain and walk in wisdom.

In the early nineteenth century, George Berry captured the themes of Proverbs as follows:

> The purpose thus stated is to teach wisdom to men, especially to the young and inexperienced, but also to those who have already some knowledge of wisdom. This is intended not only for their intellectual equipment, but for their practical guidance as well; the purpose of the book is distinctly practical. The conception of wisdom, or knowledge, as found in the book is a comprehensive one. It is this conception which gives unity to the teachings. Wisdom is a general term for all that is desirable in character, folly for all that is undesirable. Wisdom consists fundamentally in a right

---

10. Waltke, *The Book of Proverbs: Chapters 1–15*, 51.

11. Ross, "Proverbs," 30.

12. Scott, *Proverbs Ecclesiastes*, 23. Errington writes, "ethics is placed *alongside* practice" (italics in the original). He continues, "Christian ethics serves that maturity to which 'solid food' rightly belongs, which consists in a practiced ability to discern good from evil—to discern the ways of wisdom." Errington, *Every Good Path*, 226.

13. Scott, *Proverbs Ecclesiastes*, 23.

14. Scott, *Proverbs Ecclesiastes*, 23.

relation to God; the life in accordance with wisdom is one that follows God's plan.¹⁵

The importance of the themes, "Wisdom comes from God," and "Wisdom builds the relationship between God and His people," is twofold: (1) These themes help identify motifs, and (2) the themes may be compared to theological conclusions in Proverbs. For "the way" to be a motif, it must support the themes of Proverbs. In addition, the theology of "the way" should also support the themes of Proverbs.

"THE WAY" IN PROVERBS

The word "way" is used throughout Proverbs as a metaphor for the life of believers.¹⁶ Tremper Longman suggests the imagery of the way is central to the first nine chapters, although is not exclusive to those chapters.¹⁷ In Proverbs 1–9 there are thirty-nine direct references to the way,¹⁸ and an additional fifteen in Proverbs 10–31.¹⁹ Many scholars acknowledge the significance of the term in Proverbs.²⁰ However, not all scholars discuss "the way" as a literary feature as Stuart Weeks does.²¹ Bernd Schipper describes

---

15. Berry, *The Book of Proverbs*, xii–xiii.

16. Again, the terms "the way" (דֶרֶךְ) and "the path" (אֹרַח) are used interchangeably. Heim states that the way and path are a common word-pair. Knut Martin Heim, *Like Grapes of Gold Set in Silver: An Interpretation of Proverbial Clusters in Proverbs 10:1—22:16, Beihefte Zur Zeitschrift FüR Die Alttestamentliche Wissenschaft* (Berlin: De Gruyter, 2001), 197, n.77.

17. Longman, *Proverbs*, 35–36.

18. דֶרֶךְ—Prov 1:15, 31; 2:8, 12–13, 20; 3:6, 17, 23, 31; 4:11, 14, 19, 26; 5:8, 21; 6:6, 23; 7:8, 19, 25, 27; 8:2, 13, 22, 32; 9:6, 15; אֹרַח—Prov 2:8, 13, 15, 19–20; 3:6; 4:14, 18; 5:6; 8:20; 9:15.

19. דֶרֶךְ—Prov 10:9, 29; 11:5, 20; 12:15, 26, 28; 13:6, 15; 14:2, 8, 12, 14; 15:9, 19; 16:2, 7, 9, 17, 25, 29, 31; 19:3, 16; 20:24; 21:2, 8, 16, 29; 22:5–6; 23:19, 26; 26:13; 28:6, 10, 18; 29:27; 30:19–20; 31:3; אֹרַח—Prov 10:17; 12:28; 15:10, 19, 24; 17:23; 22:25.

20. O'Dowd, *Proverbs*, 240. O'Dowd discusses "the way" as a theme in an analysis of Proverbs 15:18–23. Clifford, *Proverbs*, 19–21. Clifford describes "the two ways" as a "distinctive idea" of Proverbs (19). The author uses "the way" as a metaphor to express the consequences of behavior (21).

21. Weeks, *Instruction and Imagery in Proverbs 1–9*, 73. Weeks is one scholar who considers the path as a motif. Waltke, *The Book of Proverbs: Chapters 1–15*, 591. Waltke mentions a "journey motif" when discussing Proverbs 14:12, but does not present a list or section dedicated to Proverbs' themes and motifs.

"the way" as Proverbs' terminology for the wise and foolish.[22] He continues that "the way" is meant to denote the person who chooses to either follow the way of wisdom or reject it. Schipper refers to several themes throughout his commentary, including "life and the way of insight," but he does not discuss overarching themes and motifs.[23] This author suggests "the way" is a motif, not because it is the focal point of Proverbs, but because it supports the main themes.[24] Steps four and five will provide independent support for proposing the way as a motif when its theological use is analyzed, and Freedman's method for identifying a motif is applied to Proverbs.[25]

THEOLOGY OF "THE WAY" IN PROVERBS

The theology of "the way" provides a framework for the reader for working through Proverbs.[26] The symbolism of the way in Proverbs confronts the reader in chapter one. However, Weeks identifies Proverbs 4:10–27 as having the most unambiguous expression of the path motif.[27] A theological review will show "the way" has four major characteristics: (1) it is created by the Lord, (2) it is for His people, (3) God sustains His people on the way, and (4) the way leads to life. As such, the reader should expect that the way will function in support of the key themes highlighted above.

Weeks provides a clear summary of the path imagery in Proverbs:

> Although the imagery pervades other material, the key passages can be identified quite straightforwardly. In chapter 1, the son is warned against "walking in the way" with the sinners, and admonished to keep his foot back from their path (1:15). In chapter 2,

---

22. Schipper, *Proverbs 1–15*, 25.

23. Schipper, *Proverbs 1–15*, 57. In addition, Schipper references "the theme of praising the ways of wisdom" (57), "the theme of the path of life" (74), and "the theme of the two ways" (74).

24. Longman notes imagery of the path is central to Proverbs 1–9 and is found throughout the book. Longman, *Proverbs*, 35–36. Weeks calls the path a motif. Weeks, *Instruction and Imagery in Proverbs 1–9*, 73. Waltke mentions a "journey motif" when discussing Proverbs 14:12, where "journey" appears to align with "the way." Waltke, *The Book of Proverbs: Chapters 1–15*, 591.

25. Freedman, "The Literary Motif."

26. When working through Proverbs, the reader may find it helpful to have an overview provided by a review of scholarship on the theology of "the way." The reader will notice not every passage features every component of the way.

27. Weeks, *Instruction and Imagery in Proverbs 1–9*, 73.

The True Identity of the People of the Way

God is presented as a protector of those who walk on "paths of justice," (2:8) while acceptance of instruction will protect from those who have abandoned straight paths for crooked ones (2:13, 15, cf. 19) and enable understanding of "every good path," so that the son will ultimately "walk on the way of the good and keep to the paths of the righteous" (2:9, 20). In chapter 3, acknowledgment of God will straighten the son's paths (3:6), wisdom's paths are pleasant and peaceful (3:17), and keeping wisdom will enable the son to walk safely without stumbling (3:23, 26). These ideas are brought together in chapter 4, where the father claims to have taught the "way of wisdom" and to have led his son in "straight paths," promising him that he will be able to walk without obstruction and admonishing him to avoid the path of the wicked. In 4:18–19, the paths of righteous and wicked are described and contrasted in terms of light and darkness, and the chapter finishes with an appeal for the son to walk with his eyes straight ahead, never swerving from his path.

The presentation of the path imagery in chapter 4 is the fullest expression of the motif, and the work thereafter shifts its focus to the foreign woman and to Wisdom. The initial description of the woman includes the fact, though, that she has in some way left the path of life, and is wandering down to Sheol without knowing it (5:5–6), while 5:21 famously observes that "a man's ways are before the eyes of YHWH," and 6:22–3 promises that instruction will lead the son as he walks, and in some sense be the "way of life."[28]

Weeks' summary mentions that God protects those on the path, that wisdom's way is desirable, that the son is the one on the path, and that the father encourages the son to remain so. Following his summary, Weeks writes that it is difficult to escape the importance of the way imagery, and Proverbs' use of this imagery has deeper implications than modern English use might suggest.[29] Therefore, modern readers need to make a closer examination of the imagery of the way.

The imagery has both literal and mystical or cosmic meanings attached.[30] Lady Wisdom and Dame Folly are personifications of wisdom and foolishness.[31] Proverbs portrays Lady Wisdom and Dame Folly as calling the youth down two separate paths that lead either to one or other

---

28. Weeks, *Instruction and Imagery in Proverbs 1–9*, 73–74.
29. Weeks, *Instruction and Imagery in Proverbs 1–9*, 74.
30. Bartholomew and O'Dowd, *Old Testament Wisdom Literature*, 84.
31. Perdue, *The Sword and the Stylus*, 91.

of their houses.³² A "Two-Ways" theology often captures the metaphor of the way.³³ Ernest Lucas writes, "In Proverbs 4:1–19 the 'way of wisdom' is paralleled with 'the paths of uprightness' (Prov 4:11) and is contrasted with 'the path of the wicked' and 'the way of evil men' (Prov 4:14) . . . The didactic intention of the symbolism is to set out clearly the differences between wise/foolish and righteous/wicked behavior and the consequences of each."³⁴ In ANE literature, the house metaphor describes the direction and quality of one's life.³⁵ One's life can lead to Lady Wisdom's house of life and understanding or Dame Folly's home, which is filled with death and destruction (Prov 2:7; 3:7; 5:4; 7:26).

N. C. Habel suggests "the way" functions as a baseline or nuclear symbol.³⁶ He writes, "It is our contention that among the various primary 'spontaneous' symbolic expressions in the wisdom materials of Proverbs 1–9, *derek*, 'the route,' 'the way,' 'the road,' is the basic or nuclear expression."³⁷ Similarly, Fox labels path imagery a "ground" metaphor.³⁸ Raymond van Leeuwen suggests the "nuclear symbols" proposed by Habel are characteristic of a Jewish worldview.³⁹ Also, he finds that the way and the two women (Lady Wisdom and Dame Folly) are part of a greater metaphor of liminality,⁴⁰ incorporating the imagery of water as a contributing metaphor.⁴¹ He writes, "In Proverbs 1–9, Wisdom offers love within limits, freedom within form, life within law. It is within the bounds of cosmic order

---

32. Bartholomew and O'Dowd, *Old Testament Wisdom Literature*, 84.

33. Lucas presents the "ideas of the two ways" as one with "the way" symbol (907). Nevertheless, the "Two Ways" highlights the dichotomy presented in "the way" symbol (907). Lucas, "Wisdom Theology," 901–12. When speaking of the "Two Ways," Habel highlights "three major polarities: the two ways, the two hearts, and the two female companions; the 'two ways' polarity, however, remains primary and seems to inform the imagery and language of the other binary contrasts" (135). Habel, "The Symbolism of Wisdom in Proverbs 1–9," 135.

34. Lucas, "Wisdom Theology," 907.

35. Bartholomew and O'Dowd, *Old Testament Wisdom Literature*, 84.

36. Habel, "The Symbolism of Wisdom in Proverbs 1–9."

37. Habel, "The Symbolism of Wisdom in Proverbs 1–9," 133; italics in the original.

38. Fox, *Proverbs 1–9*, 129.

39. Van Leeuwen, "Liminality and Worldview in Proverbs 1–9," 113.

40. Van Leeuwen, "Liminality and Worldview in Proverbs 1–9," 111.

41. Van Leeuwen suggests that the waters being restrained by God represent a cosmic ordering (124). Leeuwen, "Liminality and Worldview in Proverbs 1–9," 123–24.

that human freedom and fellowship are nurtured."[42] Van Leeuwen rightly connects the way and the women in Proverbs to an overarching metaphor, yet his reduction of these metaphors to "liminality" flattens them and reduces the teachings held within them. What Van Leeuwen calls "liminality," "freedom within form," "life within law," or God's cosmic boundaries, this paper classifies as living in right relationship to God.[43] Thus, the way is a nuclear symbol, and further expressions (e.g., the women) refer to the way.

As a nuclear expression (i.e., a foundational literary image), there are also satellite symbols used for the way.[44] The "two ways" are also indicated by the lighting and construction of the paths. Hence the way to Lady Wisdom's home has light shining down onto it, and is straight. The way to Dame Folly's house is crooked and shrouded in darkness. Likewise, Proverbs describes the different paths as righteous or evil and similarly presents a dichotomy between the persons who travel these paths.

The wise and foolish connect to the nuclear imagery of the path. The one taking the right path is wise, and the one taking the wrong path is foolish.[45] Further, because wisdom only comes from God, the wise person is righteous and is in a relationship with God.[46] Sun Lyu finds that the righteous and the wise are "co-referential and functionally equivalent."[47] Likewise, Waltke states that "wisdom" and "righteousness" are correlative terms that function like synonyms since they reference the same person.[48] Nevertheless, the two words are not proper synonyms, because they have different "semantic domains."[49] Proverbs patterns "wise/wisdom and righteous/righteousness" and contrasts these pairings with "their antonyms, fool/folly and wicked/wickedness."[50] The wise and the foolish are sometimes considered part of an act-consequence or character-consequence motif.[51]

---

42. Van Leeuwen, "Liminality and Worldview in Proverbs 1–9," 132.

43. Van Leeuwen mentions life within the Law. This author finds it fitting that Proverbs is teaching the Law or how to make a covenant with God. Van Leeuwen, "Liminality and Worldview in Proverbs 1–9," 117.

44. Habel, "The Symbolism of Wisdom in Proverbs 1–9," 133.

45. Longman, *Proverbs*, 56.

46. Longman, *Proverbs*, 57.

47. Lyu, *Righteousness in the Book of Proverbs*, 201.

48. Waltke, "Biblical Studies," 233.

49. Waltke, "Biblical Studies," 233.

50. Waltke, "Biblical Studies," 234.

51. Bartholomew and O'Dowd, *Old Testament Wisdom Literature*, 273.

Generally, these consequence motifs link actions to specific outcomes.[52] Bartholomew and O'Dowd prefer character-consequence, because the consequences are associated more closely with living than to individual actions.[53] This study recognizes the correlation between the characters and consequences, but considers "the way" to be the nuclear image that incorporates the consequences as satellite images.[54] This can be seen from the outcomes associated with the opposite destinations of the righteous and the wicked ways.

The righteous are likely to be protected and rewarded.[55] Proverbs evaluates the didactic choices with varying degrees of severity, and the consequences continue and become more serious as the wise or the foolish travel forward. Thus, the wise continue to gain knowledge and depart from evil (Prov 13:20; 1:5; 29:9).[56] The outcome is a completed journey whose endpoint is the home of either Lady Wisdom or Dame Folly, life or death respectively. God calls the righteous to walk in integrity and to be blameless (Prov 20:7). To be blameless, one has complete integrity, and the righteous walks in the previously completed actions of the Lord, the actions taken to make man righteous. Understanding that God produces righteousness, the newly righteous man should humbly commit his life in a consistent way that represents a total commitment to the Lord.[57] Although placed in opposition, the foolish person is not always declared evil or beyond help. Proverbs uses eight different words to describe the foolish person, and each name is associated with differing degrees of being against or far from God.[58]

The straight path suggests ease, because it is wide and free of obstruction.[59] It does not have an opening to draw the traveler aside and assumes they are not going aside of their own volition.[60] The crooked path is more devious than the translation of the English Standard Version suggests. Derek

---

52. Longman, "Book of Proverbs 1," 544.

53. Bartholomew and O'Dowd, *Old Testament Wisdom Literature*, 271, fn.22. Waltke uses "character-consequence" as well. Waltke, *The Book of Proverbs: Chapters 1–15*, 74.

54. The character-consequence motif may be subordinate to "the way" motif, and its scope (e.g., specific consequences) may include material not associated with imagery or literary devices.

55. Bartholomew and O'Dowd, *Old Testament Wisdom Literature*, 270–71.

56. Waltke, *The Book of Proverbs: Chapters 1–15*, 94.

57. Waltke, *The Book of Proverbs: Chapters 1–15*, 99.

58. Crenshaw, *Old Testament Wisdom*, 73–74.

59. Habel, "The Symbolism of Wisdom in Proverbs 1–9," 136.

60. Habel, "The Symbolism of Wisdom in Proverbs 1–9," 136.

Kidner describes the crooked path as twisted: "Various synonyms for what is 'twisted' occur throughout the book... Probably both of the main implications of the idea are to be understood: i.e., devious(ness) and *perverse*."[61] The crooked path itself is wicked, and it mimics a hard heart.[62] Moreover, a crooked path perverts truth and can imply ill-gotten gains.[63] Lucas writes about the advice of taking the straight path; "The effects of a 'perverted heart' can be avoided by taking to heart-wise teaching (Prov 6:20–22)."[64]

A brief discussion about the afterlife in Proverbs can assist in identifying allusions and motifs from OT texts in the NT. Choosing a path has consequences that lead to life or death. However, descriptions of the paths themselves do not include detail of the after-death consequences. Readers may see early indicators of a concept of an afterlife, such as the pit (Prov 1:12), which may suggest a different destination for evil people.[65] Nevertheless, there is a clear distinction between Sheol and the modern concept of the afterlife. In the early 1900s, scholars addressed the question of the afterlife, and concluded it was "highly improbable that the writers of *Proverbs* were themselves conscious of anything of the kind."[66] Rewards and punishments were expected during the lives of the righteous and the wicked.[67] Julius Greenstone finds some passages may refer to "life after death (11:7; 14:32; 15:24)" but they "are inconclusive and of doubtful meaning."[68] In brief, the concept of a spiritual or resurrected life and death is absent from Proverbs.

It is also necessary to study the word *wisdom* and its cognates, because the beginning of wisdom is the "fear of the Lord."[69] Von Rad writes, in "historical decrees and historical guidance, too, 'the fear of Yahweh' was the unalterable presupposition for knowledge."[70] The fear of the Lord also influences the metaphor of the way. John Kitchen writes how חָכְמָה in Proverbs

---

61. Kidner, *Proverbs*, 60–61; italics in the original.
62. Longman, *Proverbs*, 123. This relates to the verb, הפך, which means to "turn against."
63. Bock, *Acts*, 446.
64. Lucas, "Wisdom Theology," 907.
65. Oesterley, *The Book of Proverbs*, lxv.
66. Oesterley, *The Book of Proverbs*, lxvi; Greenstone, *The Holy Scriptures*, xxxiii.
67. Greenstone, *The Holy Scriptures*, xxxiii.
68. Greenstone, *The Holy Scriptures*, xxxiii.
69. Kitchen writes that חָכְמָה rests on the foundation of 'the Fear of the Lord.' Kitchen, *Proverbs*, 728.
70. Von Rad, *Wisdom in Israel*, 295.

focuses on the relationship between God and man.⁷¹ Alongside "wisdom" and "knowledge," Fox identifies six words in their (wisdom and knowledge) semantic field: (1) תּוּשִׁיָּה (5), מְזִמָּה (4), עָרְמָה (3), תְּבוּנָה (2), בִּינָה, and (6) עשׂה.⁷² Fox prepares lexical meanings for each word, but moreover, his list provides additional keywords for identifying allusions and motifs alongside the way for this present study.⁷³ Scott lists some of the high frequency vocabulary characteristics of the wisdom books: fool, evil/wickedness, truly, path, happy/fortunate, understand/understanding, brutish/stupid, know/knowledge, way, breath/emptiness, pay attention, inform, sinner, hasten, be wise/wise/wisdom, godless, pleasure, investigate/investigation, be silent, think, fear (of YHWH), lazy, righteous, wicked, dispute/accusation, desire, grasp, mock, and teach.⁷⁴

From an overview of the theology of the way, and its literary role in the book of Proverbs, the reader is ready to examine the concept more closely. Provided below is an analysis of selected passages that contain "the path" (דרך or אֹרַח) or imagery associated with the path.⁷⁵ This study will demonstrate an overarching image of God creating the way, as the maker of the way for His people, of sustaining His people on the way, and as the destination of the way as life.⁷⁶

---

71. Kitchen, *Proverbs*, 728.

72. Fox, "Words for Wisdom," 165.

73. Fox's list: (1) בִּינָה: "is the conceptual, interpretive activity of thought; its domain is meaning and it aims at perception and comprehension." (2) תְּבוּנָה: "designates the pragmatic, applied aspect of thought; its domain is action and it aims at efficacy and accomplishment. (3) עָרְמָה: "is the talent for devising and using adroit and wily tactics in the attaining of one's goals, whatever these may be. (4) מְזִמָּה: "is private, unrevealed thinking and the faculty for it." (5) תּוּשִׁיָּה: "is essentially deliberation—the activity, the faculty, and its products (the notion of advice is contextually determined)." (6) עשׂה: "denotes clear, proficient thinking in the exercise of power and practical operations, as distinct from thinking as an intellectual act." Fox, "Words for Wisdom," 165.

74. Scott, *The Way of Wisdom in the Old Testament*, 121–22.

75. Imagery here refers to key words and images that give a broad overview drawing attention to how the passage presents the path and its satellite images (e.g., walking, darkness, and righteous and foolish characters). This overview will not detail every individual word or image.

76. In his analysis of *halak* (walk) in Proverbs, Steinmann writes that Proverbs 3:21–35 connects the walk of the righteous one as "enabled, guided, directed, and protected by God himself." Steinmann and Eschelbach, "Walk This Way," 51.

"THE WAY" OF PROVERBS 1–9

The analysis of passages containing the path (דרך or אֹרַח), or imagery associated with the path, is divided into two main sections: Proverbs 1–9 and Proverbs 10–29. Proverbs 1–9 contains the "First Solomonic Collection," which has within it the personification of Lady Wisdom and her rival, Dame Folly. The first section of Proverbs identifies God's people as those who follow the way of wisdom, God as the creator of the way of wisdom, and God as the one who empowers the follower of wisdom on the way.

Longman writes that Proverbs 1–9 uses "the way" as a metaphor, culminating in chapter 9.[77] He suggests that the imagery is of people walking on one of two paths, straight or crooked.[78] Further, Longman writes that the path is a synonym for a person's life, and someone walking on a crooked path experiences danger and traps, which lead to death.[79] Alternately, the straight path is the right path and leads to life.[80]

Arthur Keefer suggests that Proverbs 1–9 is an interpretive guide to Proverbs 10–31.[81] Keefer's suggestion brings unity to the way as it is portrayed throughout the book. He also suggests that Proverbs 10–29 may serve to expound upon Proverbs 1–9.[82] Keefer indicates that the interpretation of Proverbs is unidirectional, where Proverbs 1–9 serves as an introduction to Proverbs 10–29, yet he also proposes interpretive reciprocity between Proverbs 1–9 and Proverbs 10–29.[83] In brief, Proverbs is designed to be read in chapter order, with the beginning chapters helping with understanding of the later chapters, and the later chapters providing clarity or elaboration on the early ones. Thus, this study will use both sections, Proverbs 1–9 and 10–29, to provide a comprehensive picture of the way. Following the passages containing the path (דרך or אֹרַח) in Proverbs 1–9, path passages from Proverbs 10–29 will be examined, and the chapter will conclude by synthesizing what Proverbs says about the way overall. Keefer proposes a system of interpretation that enables Proverbs 10–31 to assist in the understanding of

---

77. Longman, *Proverbs*, 59.
78. Longman, *Proverbs*, 59.
79. Longman, *Proverbs*, 60.
80. Longman, *Proverbs*, 60.
81. Arthur Jan Keefer, *Proverbs 1–9 as an Introduction to the Book of Proverbs*, vol. 701, Library of Hebrew Bible/Old Testament Studies, ed. Claudia V. Camp and Andrew Mein (New York: T&T Clark, 2020), 3.
82. Keefer, *Proverbs 1–9 as an Introduction to the Book of Proverbs*, 33.
83. Keefer, *Proverbs 1–9 as an Introduction to the Book of Proverbs*, 33.

Proverbs 1–9; however, Proverbs is a single literary unit, which allows every occurrence to inform the understanding of "the way."

Proverbs 1:7

In Proverbs 1:7, four main points arise. First, God's people are introduced as those who travel "the path." Second, "the fear of the Lord" is shown as the beginning of the way. Third, "the fear of the Lord" can be recognized as the phrase most closely associated with Proverbs for the study of Acts. Four, the theology of "the way" will be shown to support the main themes of Proverbs. In addition to these four points, the analysis sets the foundation for an analysis of the way as a motif in section four of this chapter.

In this verse, while "the fear of the Lord" does not refer directly to the path, the expression allows the reader to understand the relationship between God and man better. Also, because "the way" in Proverbs is associated with traveling or a journey, it is logical to associate "the fear of the Lord," with the start of the journey. Proverbs 1:7 says a person would be a fool not to fear the Lord. It also states that a person who rejects the Lord will be led away from knowledge, wisdom, and instruction. Longman writes, "the fear of the Lord inevitably leads to obedience."[84] Proverbs acknowledges that wisdom is relational and theocentric.[85] Therefore, the verse identifies the wise as those who fear the Lord, and that acquiring wisdom is a journey with the fear of the Lord as the starting point. Each main point supports the themes that "Wisdom comes from God," and "Wisdom builds the relationship between God and His people."

Further, not only does the saying about the "fear of the Lord" help identify God's people, it also acts like the book's trademark. Within Proverbs, the saying "the fear of the Lord" is used twenty-one times in association with wisdom,[86] and the saying is used strategically in the book's outline.[87] In the Old Testament, Proverbs may be the book most closely identified with the saying about "the fear of the Lord." This fact will have a bearing on the analysis of Acts 9:31.

---

84. Longman, *Proverbs*, 13.
85. Longman, *Proverbs*, 100.
86. Longman, "Book of Proverbs 1," 549.
87. Bartholomew and O'Dowd, *Old Testament Wisdom Literature*, 80–81. The saying, "the fear of the Lord," bookends the book of Proverbs.

The True Identity of the People of the Way

Proverbs 2:1–22

This passage teaches about the way of wisdom, and captures the content of chapters 1–9 like a summary.[88] Also, the passage shows that the way supports the themes of Proverbs, i.e., that: "Wisdom comes from God," and "Wisdom builds the relationship between God and His people." The passage instructs a son to pursue wisdom in order to fear the Lord.[89] As Weeks noted above, the father places the son on the path to educate him.[90] Scholars have understood chapter 2 as a single unit and perhaps a single sentence.[91] This single passage includes five uses of אֹרַח and four uses of דֶּרֶךְ, being the first passage densely populated with references to the way.[92]

George Schwab divides the passage into two: Proverbs 2:1–11 and Proverbs 2:12–22.[93] Summarizing 2:1–11, he writes, "if you cry out for discernment . . . *then* you will know YHWH . . . *then* YHWH will speak wisdom . . . *then* God will be a shield to you and will guard your blameless paths; *then* you will discern how to live rightly . . . *then* wisdom and knowledge will be internalized in you, and you will have joy and be guarded in whatever you do."[94]

Proverbs 2:12–22 teaches that the way is for God's people. God sustains His people, and the way leads to life. Believers are those on the way. The passage teaches the consequences of obedience and righteous living on the way, along with the consequences of disobedience and unrighteous living.[95] God protects the righteous on the way. Waltke makes an astute observation that "the Lord shields the lives and interests of his saints from the spears of wicked men (vv. 12–15) and the arrow of the "foreign woman" vv. 16–19) as they walk the paths (' *orḥôt*; see 1:19) of justice (*mišpaṭ*, see 1:3)."[96] Further, God's preservation of His people comes from them living a life on the way. O'Dowd writes that "God, 'knowledge' and 'discretion' all

---

88. O'Dowd considers chapter 2 a summary of the first nine chapters. O'Dowd, *Proverbs*, 76. Fox titles the chapter "The benefits of the Way of Wisdom." Fox, *Proverbs 1–9*, 117.

89. Fox, *Proverbs 1–9*, 118.

90. Weeks, *Instruction and Imagery in Proverbs 1–9*, 73.

91. O'Dowd, *Proverbs*, 76. Fox notes that the chapter is so cohesive that any division is "somewhat artificial." Fox, *Proverbs 1–9*, 118.

92. אֹרַח Prov 2:8, 13, 15, 19–20.

93. Schwab, "The Book of Proverbs," 482.

94. Schwab, "The Book of Proverbs," 482; italics in the original.

95. Schwab, "The Book of Proverbs," 482.

96. Waltke, *The Book of Proverbs: Chapters 1–15*, 225.

protect the wise."[97] Last, each way has a predictable and sure destination. Thus, one way leads to death and the other to life. Waltke writes, "These paths are protected in such a way that those on them arrive at their appointed destiny of eternal life (2:19–22; cf. Ps. 16:9–11)."[98] In sum, the passage indicates the way is for God's people, that God sustains His people, and that the way leads to either life or death. These depictions support the themes of Proverbs that "Wisdom comes from God," and "Wisdom builds the relationship between God and His people."

Proverbs 3:5–7

Proverbs 3:5–7 introduces God as the creator of "the path," and the passage demonstrates that God sustains His people on the path. The passage continues to reinforce the pattern of the way as supporting the themes in Proverbs. This information is to be later used in section four, the analysis of the way as a motif in Proverbs.

The setting of Proverbs 3:5–7 is that of a father instructing his son. The father has earned his son's obedience, and the father is now having his son dedicate himself to God.[99] However, the father knows that the teaching is only as good as God's commitment to enforcing the teaching.[100] Thus, the son needs to commit to the Lord while God continues to sustain His people on the path He created.

God guides His people on the way and through His relationship with them.[101] Within this relationship, the believer is asked to trust fully in the Lord and not lean on human understanding. The believer must understand that his wisdom is deficient, and he needs to desire and understand his need to depend on the Lord.[102] The believer will then rely on the Lord's wisdom and resources to live. In Proverbs 3:6, the believer is asked to acknowledge or know God. To know God means to be in a relationship with Him.[103] Waltke writes that the relationship of Proverbs 3 is one where

---

97. O'Dowd, *Proverbs*, 80.
98. Waltke, *The Book of Proverbs: Chapters 1–15*, 225.
99. Waltke, *The Book of Proverbs: Chapters 1–15*, 243.
100. Waltke, *The Book of Proverbs: Chapters 1–15*, 243.
101. Longman, *Proverbs*, 132. This relationship is one of covenant. Proverbs 3:1–12 uses language reminiscent of Deuteronomy 6:4–9 where the Law is bound to the person.
102. Longman, *Proverbs*, 133.
103. Kidner, *Proverbs*, 61.

God demands exclusive devotion to Himself and His will.[104] The verse then recounts the promises associated with a relationship with God: God will make one's paths straight.[105] The last verse calls believers to resist the urge to supplant God's wisdom with their own, and exhorts them to continue the attitude of living in fear of the Lord.[106]

Proverbs 3:5–7 forms a connection between the Lord and the way. God is the one who makes the path straight and guides people down it. His path is the best; His path is straight and easy to travel. It is not crooked, and it does not lead to death (Prov 9:18; 2:15).[107] William McKane observes that in Proverbs 3:5, YHWH replaces "old wisdom," and "educational discipline" with "religious illumination."[108] The new religious illumination is observable in v. 6 through the metaphor of the way.[109] The metaphor of the way indicates that knowing YHWH directs one's life, while YHWH "facilitates progress along paths which lead to a destination."[110] In sum, God is the creator of the way, and sustains His people on the way. Both of these features of the way support the two themes of Proverbs, "Wisdom comes from God," and "Wisdom builds the relationship between God and His people."

Proverbs 4:14–18

Proverbs 4:14–18 reveals the consequences of traveling the right and wrong paths. Also, the passage introduces the way as a near-synonym for the path. The conclusions create a robust understanding of the way, while the synonymous use of the way and the path provides linguistic clues for analyzing Acts. Moreover, the conclusions about the way demonstrate that the metaphor supports the themes of Proverbs.

Proverbs 4:14–18 is part of a larger portion of text, Proverbs 4:10–19, which Waltke titles "Stay Off the Wrong Way."[111] Kidner simply titles the section "Choose" and breaks down the passage as follows: "Two paths are set before us. (10–13), describe *the way of wisdom* (11) and verses 14–17

---

104. Waltke, *The Book of Proverbs: Chapters 1–15*, 244.
105. Kidner, *Proverbs*, 61.
106. Waltke, *The Book of Proverbs: Chapters 1–15*, 245.
107. Longman, *Proverbs*, 133.
108. McKane, *Proverbs*, 292.
109. McKane, *Proverbs*, 292.
110. McKane, *Proverbs*, 292.
111. Longman, *Proverbs*, 283.

the path (or *way*) *of the wicked* (14, 19), two paths are compared (18, 19)."[112] The theological implication is to persuade the reader "to pursue wisdom" and stay on the right path.[113]

The passage presents two paths: the wicked and dark path and the righteous and lighted path. However, the "two ways" do not represent absolute differences. The book of Proverbs shows varying degrees of death with the author using six imperatives to convey the importance of staying on the path of Lady Wisdom and avoiding at all costs the path of Dame Folly.[114] Evil is addictive and cumulative; those that choose the wicked way are eventually consumed day and night with evil, and Proverbs 4:14–18 warns against evil.[115]

In Proverbs 4:14, the two terms, the way and the path, are used synonymously, which happens throughout the book of Proverbs.[116] Each translation is of a different Hebrew word, yet nevertheless, no significance difference is found between the way and the path. Waltke suggests the author chose "the way" as a stylistic improvement.[117]

In sum, Proverbs 4 teaches about the interchangeable use of the way and the path and the metaphor of the way. The two ways represent God's way and the way of sin. God's way leads to life, and the way of sin leads to death. Because God's people thrive on His way, the metaphor supports the theme. "Wisdom builds the relationship between God and His people."

Proverbs 9

Proverbs 9 is considered a summary statement of Proverbs 1–8, displaying all the components of the theology of "the way": (1) the Lord creates the way, (2) the way is for God's people, (3) God sustains those on the way, and (4) the way leads to life. This conclusion affirms not only what was previously stated about the theology of "the way," but also continues to support the themes of Proverbs. Weeks finds that after Proverbs 4, the path imagery

---

112. Kidner, *Proverbs*, 64; italics in the original.
113. Longman, *Proverbs*, 151.
114. Kidner, *Proverbs*, 49.
115. Waltke, *The Book of Proverbs: Chapters 1–15*, 282–91.
116. Waltke, *The Book of Proverbs: Chapters 1–15*, 289.
117. Waltke, *The Book of Proverbs: Chapters 1–15*, 289.

"shifts its focus to the foreign woman and to Wisdom."[118] The narrative of the women in Proverbs 9 informs the reader about the way.

Proverbs 9 can be seen as three units: (1) Wisdom's Invitation (9:1–6), (2) the "Narrator's Interlude" (9:7–12); and (3) Dame Folly's Speech (9:13–18).[119] As previously noted, Proverbs 9 offers two invitations, one from Lady Wisdom and one from Dame Folly.[120] Both women are portrayed in front of their homes, but while Lady Wisdom has built her house, Dame Folly is only pictured sitting before hers.[121]

The book of Proverbs personifies Wisdom as Lady Wisdom, who, along with Dame Folly, may be understood as a satellite image[122] of "the way." As Lady Wisdom and her counterpart are discussed, their influence on "the way" becomes evident, particularly in Proverbs 9, where the two women are "competing hosts, each beckoning passers-by with an invitation to a meal."[123] The personification shows that one must choose between walking the way of Wisdom or of Folly, leading to contrasting outward living and consequences.

The rich imagery of Proverbs 9:1–6 tells of Lady Wisdom beginning a banquet. Waltke notes that Lady Wisdom's grand banquet is expected of noble or powerful figures in society.[124] The action and setting tell of Lady Wisdom's character.[125] As her grand banquet speaks of Lady Wisdom's character, so does her house.[126] O'Dowd notes Wisdom's home (Prov 8:2) is "on the heights beside the way, at the crossroads she takes her stand," and her maidens call (Prov 9:3) "from the highest places in the town," which he then associates with the "sacred temple."[127] The placement of the house is symbolic, and resembles the "building of the First Temple."[128] Later, Lady

---

118. Weeks, *Instruction and Imagery in Proverbs 1–9*, 74.

119. O'Dowd, *Proverbs*, 165. Schipper and Kitchen have identical verse breaks with similar titles. Schipper, *Proverbs 1–15*, 320; Kitchen, *Proverbs*, 201.

120. Schipper, *Proverbs 1–15*, 339.

121. Kitchen, *Proverbs*, 201.

122. Habel, "The Symbolism of Wisdom in Proverbs 1–9," 133. Satellite images reflect upon the basic symbol, here "the way."

123. Koptak, "Personification," 516–19.

124. Waltke, *The Book of Proverbs: Chapters 1–15*, 431.

125. Waltke, *The Book of Proverbs: Chapters 1–15*, 431.

126. O'Dowd, *Proverbs*, 165.

127. O'Dowd, *Proverbs*, 165.

128. O'Dowd, *Proverbs*, 165. (Exod 31:3; 35:31).

Wisdom's house is contrasted with that of Dame Folly. Wisdom's call goes out to the naïve; it goes to those who are vulnerable, but "not hardened fools."[129] Kitchen writes, "The invitation for this banquet is not prepared based upon what a person has, but on what a person lacks."[130] Upon close inspection, these two invitations could not be more different. Lady Wisdom's house and actions are based in righteousness, while Dame Folly's are founded in deceit.

The interlude of Proverbs 9:7–12 does not refer to the personified women. However, a summary is beneficial for understanding the passage. O'Dowd speaks of the context that vv. 7–12 provides: "The interlude reinforces the connection between his practical advice about life in this world and the ultimate cosmic structures of the world that lie hidden from our sight."[131] Waltke proposes that vv. 7–12 are integral to the larger passage (Prov 9:1–18).[132] Like O'Dowd, Waltke finds that the interlude reflects upon the consequences for the wise person and the fool from the perspective offered by Proverbs, that wisdom begins with YHWH.[133] This section continues to teach about the way.

Following Lady Wisdom's teaching and the interlude about God's wisdom, the section on Dame Folly's begins from a negative light. The previous section (Prov 9:1–2) displays Dame Folly's weaknesses.[134] Ironically, Dame Folly is also in the highest place, suggesting that she represents false gods.[135] Dame Folly's house and banquet reflect her character also. She does not build her house and eventually destroys it (Prov 14:1), and her banquet is filled with stolen goods.[136] The grim truth about Dame Folly is that her guests eventually find themselves in Sheol (Prov 9:18).

The "two ways" theology or imagery of the path can be seen from comparing the two women. The naïve *person must choose which way to travel.* Andrew Steinmann identifies the two women of Proverbs as a

---

129. Kitchen, *Proverbs*, 203. Waltke may best characterize the maidens' target audience as the gullible. Waltke, *The Book of Proverbs: Chapters 1–15*, 436.

130. Kitchen, *Proverbs*, 203.

131. O'Dowd, *Proverbs*, 166.

132. Waltke, *The Book of Proverbs: Chapters 1–15*, 439–41.

133. Waltke, *The Book of Proverbs: Chapters 1–15*, 431.

134. O'Dowd, *Proverbs*, 166.

135. Longman, *Proverbs*, 59.

136. O'Dowd, *Proverbs*, 166. See Fox, *Proverbs 1–9*, 301.

couplet found in Proverbs 1–9.[137] He finds that Wisdom (along with the wife and parents' instruction) contrasts with the adulteress (along with foolishness).[138] Steinmann suggests that the imagery of "the way" and the metaphor of light reinforce the teaching against adultery by contrasting the two women.[139] Wisdom has a delicious and luxurious dinner; Dame Folly serves a stolen supper. Wisdom builds her house; Folly destroys a house.[140] The symbolism grows richer when taking into consideration the location of the houses. Both Wisdom and Dame Folly live in high places, which represent divinity.[141] In Ezekiel 8:1–10, the prophet goes to Jerusalem in a vision and looks upon the temple. There he sees that "Manasseh had put a wooden image of Asherah, the Canaanite goddess, in the house of the Lord."[142] The city's highest place would have been set aside for the temple.[143] Therefore Wisdom symbolizes God's wisdom or YHWH Himself; while Folly symbolizes false idols.[144] Mirroring this stark contrast is the eventual destination portrayed by the two women: Wisdom's house leads to "wise living," and Folly's home leads to Sheol.[145]

To conclude, Lady Wisdom shows the right relationship with YHWH.[146] In fact, Lady Wisdom's way represents God's way.[147] The imagery of the two women and the way instructs the reader on a right relationship with YHWH. These conclusions align the theology of the way with the themes of Proverbs.

137. Steinmann, *Proverbs*, 180–82.

138. Steinmann, *Proverbs*, 180. (Wisdom: Prov 1:20–33; 7:4; 9:1–6; Wife Prov: 5:15–20; Parent's instruction: Prov 6:22; Adulteress: Prov 2:16–19; 5:3–6, 20; 6:24–26; 7:5–27; Foolishness: Prov 9:13–18).

139. Steinmann, *Proverbs* , 180.

140. Fox, *Proverbs 1–9*, 301.

141. Longman, *Proverbs*, 59.

142. Taylor, *Ezekiel*, 99.

143. Longman, *Proverbs*, 58–59.

144. Longman, *Proverbs*, 59.

145. Weeks points out that Folly's guests finding themselves in Sheol is the difference between Folly and Wisdom. He also notes that the path of the foreign woman leads to Sheol in Proverbs 7:27.Weeks, *Instruction and Imagery in Proverbs 1–9*, 72. "Wise living" was taken from Bartholomew. Bartholomew and O'Dowd, *Old Testament Wisdom Literature*, 89.

146. Longman, *Proverbs*, 397.

147. The discussion about Lady Wisdom and Dame Folly is limited here, but lessons learned from Proverbs 9 are used in later sections. However, when discussing the lessons from Proverbs 9, Wisdom's ways will be referred to as God's ways.

An Analysis of "the Way" in the Book of Proverbs

Proverbs 1–9 Summary

Proverbs 1–9 provides four observable features of "the way" theology. First, God's people are those who travel the way (Prov 1:7; 2:1–22; 3:5–7; 9). Establishing God's people as travelers informs both the motif and the theology of the way. The way of the people of God establishes a connection with the salvific history of Israel. Additionally, God's people as those destined for the way of wisdom implies that wisdom is associated with God. Second, God creates the way (Prov 3:5–7), which again implies wisdom requires divine revelation. Moreover, it means that God created both the beginning of the way and the destination of the way. Third, God directs and sustains His people on the way (Prov 2:1–22; 3:5–7; 9). Believers on the way of wisdom are kept from wandering far from God's path. Those on the way are ensured life. Fourth, choosing which way to follow has consequences that lead to life or death (Prov 2:1–22; 4:14–18; 9). This final point reveals that those who follow God and His revealed wisdom are guaranteed life, while death is ensured for those who travel routes outside of God's way.

These four features support the themes of Proverbs: "Wisdom comes from God," and "Wisdom builds the relationship between God and His people." Also, the four features of "the way" motif may be further affirmed by passages containing the term "the path" (דרך or אֹרַח) or associated imagery in Proverbs 10–29. Last, when the conclusions of Proverbs 1–9 are combined with Proverbs 10–29, Freedman's method for identifying motifs will be applied to the results.

"THE WAY" OF PROVERBS 10–29

The use of "the way" continues well into the second half of Proverbs. The three following examples are taken from the section of Proverbs 10–29 that contains the most occurrences of דרך and אֹרַח, and which focus most on the theology of "the way." Proverbs 10–22.16 provides the ethics that define the wicked and the righteous.[148] Next, Proverbs 13–16 is the parent unit, with an example taken from each chapter of Proverbs 14–16. Before proceeding to the analysis of the passages, an overview of Proverbs 10–29 as it relates to the study of the way is set out.

First, Proverbs 10–29 presents a worldview similar to the first nine chapters. Robert Williamson suggests it is a worldview that is predictable,

---

148. Scott, *Proverbs Ecclesiastes*, 25.

one where ethical behavior separates the eternal fates of the righteous and the wicked.[149] The contrast between righteous and wicked behavior is repeated in Proverbs 10-29. Also, these chapters similarly present the two destinations of the way. Williamson proposes that Proverbs 10-29 does not indicate a religiously-oriented eternal life (i.e., salvation or damnation), but rather a symbolic eternal existence through the "perseverance of the name, the flourishing of the biological line, the bequeathal of inheritance, and the transmission of instruction to future generations, both inside the family and in the broader community."[150]

Second, the structure of Proverbs 10-29 is radically different from chapters 1-9. However, the structure does not prevent a reliable analysis of "the way." How scholars subdivide the book attests to "the way" within this section of text, as seen with Schwab, who has three main divisions: "The Way of Wisdom and the Way of Death (13:1—14:27)," "The Wisdom of Yahweh and the King (14:28-16:15)," and "The Way of Wisdom and the Way of Death (16:16-19:12)."[151] Likewise, Waltke writes that Solomon I (Proverbs 10-15) compares the righteous with the wicked and the benefits and pitfalls associated with both.[152] Each scholar presents division summaries that showcase the role of "the way."

Rather than viewing these verses as individual proverbs, various units can be identified.[153] Viewing each proverb as part of a larger unit allows for a wider context from which to draw conclusions about passages containing "the way." Knut Heim finds the "most prominent criteria employed in the search for editorial groupings" in "chapter divisions, 'educational' sayings, paronomasia and catchwords, theological reinterpretations,

---

149. Williamson, "'In the Way of Righteousness Is Life,'" 381.

150. Williamson, "'In the Way of Righteousness Is Life,'" 381.

151. Schwab, "The Book of Proverbs," 540, 50, 62. Schipper diverges from Schwab, but the pattern of the way may still be observed through a comparison between worldly wisdom and divine wisdom: "The Sapiential Dichotomy: "The Righteous and the Wicked" (Prov 12:1-28), "A Sapiential Instruction in the Garb of Proverbial Wisdom" (Prov 13:1-25), "The Limits of Human Understanding: A Critical Perspective" (Prov 12:1-35), and "From Experiential Wisdom to Divine Wisdom" (Prov 15:1-33). Schipper, *Proverbs 1-15*, 413, 36, 60, 87.

152. Waltke, *The Book of Proverbs: Chapters 1-15*, 15. Like Waltke, Fox writes that Proverbs 10:1—15:33 is dense with antithetical sayings and comparisons between the righteous and the wicked. Fox, *Proverbs 10-31*, 509. Kidner makes a similar division of the Proverbs of Solomon (Prov 10:1—22:16). Kidner, *Proverbs,* 80.

153. Kidner, *Proverbs*; Fox, *Proverbs 10-31*. Both Kidner and Fox treat the Proverbs of Solomon as a collection of individual proverbs.

proverbial pairs and variant repetitions."[154] Roger Whybray suggests that the frequency of word repetition may be the single best way to demonstrate a group of proverbs from Proverbs 10-22.16 and 25-29 are intentionally linked.[155] Thus, analysis of the way is not limited to the analysis of the verse in which it is found. By contrast, the larger units can inform understanding of "the way."

The major scholarly divisions studied within this section are selected both for their use of the way and their literary context: Fox states that Proverbs 10:1—15:33 has a higher proportion of antithetical sayings and "places more emphasis on the antithesis between the righteous and the wicked."[156] The antithetical sayings and emphases, or the contrast between the righteous and wicked both capture satellite images of "the way." John Goldingay finds six subsections in Proverbs 10-15, with one such subsection beginning at Proverbs 14:1.[157] The main divisions to be studied are Proverbs 14:1-32; 15; 16. These divisions contain the greatest concentrations of occurrences of "the way" and reflect the literary structure of Proverbs.

Proverbs 14:1-32

Proverbs 14:1-32 has three occurrences of "the way." Waltke's divisions of this passage capture "the way" and its satellite images as follows: "Walking in wisdom (14:1-7), not by sight (14:8-15), and contrasting characterizations and consequences of social deportment (14:15-32)."[158] In what follows, the context of Proverbs 14:1-32 will be summarized. Second, Proverbs 14:8-15 will be further scrutinized. Here the second section is of the greatest importance, because it contains the three occurrences. The last section will summarize "the way" as found in Proverbs 14:1-32.

Whybray understands Proverbs 14 as presenting a choice to a student to follow or dismiss instruction and the consequences associated with that decision.[159] He does not connect all of vv. 1-32 with a unifying theme, but he does observe different groupings concerning the choice to follow

---

154. Heim, *Like Grapes of Gold Set in Silver*, 63.
155. Whybray, *The Composition of the Book of Proverbs*, 67.
156. Fox, *Proverbs 10-31*, 509.
157. Goldingay, "The Arrangement of Sayings in Proverbs 10-15," 82.
158. Waltke, *The Book of Proverbs: Chapters 1-15*, 583.
159. Whybray, *The Composition of the Book of Proverbs*, 100-01.

YHWH (1–3) and wisdom or folly (4, 6–8).[160] Similar groupings and patterns connect Proverbs 14:8–15, as discussed below.

The pericope is a unit related to ethical behavior. Whybray notes that Proverbs 14:11 may refer to the house of wisdom in Proverbs 14:1, which would suggest a parallel to Proverbs 9 and its contrasting of Wisdom and Folly.[161] He supports the division along the lines of "parallel sequences of educational, ethical, theological and pragmatic sayings."[162] Waltke similarly recognizes Proverbs 14:1 as an introduction to a new unit.[163] Uniting Proverbs 14:1–32 is its shared vocabulary and "janus verses."[164] Ronald Clements points to the repeated contrast of wisdom and foolishness as another component unifying the section.[165] Last, Waltke finds the passage concludes with mention of the consequences of behavior that supports or is contrary to the community of God.[166] The unity of the passage allows for the immediate context to assist in understanding its theology of "the way."

The first two verses establish the keywords of the section: "wisdom," "folly," "fool," and "walk" or "go."[167] Also, Proverbs 14:2 introduces the "fear of the Lord," which is the beginning of wisdom.[168] These connotations are reminiscent of Proverbs 9 and 31.[169] Specifically, Proverbs 14:1–3 teaches how a wise woman builds her house; counsels resisting Dame Folly, watching one's steps, and, more generally, the difference between wise and foolish living.[170]

Within the pericope, four verses will receive particular attention: Proverbs 14:2, 8, 12, and 14. Each verse contributes to an understanding of "the way." Proverbs 14:2 shows the relationship between faith in the Lord and a person's behavior. Proverbs 14:8 reveals the "two way" theology (i.e.,

---

160. Whybray, *The Composition of the Book of Proverbs*, 101.

161. Whybray, *The Composition of the Book of Proverbs*, 101–02.

162. Goldingay, "The Arrangement of Sayings in Proverbs 10–15," 83.

163. Waltke, *The Book of Proverbs: Chapters 1–15*, 583, 94.

164. Waltke, *The Book of Proverbs: Chapters 1–15*, 583. O'Dowd affirms Waltke's reasoning in suggesting unity in the passage, but locates the end of the unit at verse 35. O'Dowd, *Proverbs*, 227.

165. Clements, *Commentary on the Bible: Proverbs*, 67. Clements identifies the unit as Proverbs 14:1–35.

166. Waltke, *The Book of Proverbs: Chapters 1–15*, 607.

167. Waltke, *The Book of Proverbs: Chapters 1–15*, 583.

168. O'Dowd, *Proverbs*, 227.

169. O'Dowd, *Proverbs*, 227; Waltke, *The Book of Proverbs: Chapters 1–15*, 584.

170. O'Dowd, *Proverbs*, 227; Waltke, *The Book of Proverbs: Chapters 1–15*, 584.

the ways of the wicked and of wisdom). Proverbs 14:12 and 14 teach that following a particular way will lead to either death or life.

First, concerning 14:2, Fox writes that a person's conduct "is inseparable from his attitude toward God, and the former reveals the latter."[171] For Fox, Proverbs 14:2 discusses behavior, so the ways of one who fears the Lord are honest.[172] Heim finds that הלךְ is a syntagm that implies the way.[173] Fox suggests that the way of the dishonest man is to despise God.[174] Allen Ross directly relates the contrast between uprightness and perversion to Proverbs 3:32.[175] The significance of Ross' observation lies in the context of Proverbs 3:31–35, which discusses the fate of the righteous compared to the fate of the wicked.[176] The clear contrast between the fates of the righteous and the wicked demonstrates the value of living a good life and choosing the righteous way.

Second, in 14:8, scholars recognize the dichotomy between the wise and foolish, as in 14:2.[177] Waltke finds the structure of 14:8–15 similar to that of 14:1–7.[178] Particularly, Waltke writes that the prologue to each section shares catchwords that pair wisdom/folly (vv. 1, 8), the upright (vv. 2a, 9b), and way (vv. 2a, 8a).[179] Within the immediate context, O'Dowd finds a linguistic tie between vv. 7 and 8.[180] In Proverbs 14:7, the reader is admonished to walk away from the wicked, which relates to the ways of the wise and foolish in v. 8.[181] Furthermore, Heim views v. 8 as concluding vv. 6–7.[182] Proverbs 14:8 demonstrates the positive outcome for the wise while concluding the foolish will not find wisdom, as in v. 6.[183] Preceding v. 12, Proverbs 14:11 uses the imagery of the house for moral living and to

---

171. Fox, *Proverbs 10–31*, 119.
172. Fox, *Proverbs 10–31*, 119.
173. Heim, "Structure and Context in Proverbs," 152.
174. Fox, *Proverbs 10–31*, 119.
175. Ross, "Proverbs," 132–33.
176. O'Dowd, *Proverbs*, 104.
177. O'Dowd, *Proverbs*, 228; Ross, "Proverbs," 132–33.
178. Waltke, *The Book of Proverbs: Chapters 1–15*, 588.
179. Waltke, *The Book of Proverbs: Chapters 1–15*, 588.
180. O'Dowd, *Proverbs*, 228.
181. O'Dowd, *Proverbs*, 228.
182. Heim, "Structure and Context in Proverbs," 155.
183. Heim, "Structure and Context in Proverbs," 155.

suggest righteous behavior.[184] Heim notes that the house of the wicked is actually weak.[185]

Third, in 14:12, the motif of a journey continues as the proverb discusses the conclusion of wicked behavior.[186] Ross writes, "The image used is of a traveler on a straight road; it seems safe, but it is fatal, for the destination is wrong."[187] The MT indicates the destination is death, while the LXX describes the destination with the term Hades, which describes the effects of evil on "life's events."[188] This verse is knitted together with surrounding verses by the root of ישׁר and "death."[189] Interestingly the root of ישׁר is commonly used for "judgment."[190] Here in v. 12, death is linked with the destruction of the wicked one's home.[191] There is irony in that the fool judges his crooked way as straight because he uses faulty judgment. "Yasar is commonly used with 'way' and readily assumes the figurative meaning of ethical behavior that does not go outside of what is judged to be right behavior and so leads to success."[192] Waltke notes that the Hebrew words אדם and אִישׁ notify the reader of human wisdom, not godly wisdom.[193] Only God is omniscient and omnipotent (Prov 3:7; 30:1–6).[194] Thereby, the journey or way depicts "two ways" that God will judge. The path of the wicked (i.e., human/worldly wisdom) is judged guilty, and the way of the righteous (i.e., God's revealed wisdom) is just.

Fourth, in 14:14, the proverb teaches retribution.[195] The verse continues using the metaphor of "the way" to show how one's behavior connects to the future.[196] In this metaphor, the faithful are rewarded while the unfaithful are punished.[197] Similarly, Heim writes that Proverbs 14:14

---

184. Heim, "Structure and Context in Proverbs," 157.
185. Heim, "Structure and Context in Proverbs," 157.
186. Waltke, *The Book of Proverbs: Chapters 1–15*, 591.
187. Ross, "Proverbs," 134.
188. Ross, "Proverbs," 134.
189. Waltke, *The Book of Proverbs: Chapters 1–15*, 591.
190. Waltke, *The Book of Proverbs: Chapters 1–15*, 591.
191. Heim, "Structure and Context in Proverbs," 157.
192. Waltke, *The Book of Proverbs: Chapters 1–15*, 591.
193. Waltke, *The Book of Proverbs: Chapters 1–15*, 591.
194. Waltke, *The Book of Proverbs: Chapters 1–15*, 592.
195. Ross, "Proverbs," 134.
196. Waltke, *The Book of Proverbs: Chapters 1–15*, 593.
197. Waltke, *The Book of Proverbs: Chapters 1–15*, 593.

demonstrates emotional consequences and relates them to "good and bad characters."[198]

In sum, Proverbs 14:1–31 shows "the way" is for God's people and that the way of sin leads to destruction. In addition, "the way" supports the themes of Proverbs (i.e., "Wisdom comes from God," and "Wisdom builds the relationship between God and His people"). Proverbs 14:2 reveals the relationship between faith in the Lord and behavior. Proverbs 14:8 contrasts the way of the Lord (wisdom) with the way of the wicked. Proverbs 14:12 and 14 teach that the way of the Lord leads to life, while that of the wicked leads to death.

Proverbs 15

Chapter 15 focuses theologically on "the way," supports the themes of Proverbs, and contains three clustered uses of דרך and אֹרַח in Proverbs 15:9, 10, and 19. In this section, the whole passage will be discussed, before being further broken down, with particular attention given to verses directly mentioning "the way." The conclusion demonstrates that chapter 15 shows wisdom is from the Lord.

Proverbs 15 is a unified section that includes teachings of "the way." Schipper sees the chapter as accentuating wisdom, because it compares discipline and correction with "the religious dimension of sapiential behavior."[199] Schipper acutely observes that chapter 15 stands out for its explicit references to YHWH, which signals unity.[200] Likewise, Waltke finds unifying features when he locates all three uses of דרך in a single section: Proverbs 15:5–19.[201] He subdivides the unit into three sections: Prov 15:5–12, 13–17, 18–19.[202] The first division is Proverbs 15:5–12, and is based upon three factors: An inclusio with the catchword יכח in verses 5 and 19, three proverbial pairs, "the negative evaluative pattern -::-, and the motif of journey linking v. 12

---

198. Heim, "Structure and Context in Proverbs," 157–58.

199. Schipper, *Proverbs 1–15*, 489.

200. Schipper, *Proverbs 1–15*, 489.

201. Waltke, *The Book of Proverbs: Chapters 1–15*, 618; O'Dowd, *Proverbs*, 238. O'Dowd affirms this subdivision.

202. Waltke, *The Book of Proverbs: Chapters 1–15*, 616–28. O'Dowd affirms the second division, but differs over the third. For the purposes of this study, it is sufficient to note that variant divisions often still see Proverbs 15:1–33 as a unit connected by similar language and content as noted above. O'Dowd, *Proverbs*, 239.

The True Identity of the People of the Way

with vv. 10–11."²⁰³ Heim, who likewise finds Proverbs 15:5–12 to be a unit, writes the passage is on the rejection and acceptance of instruction.²⁰⁴ Waltke finds Proverbs 15:18–19 concludes the section, and observes these verses are thematically linked to the previous verses through the discussion of the two kinds of people.²⁰⁵ O'Dowd understands these final verses, Proverbs 15:18–19, are adjoined to vv. 20–23.²⁰⁶ O'Dowd determines vv. 18–23 are unified via the theme of "the way" and via similar contrasting pairs of people.²⁰⁷ Yet, O'Dowd views Proverbs 15:18–19 as phonetically connected with verse 17.²⁰⁸ Therefore, the following examination evaluates Proverbs 15:5–12 and Proverbs 15:18–23 more closely to assess the uses of דרך and אֹרַח.

The first section of Proverbs 15 (vv. 1–11) discusses the way of wisdom and discipline taught by man, but later "the way" represents the quest for righteousness (v. 9).²⁰⁹ This way of righteousness becomes the antithesis of "the 'way of the wicked' which is abomination to Yahweh."²¹⁰ Proverbs 15:5 begins the proverb cluster, vv. 5–12, by discussing the key role discipline plays "as a route to wisdom."²¹¹ The section itself, vv. 5–12, focuses on the themes of receiving counsel.²¹² In Proverbs 15:6, the wise have both "provisions or treasure" and "earnings or produce."²¹³ Provisions and earnings signify a "sapiential ideal" that contrasts with the wicked who have neither.²¹⁴ Whybray observes that in verses 8–11, all are YHWH proverbs except for v. 10, while verses 8–11 reinterpret the "wise" and "fools" under the moral categories of "righteous" and "wicked."²¹⁵ The close connection between the wise/fools and the righteous/wicked suggests that both sets of

---

203. Waltke, *The Book of Proverbs: Chapters 1–15*, 618.
204. Heim, "Structure and Context in Proverbs," 173–74.
205. Waltke, *The Book of Proverbs: Chapters 1–15*, 628.
206. O'Dowd, *Proverbs*, 240.
207. O'Dowd, *Proverbs*, 240.
208. O'Dowd, *Proverbs*, 240.
209. Whybray, *The Composition of the Book of Proverbs*, 104.
210. Whybray, *The Composition of the Book of Proverbs*, 104.
211. Longman, *Proverbs*, 313.
212. O'Dowd, *Proverbs*, 238.
213. O'Dowd, *Proverbs*, 238.
214. Schipper also notes that the Septuagint "contains two additional stichoi that should probably be understood as a duplicate translation of the Hebrew text" (497). Schipper, *Proverbs 1–15*, 496–97.
215. Whybray, *The Composition of the Book of Proverbs*, 103.

people will be under God's judgment.[216] Heim writes, "In verse 11 anyone who is not yet convinced by the preceding is reminded that the neglect of instruction inevitably suffers retribution: the Lord even knows the inner thought of men (cf. v. 7b)."[217]

In Proverbs 15:18–33 six pairs of people-types are contrasted.[218] Verse 19 employs the "sapiential thought" of contrasting the lazy person with the upright.[219] The way is a keyword in chapter 15 and is associated with two kinds of people.[220] Whybray finds Proverbs 15:20–24 and 31–33 surround the verses focusing on the righteous and the wicked.[221]

In combination with the high concentration of YHWH proverbs, three sections (vv. 20–24, 25–30, 31–33) declare YHWH as judge, that the house of the wicked will be destroyed, and that the righteous will be rewarded.[222] Schwab summarizes, "Those who rejoice in the good, however, are assured their lives will not terminate in Hades (15:24). God, who casts down the house of the proud (15:25) and is far from the wicked (15:29), hears the prayers of his saints and gives honor to those who are humble (15:33)."[223] Whybray proposes Proverbs 15:33 bridges chapters 15 and 16 and identifies wisdom with the fear of the Lord.[224] For Roland Murphy, the thorn hedge is an obstacle, similar to its use in Proverbs 16:7, thus drawing further connections between the two chapters.[225]

In sum, Proverbs 15 confirms that wisdom is from the Lord and informs the reader about the way of the wicked and the wise. Again, "the way" supports Proverbs' themes, "Wisdom comes from God" and "Wisdom builds the relationship between God and His people." The way of wisdom is associated with the Lord and leads to life. The way of the wicked is against the Lord and leads to death.

---

216. Whybray, *The Composition of the Book of Proverbs*, 103.

217. Heim, "Structure and Context in Proverbs," 175–76. See Whybray, *The Composition of the Book of Proverbs*, 104.

218. O'Dowd, *Proverbs*, 240.

219. Schipper, *Proverbs 1–15*, 505.

220. Schipper, *Proverbs 1–15*, 505.

221. Whybray, *The Composition of the Book of Proverbs*, 105.

222. Whybray, *The Composition of the Book of Proverbs*, 105–06.

223 Schwab, "The Book of Proverbs," 559.

224. Whybray, *The Composition of the Book of Proverbs*, 107.

225. Murphy, *Proverbs*, 271.

Proverbs 16

Proverbs 16 has the most occurrences of the word דרך (Prov 16:2, 7, 9, 17, 25, 29, 31). This section will first present an overview, before examining the limits and unifying features of the pericope. Uses of "the way" are examined, followed by a summary of "the way" in Proverbs 16.

Thematically, Proverbs 16 features a royal court with a concentration of synonymous sayings that focus on wise actions, wise speech, and "the theological character of the sapiential tradition."[226] Proverbs 16 highlights that YHWH is sovereign over man's plans (16:1, 9, 25).[227] YHWH is sovereign over judgment (16:2), which the wicked will experience unless "the fear of the Lord," makes it possible "to avoid evil (16:6)."[228] The chapter also portrays God as sovereign over human kingdoms, and reigning over the kings who lead those kingdoms (16:10–15).[229] Waltke writes, "Whybray argues that in its edited form the collection's initial 'righteous-wicked contrast' establishes the ethical context for Solomon I, and the Yahweh sayings that cluster the middle (chs. 15–16, especially 15:33–16:9) set theological considerations at the heart of the collection."[230] Several of these themes relate directly to the themes of the book of Proverbs.

Proverbs 16 should be understood as a unified chapter. Further subdivisions are inconsistent among scholars, but a survey of the literature demonstrates agreement that the chapter has unity. Along with a royal theme, Waltke notes the connecting language in Proverbs 15:30–16:22 of "abomination," "favor," and "wicked"/"wickedness."[231] Waltke also recognizes that the divine tetragrammaton YHWH is also prevalent in Proverbs 16:1–9.[232] Heim observers that vv. 1–7 and 9 are all YHWH sayings.[233] It is verses 8–9 that serve as an inspiration for a person to follow right (צְדָקָה) ways through the Lord's approval.[234] Heim writes, "Meinhold identifies an extended group from vv. 17–30, divided into two subunits (vv. 17–24, 25–30),

---

226. Perdue, *Proverbs*, 179–80.
227. Perdue, *Proverbs*, 180.
228. Perdue also provides 16:2 as a reference for God's judgment. Perdue, *Proverbs*, 180.
229. The verses cited are those selected by Perdue. Perdue, *Proverbs*, 181.
230. Waltke, *The Book of Proverbs: Chapters 1–15*, 17.
231. Waltke, *The Book of Proverbs: Chapters 15–31*, 5.
232. Waltke, *The Book of Proverbs: Chapters 15–31*, 8.
233. Heim, "Structure and Context in Proverbs," 186.
234. Heim, "Structure and Context in Proverbs," 190.

each introduced by a saying with reference to the 'way' concept in both cola [vv. 17 (דרך+ מְסִלָּה) and 25 (2 x דרך)]."²³⁵ He continues, "verses 31–33 display various links to what precedes and what follows."²³⁶ Heim notes that verses 20–24 are not restrictions limited to speech but include intellect.²³⁷ Whybray sees Proverbs 16:27–29 unified by its shared language and discussion of an evil nature and its consequences.²³⁸ Following verse 29, Whybray finds vv. 31 and 32 may be an antithesis to the wicked behavior mentioned again in v. 30.²³⁹ Last, he notes that 16:33 provides a reminder that YHWH is sovereign over humanity.²⁴⁰ Thus, chapter 16 should be viewed as a unified unit.

All of chapter 16 helps in understanding "the way." Murphy writes that the way of the righteous will lead to "reconciliation with one's enemies" from the Lord (Prov 16:2, 7).²⁴¹ Leo Perdue suggests that Proverbs 16:8 witnesses to YHWH as the leader of kings and kingdoms as well.²⁴² God as the leader supports the themes of "God as the source of wisdom" and "God using wisdom to build relationships with humanity." Following the way of the righteous secures success, because the Lord ensures success along His way (Prov 16:9).²⁴³ Proverbs 16:17 again brings in the image of "the way" to present evil in a moral sense.²⁴⁴ For Perdue, although the wicked may become wealthy, being righteous is worth the cost of being poor (Prov 16:19).²⁴⁵ Murphy writes, "The description of the evil type of person is continued with the notion of 'seduction,' the term that is developed in Proverbs 1:10–16. Saying the way of the wicked is 'not good' is an understatement; cf. 4:15–17."²⁴⁶ The final verse, v. 17, draws the conclusion that the wise person achieves old age, and from this it may be assumed that "the wicked

---

235. Heim, "Structure and Context in Proverbs," 197.
236. Heim, "Structure and Context in Proverbs," 197.
237. Heim, "Structure and Context in Proverbs," 198.
238. Whybray, *The Composition of the Book of Proverbs*, 109.
239. Whybray, *The Composition of the Book of Proverbs*, 110.
240. Whybray, *The Composition of the Book of Proverbs*, 110.
241. Murphy, *Proverbs*, 281.
242. Perdue, *Proverbs*, 181.
243. Murphy, *Proverbs*, 281.
244. Murphy, *Proverbs*, 282.
245. Perdue, *Proverbs*, 181.
246. Murphy, *Proverbs*, 284.

die young."[247] Proverbs 16:25–26 shows how human wisdom is limited.[248] The next occurrence of the way in v. 29 is a climax.[249] It displays the poor wisdom of a "violent person."[250] Here, the person is depicted as "violent," and using the same wisdom as anyone else outside of God's way. Nevertheless, this evil one seeks to persuade others down a path that is "not good."[251] This imagery is a rhetorical saying, denoting the way is evil and causes damage.[252] This evil way recalls Proverbs 16:25, which suggests that way leads to death.[253] Proverbs 16:31 is the final verse that uses "the way." In that verse, the way of righteousness leads to the blessing of old age.[254] Therefore, the way of the wicked is unwise, evil, and leads to death. The righteous way is wise, good, and life-giving.

In sum, Proverbs 16 employs every component of the way metaphor and demonstrates the unity of the metaphor in the book of Proverbs. Chapter 16 shows God is the creator of the way. God makes the way for believers and blesses them by directing their lives. In Proverbs 16, travelers on the way achieve life, but off the path, travelers die young. The way in chapter 16 supports major themes in Proverbs (i.e., "God is the source and giver of wisdom," and "God uses wisdom to build relationships with His people"). Last, the presentation of the way in Proverbs 16 is similar to that of Proverbs 1–9.

Proverbs 10–29: A Summary

Proverbs 10–29, although stylistically different, forms a single piece of literature unified thematically and linguistically with Proverbs 1–9. Unity between sections can be observed through the similar portrayal of the way. First, God's people are those who travel the path (Prov 16). Second, God creates the path (Prov 16). Third, God directs and sustains His people on the path (Prov 14:1–32; 16). Fourth, choosing to follow the path has consequences that lead to life or death (Prov 14:1–32; 15; 16).

247. Murphy, *Proverbs*, 284.

248. O'Dowd notes the repeating of Prov 14:12 by Prov 16:25. O'Dowd, *Proverbs*, 250.

249. Waltke, *The Book of Proverbs: Chapters 15–31*, 34.

250. Waltke, *The Book of Proverbs: Chapters 15–31*, 34.

251. Waltke, *The Book of Proverbs: Chapters 15–31*, 34.

252. Waltke, *The Book of Proverbs: Chapters 15–31*, 34.

253. O'Dowd, *Proverbs*, 250.

254. Waltke, *The Book of Proverbs: Chapters 15–31*, 34.

An Analysis of "the Way" in the Book of Proverbs

Therefore, the book of Proverbs provides a uniform use of "the way" in reinforcing the themes that "God is the revealer of wisdom" and "Wisdom teaches and forms a relationship with His people." This consistent use provides a framework for further study of the motif in Proverbs, below, and in Acts (in chapter five).

ANALYSIS OF "THE WAY" AS A MOTIF IN PROVERBS 1–29

The analysis of Proverbs 1–29 has primarily provided information about the theological use of the way. Rather than conducting an individual, passage-by-passage, analysis of "the way" as a possible motif, Freedman's method will now be applied to all of Proverbs 1–29. Freedman's method identifies five characteristics of a motif: (1) frequency, (2) avoidability, (3) occurrence in significant contexts, (4) coherency, and (5) symbolic appropriateness.[255] He considers the first two characteristics necessary for a motif to exist, while the additional three establish the strength of the motif.[256] In this brief analysis, only Freedman's two necessary criteria will be examined.[257]

The first criterion is frequency. Frequency is the rate at which the term occurs, and the term's frequency should suggest "purposiveness rather than merely coincidence."[258] Kitchen notes "the choice of two paths" is presented seventy times.[259] Direct uses of the way (דרך) and its cognate (אֹרַח) appear fifty-four times in Proverbs 1–29. Further, Proverbs has a significant percentage of occurrences of both the way (דרך) and its cognate (אֹרַח) in the OT as a whole (i.e., 11 and 31 percent respectively, see Table 6). With these numerous occurrences of the way, Proverbs fulfills the first criterion for being a motif.

The second criterion is avoidability: "The avoidability and unlikelihood of the particular uses of a motif, or of its appearance in certain

---

255. Freedman, "The Literary Motif," 126–27.
256. Freedman, "The Literary Motif," 126.
257. Another reason for the brevity of the analysis is the overwhelming consensus by scholars that the way serves an important role within Proverbs (i.e., the way is a central image, the way is listed as one of the themes). Weeks proposed previously that the way is a motif. Weeks, *Instruction and Imagery in Proverbs 1–9*, 73. Similarly, Waltke mentions a "journey motif" when discussing Proverbs 14:12. Waltke, *The Book of Proverbs: Chapters 1–15*, 591.
258. Kitchen, *Proverbs*, 126.
259. Kitchen, *Proverbs*, 734.

contexts, or of its appearance at all."[260] As the study has shown, the way has been used as a metaphor. Thus, Proverbs is not using the term the way (path, road) interchangeably with literal examples of a road or travel. Literal examples may include depictions of historical roads or travel narratives. Each example covered in this study depicts instead a metaphorical use of the way. Further, Proverbs includes "the way" and matches the two types of way with the women Lady Wisdom and Dame Folly. Also, Proverbs 9 appears to be a climax of "the way" metaphor.[261] The literary climax suggests intentionality. Therefore, because "the way" is intentionally used as a metaphor, it meets the criterion for a motif.

In sum, "the way" meets both essential criteria in Freedman's method for determining a motif. Further, "the way" as a motif supports the themes of Proverbs. As the theological analysis of "the way" has shown above, the metaphor is used to show that God grants wisdom and that God's wisdom builds the relationship between man and God.

CONCLUSION

Proverbs 1–29 provides four observable features of "the way." Moreover, these chapters use "the way" to support the themes of the book as a whole. First, God's people are those who travel the path (Prov 1:7; 2:1–22; 3:5–7; 9; 16). With God's people as travelers, Proverbs may be associated with Israel's salvific history, implying that wisdom is directly associated with divine revelation. Second, God creates the path (3:5–7; 16). Because God is the creator of the way, the nature of wisdom is again associated with God's divine revelation. Third, God directs and sustains His people on the path (Prov 2:1–22; 3:5–7; 9; 14:1–32; 16). In this third point, God is shown preserving believers in their walk of faith and ensuring they reach their destination. Fourth, choosing to follow the path has consequences that lead to life or death (Prov 2:1–22; 4:14–18; 9; 14:1–32; 15). These four features directly support significant themes in Proverbs (i.e., "Wisdom comes from God," and "Wisdom builds the relationship between God His people").

---

260. Freedman, "The Literary Motif," 126.

261. Waltke writes the "two great paired poems, chs. 7 and 8, is now brought to its apex." Waltke, *The Book of Proverbs: Chapters 15–31*, 429. Kitchen writes the "ninth chapter forms a fitting conclusion to the first eight." Kitchen, *Proverbs*, 201.

4

The Cognitive Environment of Luke-Acts

INTRODUCTION

AFTER IDENTIFYING A LACUNA in the research concerning the referent or literary use of "the Way" in Acts, the previous chapter examined the use of the way metaphor in Proverbs, showing the term is a motif of Proverbs with four proposed features. Also, chapter 3 suggested Proverbs as a referent and literary example for Luke's use of "the Way." Chapter 4 will show how Wisdom literature influenced the cognitive environment of the first-century authors by surveying the use of "the Way" in other Old Testament books and related texts until the writing of Acts. First, the term "cognitive environment" is defined. Second, the author and audience of Acts is reviewed. Third, the use of "the Way" within each text is summarized. Four, synthesizing the three previous points, "cognitive environment," author and audience, and the uses of "the Way," the influence the Wisdom literature, and particularly the theology of "the Way," may have had on Luke is suggested.

THE COGNITIVE ENVIRONMENT

An understanding of Luke's cognitive environment provides the information needed to demonstrate the influence Wisdom literature had on the author of the book of Acts.[1] John Walton defines "cognitive environment

---

1. The many arguments for the dating of Acts will not be discussed. This paper

criticism" as the discipline that explores the OT's relationship (the NT in this study) with its cultural milieu.² Cognitive environment criticism aims to "recover the world's cultural layers behind" the writing with external texts and iconography.³ Walton developed five models to associate one text with another text: borrowing, polemics, counter-texts, echoes, and diffusion.⁴ In this analysis of the cognitive environment of Acts, Walton's method of echoes is applied.⁵ Walton's echoes model seeks to understand similarities between texts by identifying allusions, citations, or references to an older text. While Beale's method of analyzing allusions within Acts is employed in chapter 5, Walton's cognitive environment criticism model nevertheless assists in understanding and determining the plausibility of the "Way" motif from Wisdom literature influencing Luke. In this chapter, the use of "the Way" is traced through biblical history to demonstrate that authors from the cognitive environment of the NT were "echoing" the theology of "the Way" as present in the OT.

Two parameters are helpful in identifying the influence of Wisdom literature on the New Testament. First, it must be determined if it is plausible that Wisdom literature influenced the NT authors, especially Luke who was not Jewish.⁶ Second, it must be determined if the context of the book of Acts supports the view that Luke was influenced by the Wisdom literature. This second determination will be addressed in chapter 5, where Acts is

---

agrees with Keener's assessment. Keener writes, "Because I [Keener] believe that the arguments are compelling in favor of the author having been one of Paul's traveling companions (probably for a brief time as early as ca. 48 C.E.), I would restrict any date estimate I would offer to within the probable lifetime of such a companion . . . The date of Acts is uncertain, buy my [Keener's] best guesses, for reasons that follow, are in the early 70s, with dates in the 80s and 60s still plausible, and a date in the 90s not impossible" (400). Keener, *Acts: 1:1—2:47*, 400.

2. Walton, "Interactions in the Ancient Cognitive Environment," 333.

3. Walton, "Interactions in the Ancient Cognitive Environment," 333.

4. Walton, "Interactions in the Ancient Cognitive Environment," 333–35.

5. Here the echoes model is not to be confused with the technical term that denotes a less strong allusion.

6. According to Walton, the Greek philosopher Carneades provides the best definition of plausibility: "something is plausible if it appears to be true, or (is even more plausible) if it appears to be true and is consistent with other things that appear to be true. Or thirdly, it is even more plausible if it is stable (consistent with other things that appear to be true) and is tested. According to the epistemological theory of Carneades, everything we accept, or should accept, as reasonably based on evidence, is subject to doubt and is plausible only, as opposed to being known (beyond all reasonable doubt) to be true" (152). Walton, "Abductive, Presumptive and Plausible Arguments," 152.

examined using the methods of Freedman and Beale. This present chapter addresses the first parameter by examining the author and audience of Acts and uses the echoes model to show that it is plausible that the Wisdom literature influenced the authors of the NT.

AUTHOR AND AUDIENCE

Although some may argue that the "identity of the author is not critical to our reading"[7] a basic understanding of both the author and audience is crucial in this study to determine if Wisdom literature influences the book of Acts. This work proposes the physician as the author of Luke-Acts and the primary audience to be Theophilus, along with fellow believers. By establishing the author and audience of Acts, later arguments concerning the cognitive environment and establishing the possibility that Acts references Proverbs requires Luke and his audience to be more than Gentiles unfamiliar with Judaism and the OT.

The physician Luke was likely a God-fearer and knowledgeable in Jewish History (i.e., the Old Testament and Judaism).[8] Further, the audience has comparable knowledge of the Old Testament and Judaism. Keener looks to Luke-Acts for internal evidence of authorship: (1) Luke's Greek and Hellenistic education, (2) the "we" passages, and (3) his knowledge of Judaism.[9] His argument is accumulative, for even by his own admission, Luke's Greek and Hellenistic education is not conclusive.[10] But, he finds that it points to Luke being "immersed in Diaspora synagogue Judaism."[11] Keener finds the "we" passages suggest "Luke traveled with Paul to Jerusalem as a representative of the Gentile churches (Acts 20:4–5; cf. Rom 15:27; 2 Cor 8:23), he was probably ethnically Gentile."[12] Moreover, Keener suggests Luke was likely a God-fearer or a "long-standing member of the

---

7. Green is speaking here about the need to know the author of the Gospel of Luke to interpret the book. Green, *The Gospel of Luke*, 20.

8. Bovon supports the claims that Luke was a God-fearer. Also, he suggests Luke is in the "higher strat of society," has a good education, and is a "second or third generation of the church." Bovon and Koester, *Luke 1*, 8.

9. Keener, *Acts: 1:1—2:47*, 404.

10. Keener, *Acts: 1:1—2:47*, 404.

11. Keener, *Acts: 1:1—2:47*, 404. See Sterling, *Historiography and Self-Definition*, 327–29.

12. Keener, *Acts: 1:1—2:47*, 327–29.

Hellenistic Jewish Christian movement."[13] Hemer concludes the "we" passages are the most significant testament to the author's identity."[14] Moreover, Hemer states the "we" passages affirm the external evidence of Luke as the author.[15] Last, Luke's extensive knowledge of Judaism leans to understanding Luke as a God-fearer or at minimum a learned Christian.[16] Luke's use of the LXX and "biblical speech" is also suggestive thorough education prior to authoring Luke-Acts, according to Keener.[17] Leifeld and Pao also find the "Semitic elements of style" in Luke-Acts suggests Luke was a Jewish Christian.[18] Luke's use of the LXX is fitting given promise-fulfillment in Luke-Acts. Speaking of Luke's purpose in his Gospel, Hays writes, "The overall design of Luke's two-volume work, accordingly, highlights God's purpose in fulfilling the promise of redemption for his people Israel"[19] and "Luke is seeking to reassure his implied readers . . . that the story of Jesus constitutes the fulfillment of the story of Israel."[20]

The audience of Acts was likely a "literate, Greco-Roman, gentile."[21] However, as Keener recognizes, Acts is likely written to a wide audience.[22] The internal evidence within Luke-Acts provides support by Luke's address to Theophilus and the Jewish content (e.g., reference to the LXX). Moreover, external evidence suggests the Church was composed of both Gentile and Jewish Christians.

Luke addresses Luke-Acts to Theophilus (Luke 1:3; Acts 1:1). Keener suggests Theophilus was probably a wealthier individual, well educated, and held a higher rank amongst the people.[23] Bock also proposes Theophilus is a Christian.[24] Further, Theophilus may have commissioned Luke's writings.[25] Regardless of Theophilus' role, Luke addresses Theophilus as the recipient.

13. Keener, *Acts: 1:1—2:47*, 404–05.
14. Hemer, *The Book of Acts in the Setting of Hellenistic History*, 413.
15. Hemer, *The Book of Acts in the Setting of Hellenistic History*, 413.
16. Keener, *Acts: 1:1—2:47*, 405.
17. Keener, *Acts: 1:1—2:47*, 405.
18. Liefeld, "Luke," 24.
19. Hays, *Echoes of Scripture in the Gospels*, 191.
20. Hays, *Echoes of Scripture in the Gospels*, 192.
21. Stevens, *Acts*, 32.
22. Keener, *Acts: 1:1—2:47*, 423.
23. Keener, *Acts: 1:1—2:47*, 423–24.
24. Bock, *Luke: Volume 1*, 14.
25. Bock, *Luke: Volume 1*, 63.

Yet, Bock writes:

> Luke did not write, however, just for this one person, but for any who felt this tension. Any Gentile feeling out of place in originally Jewish movement could benefit from the reassurance Luke offers. Any Jew (or Jewish Christian) troubled by the lack of Jewish response to the gospel or by the Gentile openness to the gospel could see that God directed the affair and that he gave the nation multiple invitations to join in God's renewed work.[26]

Bock does well in understanding the audience to share in a similar background (specifically as a reader) to Theophilus. In fact, this approach may be preferred over narrowing the audience down to a specific people group based upon external evidence. Keener writes that by the time of Greek churches, the congregation make-up contained great numbers of Gentiles, and with Philippi, the church "never had a large Jewish population to begin with."[27] Keener notes that most churches began with a Jewish base derived from the synagogues.[28] Nevertheless, the external evidence suggests Jewish and Gentile churches.

The internal evidence also supports an audience familiar with Judaism. One example is the audiences understanding of the LXX. Pao suggests the audience knew about the LXX for four reasons: "(1) the prevailing use of Isaiah in other early Christian works as shown above; (2) the Lukan focus on synagogues and therefore the possibility of his audience being God-fearers; (3) the Lukan text itself reflects the training of Christian converts in Israel's scripture; and (4) the pervasive use of scriptural quotations, allusions, and patterns in the narrative itself."[29] Pao recognizes both the external facts listed by Keener (i.e., the synagogues), but he also highlights Luke's use of specific Old Testament citations, allusions, and patterns.

In sum, the author and audience were likely familiar with Jewish history and the Septuagint. Luke, himself, was probably a former God-fearer with previous knowledge of the LXX. Moreover, Luke was a member of the Church—dating back to the "we" passages—prior to authoring Luke-Acts. The recipients of Luke-Acts were equally familiar with Jewish history and the LXX, as the composition of Greek churches and Luke's writings evidence. Thus, if the summary below shows the potential influence of OT

---

26. Bock, *Luke: Volume 1*, 15.
27. Keener, *Acts: 1:1—2:47*, 426.
28. Keener, *Acts: 1:1—2:47*, 426.
29. Pao, *Acts and the Isaianic New Exodus*, 35.

Wisdom literatures during Luke and his audience's life, they would likely be influenced by its content.

WISDOM LITERATURE: PROVERBS, ECCLESIASTES, JOB

To determine if the cognitive environment of Acts was influenced by the Wisdom literature of the OT, there needs to be a baseline understanding of OT Wisdom literature. There is, however, difficulty deciding what constitutes Wisdom literature. In *Wisdom in Israel*, Gerhard von Rad notes this difficulty, because the word "wisdom" can be interpreted broadly, and the Wisdom literature has an indeterminate literary form.[30] Because of these two characteristics, scholars disagree which passages in the Bible are part of the Wisdom literature. Thankfully, there is a general consensus around the starting point for identifying Wisdom literature: hence, many scholars agree that Ecclesiastes, Proverbs, and Job provide guidance for identifying Wisdom literature or Israel's concept of wisdom.[31]

Ecclesiastes and Job join Proverbs to complete the gold standard for identifying Wisdom literature.[32] Thus, these books will be explicitly reviewed where extra-biblical texts will be overviewed. This section discusses a theology of "the way" in Ecclesiastes and Job, specifically in terms of the use of דרך.

---

30. Von Rad, *Wisdom in Israel*, 291.

31. The recent work by Kynes calls into question the Wisdom literature genre (244). Kynes suggests that wisdom is a concept and not a form or origin (57). Will Kynes, *An Obituary for "Wisdom Literature": The Birth, Death, and Intertextual Reintegration of a Biblical Corpus* (New York: Oxford University Press, 2019). Andrew Judd responds to Kynes, writing, "Rather than follow Will Kynes in seeing genre as a subjective tool for reader response, it is best to see genres as conventions . . . that involve both readers and writers . . . The fact that smaller genres like 'saying' and 'riddle' exist and have similar themes and social function seems beyond doubt. It also seems clear that certain 'instructional books'—like Proverbs, Ecclesiastes, and Job—might have a particular interest in those themes and be designed to pull together genres for instructional ends." Andrew Judd, *Modern Genre Theory: An Introduction for Biblical Studies* (Grand Rapids, MI: Zondervan Academic, 2024), 198. Collins notes that Wisdom literature does manifest a shared worldview or particular literary forms. John J. Collins, *Jewish Wisdom in the Hellenistic Age*, The Old Testament Library (Louisville, KY: Westminster John Knox, 1997), 1. This paper finds literary forms are helpful in identifying Wisdom literature as Collins suggests.

32. See introductions to OT Wisdom Literature, such as Bartholomew and O'Dowd's *Old Testament Wisdom Literature* and Crenshaw's *Old Testament Wisdom*.

Ecclesiastes and "the Way"

Ecclesiastes does not mention "the way" often.[33] There are two occurrences of דרך in Ecclesiastes 11, and both times the author uses the term metaphorically. This sparse mention in Ecclesiastes eliminates "the way" as a theme or motif in the book. However, readers may observe similarities between the two occurrences.

First, Ecclesiastes 11:5 demonstrates humanity's inability to control the future, and the author explains God's control of creation through the formation of the unborn.[34] Further, "the way" in 11:5 references humanity's "life-breath" or spirit.[35] George Athas writes, "God is in control of the world, and his ways are inscrutable to humans as the way a baby forms in the womb (11:5)."[36] Ecclesiastes 11:5 depicts God as the one in control of humanity.

The second use of דרך is in 11:9. Michael Eaton writes that here the metaphor to walk refers to a person's manner of life.[37] Athas paraphrases verse 9 as follows: "First, he urges the man to follow the desires of his heart while he is young (11:9)."[38] Both scholars understand the way as a metaphor for a manner of life.

Job and "the Way"

The word דרך appears twice in chapter 28 and contains the wisdom phrase "Fear of the Lord," which provides excellent and representative insight into Job's use of "the way." Job 28:12 asks: "Where shall wisdom be found? And where is the place of understanding?"[39] The poem captures God's relation-

---

33. "דרך" in Eccl 10:3; 11:5, 9; 12:5. Ecclesiastes does not contain the cognate אֹרַח.

34. George Athas, *Ecclesiastes, Song of Songs*, Story of God Bible Commentary (Grand Rapids, MI: Zondervan, 2020), 208.

35. Roland E. Murphy, *Ecclesiastes*, Accordance electronic ed., vol. 23A, Word Biblical Commentary (Grand Rapids: Zondervan, 1992), 109. Murphy references "life-breath"; Michael A. Eaton, *Ecclesiastes: An Introduction and Commentary*, vol. 18, Tyndale Old Testament Commentaries (Downers Grove, IL: InterVarsity, 1983), 162. Eaton references the Spirit.

36. Athas, *Ecclesiastes, Song of Songs*, 208.

37. Eaton, *Ecclesiastes*, 165.

38. Athas, *Ecclesiastes, Song of Songs*, 210.

39. Francis I. Andersen, *Job: An Introduction and Commentary*, vol. 14, Tyndale Old Testament Commentaries (Downers Grove, IL: InterVarsity, 1976), 242.

ship with man, reflects on wisdom, and identifies the origin of wisdom. In vv. 1–12, "the way" is used to describe the discovery of ore and precious metals in the earth. Interestingly, animals are incapable of finding the way to these treasures.[40] David Clines understands this usage as the path cut by miners, although the text may also refer to the ability of animals, so perhaps the way is both literal (e.g., the path cut in rock) and a metaphor for wisdom.[41] The second pericope (vv. 13–20) does not explicitly describe "the way" but asks where "the way" resides and its price. The answer to these questions is that wisdom cannot be purchased or found by humans.

The third stanza (21–28) uses "the way" as a metaphor for the realm of wisdom.[42] Indeed, the realm of wisdom is not merely in God's mind, but is observable in all creation.[43] However, only God can reveal wisdom through the universe.[44] Barry Webb finds that vv. 23–27 explains why one must find God to find wisdom, i.e., "Only 'God understands the way to wisdom, and he knows its location' (v. 23)."[45] Accordingly, the poem concludes by declaring that one finds wisdom in "the fear of the Lord." The conclusion shows that humanity can acquire the wisdom of God if they have a fear of the Lord.[46] Along with having a fear of the Lord, Clines suggests that the revelation of Job 28:28 involves living life in the right way, which consists in turning from evil paths.[47] Human beings cannot obtain wisdom themselves. John Hartley writes, "no human being can bring wisdom into his own service."[48] Thus, God gives wisdom, while humanity can only receive wisdom. Webb provides a particularly relevant biblical theology concerning Job 28,

---

40. Tremper Longman, III, *Job*, Baker Commentary on the Old Testament Wisdom and Psalms (Grand Rapids, MI: Baker Academic, 2012), 327.

41. Clines understands the path literally connecting to the assumption that all paths on earth are known to animal wisdom, and that those underground are hidden from them (913). David J. A. Clines, *Job 21–37*, vol. 18A, Word Biblical Commentary (Nashville, TN: Thomas Nelson, 2006), 913. Andersen, *Job*, 242.

42. Clines, *Job 21–37*, 919–920.

43. Andersen, *Job*, 245.

44. Andersen, *Job*, 245.

45. Barry G. Webb, *Job*, ed. T. Desmond Alexander, Thomas R. Schreiner, and Andreas J. Köstenberger, Evangelical Biblical Theology Commentary (Bellingham, WA: Lexham Academic, 2023), 314.

46. Longman III, *Job*, 333.

47. Clines, *Job 21–37*, 924, "So what exactly does wisdom consist of?"

48. John E. Hartley, *The Book of Job*, New International Commentary on the Old Testament (Grand Rapids, MI: Eerdmans, 1988), 380.

> The special contribution of this chapter is the way it points us directly to the only source of true wisdom, especially the wisdom we need to cope rightly with the mystery of undeserved suffering . . . The New Testament, too, tells us of a wisdom that is "from above," and utterly different from the wisdom of this world that leads to disorder and every kind of evil (Jas 3:17). [T]he earliest Christian churches, for example, had peace and were built up, "living in the fear of the Lord" (Acts 9:31). The only difference is that the title "the Lord" has taken on a deeper and richer meaning here—no longer just the mighty Creator, but also the God who became incarnate for us in Jesus Christ; no longer just the God who spoke from above, but the One who came to show us the wisdom from above lived out in perfect obedience to God and to love us, and who plumbed the depths of undeserved suffering for us in order to bring us home to God.[49]

Webb's insights point to God as the source of wisdom, the connection between biblical wisdom to the book of Acts, and to the metaphor of the way being developed in view of Christ.

Job and Ecclesiastes: Summary

Job and Ecclesiastes use "the way" as a metaphor for life. Also, both books associate "the way" with the Lord. When these books are compared with Proverbs, one can see all three biblical texts use "the way" to describe conduct, future outcomes based on conduct, and the personification of wisdom. Often, these uses have overlapping theological implications.[50] Last, the three books give a framework for the use of "the way" in the OT. This framework provides a foundation for comparing OT uses of "the way" with the intertestamental period, and the NT.

The "gold standard" also provides valuable information because of its place within ancient Israel. Wisdom literature is not an isolated or removed set of texts from Israel's culture. Van Leeuwen considers "wisdom and covenant as linked by their common root in creation."[51] Kahtrine Dell shares a similar sentiment, "wisdom does demonstrate links to covenantal ideas,

---

49. Webb, *Job*, 319–20.

50. Habel calls these overlapping concepts satellite symbols gravitating around "the way," which is a nuclear symbol.

51. Van Leeuwen, "Theology: Creation, Wisdom, and Covenant," 65.

broadly defined."[52] Similarly, the Psalms also support examples of broad contextual connecions between covenant and wisdom, but the following sections focus predominantly on the continued use of Wisdom literature and more specifically, the continual use of "the Way" metaphor.[53]

"THE WAY" IN THE PSALMS, THE DEAD SEA SCROLLS, AND THE SEPTUAGINT

Studying the history of Wisdom literature is necessary for understanding its use in the Bible, especially the NT.[54] As noted above, both Luke and his audience were familiar with the LXX, so they would have been influenced by Wisdom literature from the Septuagint. Besides the gold standard of Proverbs, Job and Ecclesiastes, the book of Psalms, Wisdom, Ben Sira, and the Dead Sea Scrolls contribute to an understanding of wisdom from Ancient Israel through to Second Temple Judaism.[55] That is, the examination of these texts covers a time that ranges from the OT to the NT. These works relate to OT Wisdom literature because of their close theological and literary connections with Proverbs, Ecclesiastes, and Job. In addition to analysis of the texts, an overview is given of the afterlife in Second Temple literature. This summary is necessary for better understanding how "the way," when used as a metaphor for a destination, relates to the cognitive environment of the NT, the author and audience of Luke-Acts, who knew the Septuagint.

Psalms: "The Way"

Psalms containing wisdom contribute to the understanding of the cognitive environment of Acts by demonstrating how the Israelites understood the wisdom tradition. Further, the psalmists' use of parallelism helps define and clarify the vocabulary and ideas of the tradition. Hence, the

---

52. Dell, *The Lord by Wisdom Founded the Earth*, 196.

53. Although not providing a case for the present argument of cultural milieu or cognitive environment but more in support of continued use of Wisdom literature, Walter T. Wilson's *Ancient Wisdom* presents proverbial and gnomic texts spanning ancient Near East and the Greco-Roman world and both Jewish and Christian contexts. Wilson, *Ancient Wisdom*.

54. Crenshaw, "Method in Determining Wisdom Influence," 135.

55. See Longman and Dillard, *An Introduction to the Old Testament*; Murphy, *The Tree of Life*, 2nd ed.; Perdue, *The Sword and the Stylus*.

Psalms contribute to identifying common features of Wisdom literature in Scripture.

There is no agreement about which psalms can be considered wisdom psalms,[56] although scholars frequently identify Psalms 1, 19, 37, 39, 49, 73, and 119.[57] Goldingay uses two qualifiers to identify wisdom in the Psalms. Wisdom psalms must use the language of wisdom, and reflect the insights of the Wisdom literature.[58] Similarly, Murphy looks for wisdom diction (i.e., blessing formulas, numerical sayings, etc.) and wisdom themes (i.e., two-ways theology, "fear of the Lord," etc.) to identify wisdom psalms.[59] Psalm 1, to be examined below, meets the criteria proposed by Goldingay and Murphy.

The Psalms include many uses of "the way."[60] One example is found in Psalm 1, which provides an introduction to the Psalter and a rough framework to help in understanding the book.[61] Psalm 1 "teaches that the psalms are God's instruction—they are *the way* of the Lord."[62] The word דרך translates as "the way" in both verses 1 and 6.[63] Moreover, the context establishes "the contrasting of two *ways*," a common theme in Scripture.[64] In verse one, "the way" describes all the characteristics of the wicked, which the righteous should avoid.[65] In Psalm 1:6, "the way" refers to the actions and thoughts of the righteous. Also, the Lord protects the way of the righteous, for they are not walking in their own lordship, but that of God (v. 6).[66]

56. The classification of wisdom psalms is rightly called into question. Kynes states that identifying a psalm as wisdom involves circular reasoning. In this study, the use of wisdom psalms here reflects vocabulary used by scholars, with wisdom psalms being those exhibiting the concepts of wisdom. Kynes, *An Obituary for "Wisdom Literature,"* 32.

57. Longman, *The Fear of the Lord Is Wisdom*, 67–68. Crenshaw, *Old Testament Wisdom*, 192. Murphy, *The Tree of Life*, 103.

58. Goldingay, *Psalms, 1–41*, 57.

59. Murphy, *The Tree of Life*, 103.

60. Occurrences of "דרך" in the Psalms: 1:1, 6; 2:12; 5:9; 7:13; 10:5; 11:2; 18:22, 31, 33; 25:4, 5, 8, 9; 27:11; 32:8; 35:6; 36:5; 37:5, 7, 14, 23, 34; 39:2; 49:14; 50:23; 51:15; 58:8; 64:4; 67:3; 77:14, 20; 80:13; 81:14; 85:14; 86:11; 89:42; 91:11, 13; 95:10; 101:2, 6; 102:24; 103:7; 107:4, 7, 17, 40; 110:7; 119:1, 3, 5, 14, 26, 27, 29, 30, 32, 33, 35, 37, 59, 168; 128:1; 138:5; 139:3, 24; 143:8; 145:17; 146:9.

61. Craigie, *Psalms 1–50*, 58.

62. Jacobson and Tanner, "Book One of the Psalter," 56.

63. Craigie, *Psalms 1–50*, 58.

64. Craigie, *Psalms 1–50*, 58; italics in the original.

65. Craigie, *Psalms 1–50*, 60.

66. Craigie, *Psalms 1–50*, 61; Jacobson and Tanner, "Book One of the Psalter," 63.

Here, the parallel of "the way" in verse six strengthens the motif of the way as a metaphor for living.[67] Concerning Psalm 1, Waltke and Zaspel observe that like Proverbs, the way metaphor governs.[68] They write, "'The way' in 1:1 and 1:6 brackets Psalm 1 (an *inclusio*), and by this metaphor life is pictured as a journey—a common figure in both Psalms and Proverbs. 'Way' connotes the context, conduct, and consequences of a particular direction taken in life, and this psalm stresses that the 'way' of the righteous differs from the 'way' of the wicked in these respects."[69] The way metaphor is easily observed in this psalm, both in its presence and function.

Ben Sira and "the Way"

Ben Sira is an intertestamental text that provides a chronological bridge to observe the use of Wisdom literature between the OT and the NT, contributing to an understanding of Luke's cognitive environment. Ben Sira is found within the DSS and is recorded in both Hebrew and Greek.[70] Luke and his audience, knowledgeable in Judaism, were likely exposed to Ben Sira. Scholars date the Wisdom of Joshua Ben Sira, known as Sirach or Ben Sira, to around 200 BC.[71] Compared to the Wisdom literature of the Bible, Ben Sira is like the book of Proverbs.[72] Wilson writes, "Given how he

---

67. Goldingay translates the way as the path. In addition, he finds that the use of ashre in verse one, "immediately introduces the idea of the walk of life" (82). Goldingay, *Psalms*, 89.

68. Bruce K. Waltke and Fred G. Zaspel, *How to Read and Understand the Psalms* (Wheaton, IL: Crossway, 2023), 12.

69. Waltke and Zaspel, *How to Read and Understand the Psalms*, 12; italics in the original.

70. John Kampen, *Wisdom Literature*, Eerdmans Commentaries on the Dead Sea Scrolls (Grand Rapids, MI: Eerdmans, 2011), 342–343. Athas has a more specific comment, "He wrote originally in Hebrew (a nationalistic choice), and his grandson translated the work into Greek at Alexandria in 132 BC, adding an introductory preface to it. The book is a discourse on wisdom, which gives us insight into Judaism when sovereignty over Judea passed from the Ptolemies to the Seleucids." George Athas, *Bridging the Testaments: The History and Theology of God's People in the Second Temple Period* (Grand Rapids, MI: Zondervan Academic, 2023), 291–92.

71. Skehan and Di Lella date the book to the first quarter of the second century B.C. Patrick W. Skehan, and Alexander A. Di Lella, *The Wisdom of Ben Sira*, The Anchor Bible 39 (New York: Doubleday, 1987), 10. Longman supports this dating. Longman III, *The Fear of the Lord is Wisdom*, 221. Wilson places the date "between 195 and 175 BCE." Walter T. Wilson, *The Wisdom of Sirach* (Grand Rapids, MI: Eerdmans, 2023), 5.

72. Collins, *Jewish Wisdom in the Hellenistic Age*, 226.

presents himself as both a sage and a font of wisdom, it is not surprising that the traditions to which Ben Sira most often turns can be traced back to the book of Proverbs, which provided him with models of both form and content."[73] Indeed, Ben Sira continues to deliver wisdom for everyday living through maxims. Furthermore, Ben Sira also believes the fear of the Lord is the beginning of knowledge (Sir 1:7).

Nonetheless, Ben Sira differs from Proverbs, Ecclesiastes, and Job by explicitly incorporating the Mosaic Law.[74] By integrating the Mosaic Law, the book combines traditional wisdom with the salvation theology found within the context of Israel's history.[75] The wisdom of Ben Sira demonstrates the importance of both the Torah and Wisdom literature in Second Temple Judaism.

Ben Sira includes twenty-five uses of ὁδός (the way).[76] Most of these occurrences of ὁδός can be understood metaphorically. "The way" may describe the conduct of a person, the personification of wisdom, or (rarely) a literal road or path.[77] The continued use of "the way" as a metaphor contributes most to an understanding of the motif, both because a metaphor has a more flexible range of meanings in comparison to a literal use and because metaphors are more likely to change in meaning over time.

Metaphors about conduct are uses of ὁδός that depict the thoughts and actions of a person, animal, or God.[78] "The way" metaphor can capture the dichotomy between sin and righteousness.[79] Two examples demonstrate ὁδός used as a metaphor for personal conduct: Sirach 2:6, 15 and 37:9, 15. First, in Sirach 2:6, 15, Ben Sira describes how God can guide one's ways. Alexander Di Lella and Patrick Skehan compare Sirach 2:6 to Proverbs 3:5-6,[80] which recommends placing all one's faith in God, who can make all one's ways straight. Sirach 2:6 likewise advises putting faith in God, who

---

73. Wilson, *The Wisdom of Sirach*, 20.

74. Crenshaw, *Old Testament Wisdom*, 155.

75. Perdue, *The Sword and the Stylus*, 285.

76. Sir 2:6, 15; 6:26; 8:15; 11:26; 14:21, 22; 16:20; 17:15, 19; 21:10, 16; 23:19; 32:20, 21; 33:11, 13, 33; 37:9, 15; 19:21; 47:23; 48:22; 49:6, 9.

77. The direction in which a slave ran (Sir 32:33) and the burning of physical streets (Sir 49:6) are two examples of literal uses of the way in Sirach.

78. Sir 2:6, 15; 8:15; 11:26; 16:20; 17:15, 19; 23:19. Sirach 48:22 uses a ὁδός as a metaphor for actions in keeping with the character and tradition of David.

79. Sirach 21:10, 16; 39:24; 47:24; 49:9.

80. Di Lella and Skehan, *The Wisdom of Ben Sira*, 151.

will make one's path straight.[81] Another common use of the metaphor is to describe possible futures, which relate to a person's conduct.[82] Second, Sirach 37:9 is set within a context warning the reader to take care to find good counsel and to remember that expert advice is not self-interested.[83] Sirach 37:9 also points out that great counsel is to be found in a religious person who keeps God's directives.[84]

Wisdom is personified in Sirach 14:21, 22,[85] with Sirach 14:20–15:10 pondering Wisdom's ways and paths, and 14:20–27 focusing on imagery of a person seeking wisdom.[86] The passage uses ὁδός to describe Wisdom's ways and paths, which is similar to Proverbs 3:17's use of דרך and נְתִיבָה.[87] The passage compares the pursuit of wisdom "to the clandestine activity of 'a scout'" and, like Proverbs 8:34, depicts Wisdom's dwelling place as a house that can be located and gazed upon.[88] As can be seen, Ben Sira was a Jewish text despite the author's Hellenistic culture. Athas writes about Ben Sira, "He was open to Greek thought, as long it could be 'Judaized,' and opposed those elements that could potentially dismantle Judaism."[89]

Wisdom and "the Way" in the Wisdom of Solomon

Like Ben Sira, this intertestamental text provides information on "the way" as a metaphor that can inform understanding of the influence of the Wisdom literature on the authors of the NT, including Luke, the author of Acts. The Wisdom of Solomon is dated between the first century BC to 50 AD,[90]

---

81. Sirach 2:15 also mentions the fear of the Lord, which will be discussed later as a connection between "the way" and Proverbs.

82. Sirach 32:20, 21; 33:11, 13; 37:9, 15. Stekan and Lella find that ὁδός is used as a metaphor to describe the destiny of different people in 33:11–13 (400), and the future direction of a person's life in 37:9, 15 (406). Di Lella, and Skehan, *The Wisdom of Ben Sira*, 400, 406.

83. Di Lella and Skehan, *The Wisdom of Ben Sira*, 432.

84. Di Lella and Skehan, *The Wisdom of Ben Sira*, 433.

85. Sirach 6:26; 14:21, 22.

86. Di Lella and Skehan, *The Wisdom of Ben Sira*, 263.

87. Di Lella and Skehan, *The Wisdom of Ben Sira*, 263.

88. Di Lella and Skehan, *The Wisdom of Ben Sira*, 264.

89. Athas, *Bridging the Testaments*, 295.

90. Winston dates the book from 30 BCE to 41 CE, but notes scholars place the book as early as 220 BCE to 50 CE (20). Winston, *The Wisdom of Solomon*, 23–24. Longman dates the book between the second century BC and 50 AD. Longman, *The Fear of the*

and was written during a time of Jewish persecution to encourage those of the faith to remain faithful.[91] The book was written in Greek and was intended to serve as an apologetic. The author's personification of Wisdom is much like Proverbs, although Wisdom's author removes the focus from practical wisdom, placing it on ethical wisdom.[92] The Wisdom of Solomon also explicitly incorporates the history of God's people.[93] The book's style includes Greek rhetorical and literary forms. This incorporation of Greek rhetoric and literary style shows that the Wisdom literature was in some ways influenced by Greek culture. Notwithstanding, it also indicates that the understanding of Wisdom literature, the theology of Scripture, was not affected by Greek culture. Hence, the author Wisdom rejected assimilation into Hellenistic culture.[94] Mark Giszczak iterates, "While these books collect everyday advice on self-discipline, daily work, and personal relationships, they are fundamentally oriented toward God."[95] The intertestamental Wisdom literature remained Jewish, much like the OT, continuing to inform the use of the "the way" metaphor in the NT. The Wisdom of Solomon, therefore, strengthens the likelihood that the cognitive environment of Luke and his audience included "the way" metaphor, as depicted in the book of Proverbs.

The Wisdom of Solomon uses the word ὁδός eight times.[96] The author also uses several words that may be etymologically related to ὁδός,[97] both literally and metaphorically, to describe right conduct and wisdom's personification.[98] The book uses ὁδός as a metaphor to describe the truth and the way of the Lord. Also, the metaphor of the light of justice may apply to Lady wisdom.[99] A metaphor more closely related to the personi-

---

Lord Is Wisdom, 228. Perdue places the book between the first century BC and 40 AD. Perdue, *The Sword and the Stylus*, 292.

91. Perdue, *The Sword and the Stylus*, 293.

92. Longman, *The Fear of the Lord Is Wisdom*, 232.

93. Crenshaw, *Old Testament Wisdom*, 182.

94. Perdue, *The Sword and the Stylus*, 309.

95. Giszczak, *Wisdom of Solomon*, 17–18.

96. Wisdom 2:16; 5:6, 7; 10:17; 12:24; 14:3; 18:23; 19:7.

97. Examples include παροδεύω found in Wisdom 1:8; 2:7; 5:14; 6:22; 10:8 and πάροδος found in Wisdom 2:5, 16.

98. Literal remaining uses of ὁδός include Wisdom 18:23; 19:7.

99. Winston suggests that the imagery of the light of justice, or righteousness, can be metaphorically applied to Lady Wisdom, the personification of wisdom, as he cites FPG:224 (*Fragmenta Pseudepigraphorum Quae Supersunt Graeca*) (1970). Winston, *The*

fication of wisdom is found in Wisdom 10:17, where Lady Wisdom guides behavior and actions, and, as David Winston shows, provides shelter and salvation.[100] Additionally, the Wisdom of Solomon depicts Lady Wisdom as a divine agent who is eternal, immanent and transcendent, and one who enables seekers of wisdom to be "friends with God."[101] Throughout the book, it is easy to observe that divinity and wisdom intersect and can muddle the distinction between God and wisdom's identity, for at times, "wisdom is the *path* to God" and at other times, "wisdom is the *destination*," but lady wisdom and God are not the same in Wisdom.[102]

Next, Wisdom 12:24 and 14:3 use ὁδός to describe the actions and thoughts of the foolish and God's providence or direction in life.[103] In Wisdom 12:24, Egypt is depicted as venturing too far down the wrong path by worshipping false gods, becoming fools in the eyes of God and subjected to His judgment.[104] Wisdom 14:3 uses both ὁδός, and a cognate, τρίβος, to describe both the literal path made through the Red Sea and the metaphorical path of the Lord's providence. Continuing, Wisdom 18:23 and 19:7 use ὁδός in a literal sense to describe the path death takes to overcome the living, and the path made by the division of the Red Sea.

The Dead Sea Scrolls and "the Way"

The Dead Sea Scrolls provide a history of interpretation of "the way." Even before the publication of the Qumran cave four materials, known for its Wisdom literature, it was evident that wisdom was fundamental in the Qumran documents.[105] The texts classified as wisdom among the Dead Sea Scrolls share commonalities with Job, Proverbs, and Ecclesiastes, such as "terminology related to wisdom and knowledge, literary forms associated with pedagogy, and a worldview that centered on the notion of a perfectly ordered creation."[106] The DSS continue to educate about the influence

---

Wisdom of Solomon, 147.

100. Winston, *The Wisdom of Solomon*, 221.

101. Sidnie White Crawford, "Lady Wisdom and Dame Folly at Qumran," *Dead Sea Discoveries* 5, no. 3 (1998): 358.

102. Giszczak, *Wisdom of Solomon*, 18; italics in the original.

103. Wisdom 12:24 includes the use of hyperbaton.

104. Mazzinghi, *Wisdom*, 319.

105. Bakker, "Wisdom in the Dead Sea Scrolls," 141.

106. Bakker, "Wisdom in the Dead Sea Scrolls," 142.

wisdom had upon the NT through the development of the Wisdom tradition, the continuing use of biblical Wisdom literature in general (e.g., the inclusion of biblical books and intertestamental wisdom books such as Ben Sira), and the continuing use of "the way" as a metaphor. Of course, the Qumran community is the only known entity to reference itself as "the Way" prior to Luke referring to the Church as the Way in Acts. First, to be discussed are two developments in Wisdom literature reflected in the DSS, i.e., the associations between Wisdom literature and the Mosaic Law and between Wisdom literature and apocalyptic literature, and second, the use of "the way" in the DSS.

Wisdom texts among the DSS reflect "a reinterpretation of biblical Wisdom Literature within new conceptual frameworks and within the broader context of the interpretive culture of Second Temple Judaism."[107] Such broader contexts would allow or provide a new concept for Luke to use the way metaphor of Proverbs to describe the Church in Acts. One such development is the incorporation of the Mosaic Law, as observed in Ben Sira. The incorporation of the Mosaic Law comes in part because the Dead Sea Scrolls contains Sirach. Additional support for the trend to merge the Mosaic Law with the Wisdom literature came from the discovery of 4Q525. This manuscript, titled the "Beatitudes," resembles the Beatitudes of Matthew 5. The manuscript directly correlates wisdom and the Law, because it discusses a man who obtains wisdom and walks in the Law.[108] Moreover, the author of the Beatitudes self-identifies the text as Wisdom literature, and the literary style closely relates to biblical wisdom texts, as in the personification of wisdom and use of macarisms.

Next, the relationship between wisdom and apocalyptic writing is observable between 330 BC to 135 AD,[109] with the DSS showing an additional association between the two.[110] Potentially, the most influential wisdom text from Qumran is the 4QInstruction text, which combines apocalyptic and wisdom writing (e.g., Proverbs). 4QInstruction discusses the hidden wisdom that is made known to believers.[111] The DSS thus contribute to an

---

107. Bakker, "Wisdom in the Dead Sea Scrolls," 145.

108. Kampen, *Wisdom Literature*, 307.

109. Kampen, *Wisdom Literature*, 16; Purdue references a time between the "third century B.C.E. to the late first century C.E." Perdue, *The Sword and the Stylus*, 357. See Von Rad, *Old Testament Theology*, 2: 303–08.

110. Perdue, *The Sword and the Stylus*, 372.

111. Perdue, *The Sword and the Stylus*, 417.

understanding of the cognitive environment of Luke and his audience by confirming the continued use of Proverbs and through the new relationships between the Wisdom literature, the Law, and apocalyptic literature.

The DSS uses דרך with a similar semantic range as the Psalms.[112] The DSS uses דרך as a metaphor, but unlike the OT Wisdom books, here "the Way" is nomenclature for a sect or community. Concerning this metaphor, David Seely notes the Lord is the one who instills pious qualities as He opens His people's eyes to His ways, their ears to His teaching (4Q434 1 i 3–4), and sets their feet on "the way" (4Q434 1 i 4).[113] John Kampen finds 4Q473 ("The Two Ways") reflects the importance of the imagery of the two ways in Second Temple Judaism, as found in Proverbs and Deuteronomy.[114] These two instances capture how the Qumran community would use "the way" to discuss a way of life.

Regarding דרך as a designation for a people group, Craig Evans writes, "That early 'Christianity' would regard itself as the 'Way,' the same self-designation employed by their contemporaries and rivals who made up the *Yaḥad*, is an important point that must not be underrated."[115] Evans finds that Luke's use of the way metaphor is nearly identical to the self-referential use of דרך in the DSS.[116] He considers the "Rule of the Community" the best text for displaying the similarities between Luke and the DSS.[117] The "Rule of the Community" claims that those of "the way" follow the Most High and that they will one day prepare the way (e.g., Isa 40:3).[118] Conversely, Jörg Frey finds that the use of "the way" is not similar:

> Completely different is the reference to Isa 40:3 in the *Rule of the Community* (1QS 8.14–16): "In the wilderness prepare the Way of the Lord, make level in the desert a highway for our God. This (alludes to) the study of the Torah wh[ic]h he commanded through Moses to do, according to everything that has been revealed

---

112. Tread or trample (1QM 11:6); cause to tread (CD 1:11); way or passage (1QH 6:24); journey (1QM3:10). The Dictionary of Classical Hebrew. vol. 2, ed. David J. A. Clines, s.v. "דרך." The shared use comes from shared content with Scripture, such as the book of Isaiah, and non-biblical entries.

113. Seely, "Barki Nafshi," 416–17.

114. Kampen, *Wisdom Literature*, 287.

115. Evans, "The Synoptic Gospels and the Dead Sea Scrolls," 92.

116. Evans, "The Synoptic Gospels and the Dead Sea Scrolls," 91.

117. Evans, "The Synoptic Gospels and the Dead Sea Scrolls," 91. Evans cites 1QS 4:22; 8:13–14; 9:6–22; 11:17; 1QH 12:4.

118. Evans, "The Synoptic Gospels and the Dead Sea Scrolls," 91.

(from) time to time, and according to that which the prophets have revealed by his holy spirit."[119]

Frey finds that the Qumran community understands preparing "the way" as communal study of the Torah. Also, the desert highway from Isaiah 40:3 influenced the physical settlement of the Qumran community. Frey writes, "There the Essenes could study the Torah in complete segregation from the world outside, and they saw this as fulfillment of Isa 40:3 (cf. 1QS 8.13–14)."[120] Frey concludes that the NT and Qumran understanding of the prophecy of Isaiah 40:3 were different.[121] In brief, the DSS perhaps uses "the Way" as a self-designation describing the ushering in of the Messiah (i.e., Evans' suggestion), or as a self-designation describing a group focused on segregation and Torah observance (i.e., Frey's proposal). However, if Luke is perpetuating the way metaphor as Evans suggests, he is perpetuating an understanding of Isaiah that is incongruent with the NT, as Frey proposes. Peter Lanfer writes that the language of "the way" may be interpreted as a polemic, insider or outsider language, or anti-language. Anti-language was employed by Hebrew groups or sects to differentiate themselves from other Jews, particularly evident with the Qumran society and the DSS.[122] He recognizes that such anti-language persisted into the first century with the early Christian community self-referencing themselves as "the way."[123]

Finally, by examining three Qumran texts (4Q184, "The Wiles of the Wicked Woman," 4Q185, "A Sapiential Work," and 4Q525, "Beatitudes"), Sidnie Crawford finds several themes from the OT representation of Lady Wisdom and Dame Folly.[124] She sees the Qumran community still portrays "wisdom as a divine creation, female in gender, with a particular role in creation and particular relationship with humanity (or, more probably, men)," while Dame Folly is associated chiefly with sinful sexuality in women.[125] These similarities include depicting Dame Folly as leading a person to death

---

119. Frey uses the translation from Elisha Qimron and James H. Charlesworth, "Rule of the Community," in *The Rule of the Community and Related Documents* (PTSDSSP 1), 37. Frey, "The Impact of the Dead Sea Scrolls on New Testament Interpretation," 449.

120. Frey, "The Impact of the Dead Sea Scrolls on New Testament Interpretation," 449.

121. Frey, "The Impact of the Dead Sea Scrolls on New Testament Interpretation," 449.

122. Lanfer, "Anti-Language," 113.

123. Lanfer, "Anti-Language," 113.

124. Crawford, "Lady Wisdom and Dame Folly at Qumran," 359.

125. Crawford, "Lady Wisdom and Dame Folly at Qumran," 359.

and Sheol.[126] Yet, Crawford observes differences between the Qumran's depiction of Lady Wisdom and Dame Folly and their depiction in the OT.

First, in 4Q184, Dame Folly is portrayed as "more cosmic in scope."[127] This increase in scope reflects a greater struggle between good and evil, or God and Satan.[128] Second, Lady Wisdom becomes portrayed as an object to be obtained for a blessing with undertones of equating wisdom with the Torah.[129] In short, these changes remove individual personhood from the personification of Lady Wisdom while elevating Dame Folly to "a semi-divine being (1 Enoch 42), to chthonic night demon (4Q184)."[130]

The Afterlife in the Second Temple Literature

The views of the afterlife in the Second Temple literature influence how the consequences, or final destinations, of "the way" may have been understood in the cognitive environment of Luke's day. The time period covered by Second Temple literature ranges from Ben Sira beyond the authoring of the NT. Although the concept of the afterlife was not fully developed in, or at times even absent from the books of the OT, by the time of the first century, the concept of an afterlife had expanded. Therefore, Second Temple ideas about an afterlife may have altered how the authors of first-century texts, or the NT understood the destination of the way (i.e., death, life, or afterlife).

Jan Sigvartsen has worked through the Apocrypha and Pseudepigrapha, recording views of the afterlife,[131] of which he found eighteen.[132] There appears to be no progression within these views of the afterlife, nor is there an observable shift from a bodily or spiritual resurrection.[133] In fact, the Second Temple literature predominantly shares a "bipartite view (Body + Soul)" of resurrection.[134] Also, Second Temple literature mostly reflects a

---

126. Crawford, "Lady Wisdom and Dame Folly at Qumran," 360.

127. Crawford, "Lady Wisdom and Dame Folly at Qumran," 360.

128. Crawford, "Lady Wisdom and Dame Folly at Qumran," 361–62.

129. Crawford, "Lady Wisdom and Dame Folly at Qumran," 363–65.

130. Crawford, "Lady Wisdom and Dame Folly at Qumran," 365–66.

131. Sigvartsen, *Afterlife and Resurrection Beliefs in the Apocrypha and Apocalyptic Literature*; Sigvartsen, *Afterlife and Resurrection Beliefs in the Pseudepigrapha, Jewish and Christian Texts in Contexts and Related Studies*.

132. Sigvartsen, *Afterlife and Resurrection Beliefs in the Pseudepigrapha*, 209.

133. Sigvartsen, *Afterlife and Resurrection Beliefs in the Pseudepigrapha*, 209.

134. Sigvartsen, *Afterlife and Resurrection Beliefs in the Pseudepigrapha*, 210.

concept of "postmortem evaluation of the soul" where the righteous are rewarded and the wicked are punished.[135] The End of Days also became associated with divine judgement of the righteous and the wicked.[136] This development in the understanding of wisdom led to the concept of "delayed retribution," which provided a solution for the "crisis of theodicy" that was manifest in "the Second Temple era."[137]

The Second Temple literature depicts an afterlife that is more robust than that found in the OT. Within Second Temple literature the concept of a bodily or spiritual resurrection appears, while the End of Days becomes associated with the judgment of humanity.

"The way" in the Psalms, the Dead Sea Scrolls, and the Septuagint give rise to several observations that impact understanding of the influence of Wisdom literature and the use of "the way" as a metaphor in the NT. First, "the way" functions as a metaphor in the Psalms, the DSS, and other intertestamental texts, just as it functioned in Proverbs, Ecclesiastes and Job. Second, the Wisdom literature develops or shows associations with the Law and apocalyptic literature. Third, "the way" is used to describe a people group. Fourth, the culture surrounding these texts is unlikely to have supported the view of an afterlife that is found in the NT.

CONTEMPORANEOUS FIRST-CENTURY USES OF "THE WAY"

Texts from the first century that are contemporaneous with the NT provide further examples of "the way" that can be compared both to texts dated earlier (e.g., the OT texts) and to the use of "the Way" in Acts. Hellenistic sources, the Apostolic Fathers, and NT co-authors stand as contemporaries of the author of Luke-Acts. So far, the texts examined have either been part of the Christian heritage or have close associations (i.e., DSS). The contemporaneous first-century texts include both those with shared or similar heritage (i.e., the two-way tradition and the NT co-authors) and texts that do not share a similar heritage (i.e., the Hellenistic sources). However, each of these sources' use of "the way" provides insight into the cognitive environment of Luke.

---

135. Sigvartsen, *Afterlife and Resurrection Beliefs in the Pseudepigrapha*, 212–13.
136. Alouf-Aboody, *Through the Prism of Wisdom*, 137.
137. Alouf-Aboody, *Through the Prism of Wisdom*, 138.

Hellenistic Sources

Hans Conzelmann writes that Luke's unique use of "the Way" cannot be derived from the Greek background of the term.[138] Here, Conzelmann references "the Way" as a descriptor for early Christians (Acts 19:1–2, 9; 22:4; 24:14, 22).[139] This study affirms Conzelmann's conclusions and presents uses of "the Way" from Hellenistic sources in Table 8 in the appendix.

Two-Ways Tradition

The two-ways tradition is an important collection of works because they are similar to Wisdom literature and share a Christian or Jewish ancestry. The two-ways tradition includes several works thought to be written between the first and second centuries: *The Didache, The Epistle of Barnabas, Doctrina,* the *Canons,* and the *Epitome*.[140] J. A. Robinson proposed in 1912 that the *Didache* was dependent on *Barnabas*.[141] Following the discovery of the Dead Sea Scrolls, Robinson's proposal was dismissed because the two-ways tradition was seen to have originated outside of either the *Didache* or *Barnabas*.[142] John Kloppenborg suggests the two-ways tradition produced three independent tracts which created *Barnabas, Doctrina* and the *Didache,* and the *Canons and Epitome*.[143] He concludes *Barnabas* is more likely derived from an older two-ways source than the *Didache*.[144] Kloppenborg finds almost no trace of any distinct Christian feature in *Barnabas*.[145] Still, *Barnabas* has exegetical value for the NT scholar because of its use of the OT.[146] How much more so the *Didache,* which is clearly a Christianized two-ways text.[147]

---

138. Conzelmann, *Acts of the Apostles,* 71.
139. Conzelmann, *Acts of the Apostles,* 71.
140. Kloppenborg, "The Transformation of Moral Exhortation in Didache 1–5," 92.
141. Robinson, "The Problem of the Didache," 339–56.
142. Kloppenborg, "The Transformation of Moral Exhortation in Didache 1–5," 92.
143. Kloppenborg, "The Transformation of Moral Exhortation in Didache 1–5," 92.
144. Kloppenborg, "The Transformation of Moral Exhortation in Didache 1–5," 88–109; Rhodes, "The Two Ways Tradition."
145. Kloppenborg, "The Transformation of Moral Exhortation in Didache 1–5," 97.
146. Olbricht, "Apostolic Fathers," 81–85.
147. Kloppenborg, "The Transformation of Moral Exhortation in Didache 1–5," 98. Kloppenborg states that the *Didache* is Christian.

The *Didache* offers two potential contributions to this study. First, the author was influenced by Wisdom literature. Second, an early dating of the *Didache* to 80 AD may suggest contemporaneous writing.[148] Contemporaneous writing would provide more support for the *Didache* and Acts being similarly affected by Wisdom literature.[149] However, a later dating of the *Didache* would still allow for both books to be similarly influenced by Wisdom literature. The connections are not clear, although C. K. Barrett says that there is enough evidence in the *Didache* to suggest there is a shared tradition between Acts and the *Didache*.[150]

New Testament

While the NT has no books written in the wisdom genre,[151] it has been observed that wisdom nevertheless influences the Synoptic Gospels, the Pauline epistles, and, most obviously, the letter of James.[152] Within the NT, wisdom manifests in advice on how to live for the kingdom of God.[153] Two authors who best reflect the influence of wisdom for this study are James and Paul.

The book of James is commonly associated with Jewish Wisdom.[154] Richard Bauckham classifies the genre as wisdom paraenesis.[155] James shares several common literary techniques with Wisdom literature.[156] Furthermore, James is recognized as referencing several passages from the

---

148. Kurt Niederwimmer proposes a reasonable approximate date range from 110 to 120 AD, and cites a wide variety of scholars who have dated the *Didache* from 80 to 250 AD. The hypotheses have an even distribution of dates. Niederwimmer and Attridge, *The Didache*, 53.

149. Jefford writes, "it seems clear that the teachings of Sirach held a central place of concern for both Matthew and the Didachist." Jefford, "The Wisdom of Sirach and the Glue of the Matthew-Didache Tradition," 18.

150. Barrett, *Acts of the Apostles*, 35–36.

151. Kovalishyn partially attributes this to the apocalyptic overtones the Wisdom literature had acquired by the time the New Testament was written. Kovalishyn, "Wisdom in the New Testament," 173.

152. Kovalishyn, "Wisdom in the New Testament," 173.

153. Kovalishyn, "Wisdom in the New Testament," 184.

154. McCartney, *James*, 280.

155. Bauckham, *James*, 41–42; Moo recognizes paranesis as the most probable genre, with wisdom as a runner-up. Moo, *The Letter of James*, 8.

156. Bauckham, *James*, 46–62. Bauckham identifies aphorisms (i.e., beatitudes, antithetical and paradoxical aphorisms), similitudes and parables, and diatribe.

Wisdom literature.[157] Although saturated in Wisdom literature, James does not clearly reference "the way" of Proverbs. Yet, Martin Dibelius and Heinrich Greeven see a connection between James 5:20 and "the way" from Proverbs.[158] Dibelius and Greeven observe that πλανᾶσθαι (to wander) and the way (ὁδός) are often associated (Deut 11:28; Prov 21:16; Isa 53:6; Wis 5:6).[159] They suggest the close association with "truth" may have led the reading "(ἀπὸ τῆς ὁδοῦ τῆς ἀληθείας, 81 33 ℵ et al.) in v. 19."[160] Peter Davids sees a similar connection between James 5:19–20 and the Wisdom literature. He perceives parallels between James 5:19–20 and Wisdom 12:24; Proverbs 2:15 (cf. Isa 9:15; Ezek 34:4; Wis 5:6).[161] He also understands James' use of "the truth" in v. 19 as shorthand for "the way of truth."[162] While there is no definitive evidence that James is referencing "the way" from Proverbs, his references to wisdom and the use of similar language suggest that a contemporary of Luke within the NT came from a cognitive environment influenced by Wisdom literature.

Andrew Steinmann and Michael Eschelbach propose, "The way in Proverbs becomes the walk in Paul, because in Christ's suffering and death the one who is 'the Way' gives his people the power to walk, guides them on his path, and leads them to his righteousness."[163] However, Paul rarely uses "way" language.[164] Steinmann and Eschelbach find that Paul's Rabbinic training and interactions with Judaizers influenced his use of *halakah* (to walk).[165] Jewish people and Judaizers placed an emphasis on *halakah* where

---

157. Eberhard Nestle, Erwin Nestle, B. Aland, K. Aland, Karavidopoulos, Martini, and Metzger, ed., *Novum Testamentum Graece*, 28th rev ed.: Jas 1:2 [Sap 3.4; Sir 2.1], 1:5 [Prov 2:3–6; Sap 7:7], 1:8 [Sir 1:28], 1:11 [Job 14:2], 1:13 [Sir 15:11–20], 1:19 [Sir 5:11, 26; 3:1–8; Eccl 5:1; Prov 29:20; Eccl 7:9; Prov 15:1]; 1:22 [Sir 1:22]; 1:21 [Sir 3:17]; 1:26 [Sir 4:10]; 2:6 [Prov 14:21]; 2:13 [Prov 19:17]; 2:23 [Sap 7:27]; Jas 3:3,2 [Eccl 7:20; Sir 14:1; 19:16; 1:26]; 3:5 [Prov 18:21]; 3:16 [Sir 5:13; Prov 16:27]; 3:9 [Sir 23:1, 4]; 3:10 [Sir 28:12]; 4:2 [Sir 34:25–27]; 4.6 [Prov 3:34 LXX; Job 22:29]; 4:11 [Sap 1:11]; 4:14 [Prov 27:1]; 5:2 [Job 14:28]; 5:3 [Sir 29:10]; 5:6 [Sap 2:10, 12, 19]; 5:11 [Job 1:21; 2:10; 42:10–17].

158. Dibelius and Greeven, *James*, 257.
159. Dibelius and Greeven, *James*, 257.
160. Dibelius and Greeven, *James*, 257.
161. Davids, *The Epistle of James*, 199.
162. Davids, *The Epistle of James*, 198.
163. Steinmann and Eschelbach, "Walk This Way," 61.
164. Steinmann and Eschelbach, "Walk This Way," 52.
165. Steinmann and Eschelbach, "Walk This Way," 52.

it describes the Jewish pursuit of upholding the OT in their lives.[166] Steinmann and Eschelbach suggest Paul expounds on the Walk in Proverbs to illustrate that Jesus is Himself the path.[167] Steinmann and Eschelbach write, "The way in Proverbs becomes the walk in Paul, because in Christ's suffering and death the one who is 'the Way' gives his people the power to walk, guides them on his path, and leads them to his righteousness."[168] Steinmann explains it is Jesus' revelation to Paul that enables Paul to "explain the full implications that were latent in Proverbs' words."[169]

Contemporaneous New Testament Texts: Summary

Writings contemporaneous with the NT contribute the most to identifying the cognitive environment of Acts. First, these writings reflect two traditions: (1) Hellenistic and (2) Jewish Christian. Texts with a Jewish Christian heritage shared more in common with OT Wisdom literature and "the Way" theology of the OT. In contrast, the Hellenistic texts have little in common with OT Wisdom literature and "the Way" theology of the OT. Second, contemporary writings are chronologically close. Thus, the NT contemporaries share a similar cognitive environment with Luke.

CONCLUSION

Determining Luke's cognitive environment required an analysis of Wisdom literature and "the way" in the OT. Following that analysis, uses of "the way" were examined in texts ranging from the intertestamental period to Luke's time. The analysis showed that these texts "echo" the Wisdom literature and "the way" theology of the OT. In fact, with little theological development from the OT, "the way" metaphor was prevalent in Luke's day. It is therefore plausible to argue that Luke draws on "the way" metaphor found in the OT. Luke and the audience of Acts were familiar with Proverbs. Wisdom was taught throughout Israel's history. Wisdom was how YHWH acted, and Israel was called to act similarly.[170] The analysis did reveal some subtle

---

166. Steinmann and Eschelbach, "Walk This Way," 52.
167. Steinmann and Eschelbach, "Walk This Way," 61.
168. Steinmann and Eschelbach, "Walk This Way," 61.
169. Steinmann and Eschelbach, "Walk This Way," 62.
170. Wright, *The New Testament and the People of God*, 264–65.

developments in both the Wisdom literature and in the understanding of an afterlife. However, the Wisdom literature and the theology of "the way" of the OT were preserved into the first century. The next chapter will examine the use of "the Way" in Acts to determine both its use as a motif and whether Acts "echoes" the way in the OT, as Luke's contemporaries do.

5

An Analysis of "the Way" in the Book of Acts

INTRODUCTION

THIS CHAPTER EXAMINES LUKE'S use of "the Way" as a possible literary motif and allusion to Proverbs. Previous chapters found no consensus about a satisfactory referent or literary function of the Way in Acts, while at the same time Proverbs was shown to have a well-developed concept of "the way" motif and theology. In the previous chapter, Luke's first-century contemporaries were found to be influenced by Wisdom literature, with some influenced by Proverbs' use of "the way" metaphor. Here the Way in Acts (1–8; 9:1–31; 13:4–12; 14:8–20; 16:11–40; 18:24–28; 19; 22:1–22; 24:1–27) will be subject to a three-fold examination in terms of first, the possible function of the Way as a motif; second, the use of the Way as a possible allusion; and third, the metaphorical use of the Way.

THE STRUCTURE OF THE ANALYSIS

This analysis will generally follow three-stages: specific passages will be overviewed, followed by a literary, and then a theological analysis. The repetition that stems from applying the methods of Freedman and Beale can result in the same or similar material being presented several times. Three strategies reduce the amount of repetition, however: (1) Each passage is analyzed just once, using both methods; (2) in some cases the conclusions apply to all the subsequent passages also, and so in these cases the initial analysis will simply be referenced thereafter; and (3) some of Beale and Freedman's criteria will primarily be handled in the summary. An example of a criterion that will be mentioned once and thereafter simply referenced is "avoidability," while an example of a criterion best handled in summary is that of frequency, which is best observed through the accumulation of references.

THE "WAY" IN ACTS

The word ὁδός (the way) occurs 101 times in the NT.[1] Forty of these occurrences are found within Luke-Acts, twenty in Acts.[2] These forty occurrences can helpfully be sub-categorized by their location in the book and by their literary function. First, Acts can be divided into two sections for the purpose of this study as will be discussed below: Acts 1–8 and Acts 9–28. Second, the uses of "the way" can be categorized as literal or metaphorical. Therefore, the analysis proceeds as follows: (1) Acts 1–8, (2) the literal occurrences of the Way in Acts 9–28, and (3) Luke's metaphorical uses of the Way in Acts 9–28.

There are three reasons why it is logical to separate Acts 1–8 from 9–28. First, fifteen of the twenty uses of ὁδός in Acts occur in Acts 9:2–26:13.[3] Second, as Ben Witherington observes, "the overwhelming impression left by the speech material in the last quarter of Acts is that 'the Way's' relationship to non-Christian Judaism is still very much a live issue for the author, requiring repeated instruction to his audience on this subject."[4] Indeed, a shift happens within the speech material and in the occurrence of ὁδός before and after Acts 9. Third, Acts 9 is where Luke first uses ὁδός to describe the Church. Therefore, the three-fold approach will only be applied to uses of ὁδός following Acts 9 (i.e., the application of Freedman's and Beale's methods, and analysis of "the way" as a metaphor). Nevertheless, Acts 1–8 is still discussed, in order to observe "the way" metaphor prior to the shift in Acts 9.

---

1. List generated using Accordance Bible Software and the NA28.

2. Concerning the twenty uses of ὁδός in Luke, Denaux and Corsjens provides a lexical entry for the gospel here in part, "1. road (Lk 9, 57); 2. Journey (Lk 2, 44); 3. Way of life; 4. Christian way of life (Acts 9,2)" (426). Denaux and Corsjens, *The Vocabulary of Luke*, 426–27.

3. There are no additional uses of ὁδός in Acts 26:14–28:31.

4. Witherington III, *The Acts of the Apostles*, 659–60.

Acts 1–8

The analysis of Acts 1–8 establishes how Luke uses ὁδός prior to Acts 9. This section has five of the twenty occurrences of ὁδός to be considered when determining Luke's use of "the way." Four of these refer to travel and are not metaphors (Acts 1:12; 8:26, 36, 39).[5] The only explicit metaphorical use is in Acts 2:28, where Peter's speech references Psalm 16,[6] in which David prays YHWH will "lead him on the 'path of life.'"[7] Thus, Acts 2:28 with its metaphorical use of "the way" is discussed.

By applying Psalm 16 to his context in this manner, Peter is proclaiming that Jesus is the Messiah.[8] Keener suggests that "if the principles in the psalms of righteous sufferers applied to Jesus par excellence, so did the vindication they usually promised."[9] Thus, as David likely prayed for salvation from death (before dying), Peter seeks deliverance from the permanence of death. Keener also proposes that Luke is either envisioning the "'ways of life' as the 'ways of the Lord'" or is suggesting that the way contrasts "safe, as opposed to dangerous, behavior (Prov 5:6; 6:23; 10:17; 12:28; 15:24; cf. 4:10; 16:17; 21:21), applicable to the 'two ways' tradition."[10] Alternatively, Grant Osborne writes, "Jesus the Davidic Messiah has experienced 'the paths of life.' He now will never die, and his eternity is certain."[11] Although both Keener and Osborne understand Jesus as the fulfillment of the prophecy, Osborne considers that "the paths of life" refers to "all the benefits of eternal life as he [Jesus] now will spend eternity."[12] Without drawing a definitive conclusion, it appears that here Luke is employing the way as a metaphor for living.

---

5. The only possible exception may be Acts 8:26. This passage is similar to Acts 9:6, a passage relating to the calling of Paul and Ananias. Both passages contain a literal use of the Way, but the greater context bolsters the possible use of a motif of the Way alongside the literal use.

6. Bruce, *The Book of Acts*, 64.

7. Schnabel, *Acts*, 144.

8. Schnabel, *Acts*, 144.

9. Keener, *Acts: 1:1—2:47*, 945.

10. Keener, *Acts*, 950.

11. Osborne, *Acts*, 53.

12. Osborne, *Acts*, 53.

Acts 9–28: Non-metaphorical Uses of "The Way"

Luke's non-metaphorical uses of ὁδός provide data to contrast with his metaphorical uses. The non-metaphorical data provides context within Luke's narrative that is different from the context where Luke employs ὁδός as a metaphor. Of the fifteen usages of ὁδός that occur between Acts 9:2 and 26:13, four are non-metaphorical (Acts 9:17, 27; 25:3; 26:13). These non-metaphorical uses of ὁδός are now discussed briefly to provide data for later comparison.

In the first non-metaphorical uses, Acts 9:17 and 27, ὁδός means a literal, existing road. Both part of the narrative discussing Paul's trip to Jerusalem, his conversion, and his time in Jerusalem.[13] In these two verses, Luke tells of Saul meeting the Lord on the Damascus Road. In v. 17, Ananias goes to commission Saul.[14] Luke records Ananias' words as he speaks of Saul's encounter with Jesus on the road, the ὁδός, while traveling to Jerusalem (Acts 9:17). Similarly, in Acts 9:27, Barnabas tells the apostles about Paul meeting the Lord on the road (ὁδός). In both instances, Luke is describing a physical road traveled by Paul and his companions.

The third use of ὁδός in Acts 25:3 is also literal or non-metaphorical description of a road. The context is Paul's case before Festus. The Jewish leaders propose a plan to move Paul, thereby creating an opportunity to ambush and kill him (Acts 23:12–22).[15] Bruce notes that Luke is writing about the Jewish leaders' ambitions and how they "might find a better opportunity to do away with him on the road from Caesarea to Jerusalem."[16] As can be seen from the context and Bruce's translation, here Luke is using ὁδός to describe the physical road or route that Paul would travel.

The last occurrence is in Acts 26:12–15 and continues to illustrate how Luke uses ὁδός in a literal manner to describe an actual road. Here Saul is heading to Damascus to persecute Christians.[17] Again Luke uses ὁδός to describe the physical road that Saul and his companions are traveling on,[18] and hence this too is a literal usage.

---

13. Bock, *Acts*, 353, 63, 68.
14. Bruce, *The Book of Acts*, 189.
15. Bock, *Acts*, 700.
16. Bruce, *The Book of Acts*, 450.
17. Bock, *Acts*, 716.
18. Bock, *Acts*, 716.

In sum, these four verses have ὁδός depicting a literal road traveled by Paul, with Luke primarily using "the way" in a non-metaphorical sense. Because these uses are suggestive firstly of a literal meaning for ὁδός, and because here ὁδός is not describing a people group, these occurrences are separated from the metaphorical or allusive uses of the Way that are the focus of this study.[19]

Acts 9:1–31

Acts 9 introduces the first distinct case of ὁδός as a metaphor, which is to be analyzed for consideration as a literary motif and a possible allusion to Proverbs. Acts 9:1–31 contains two passages of particular interest concerning Luke's use of the Way. Acts 9:1–2 discusses ὁδός, while Acts 9:31 talks about the beginning of wisdom, which indirectly teaches about the way. Overall, the entire passage provides information about the way metaphor (and will be analyzed using both Freedman and Beale's methods).

The passage can be subdivided into three sections: Acts 9:1–19a "Saul's Conversion,"[20] Acts 9:19b–30 "Saul from Damascus to Jerusalem,"[21] and Acts 9:31 "The Church in Judaea, Galilee, and Samaria: A Summary."[22] Acts 9:1–2 uses ὁδός as a metaphor; here it is used to describe the Church in Acts. Additionally, Acts 9:31 incorporates the proverbial saying, "the fear of the Lord." Therefore, both Acts 9:1–2 and Acts 9:31 will be examined in the most detail, and the two sections will be treated as an *inclusio*.

Acts 9:1–2 tells of Saul's zeal for the Torah and his desire to uphold spiritual purity and resist Gentile defilement.[23] Here Luke identifies Saul as being against the disciples of the Lord, and the disciples as the people of the Way.[24] Paul finds himself on the wrong path, but later Paul presents the way of Jesus as correct.

---

19. Similarly, this study will not focus on the literal uses of the way found in Acts 1:12; 8:26, 36, 39.

20. Barrett, *Acts of the Apostles*, 437.

21. Barrett, *Acts of the Apostles*, 459.

22. Barrett, *Acts of the Apostles*, 472.

23. Wright, *The New Testament and the People of God*, 187–189; Witherington III, *The Acts of the Apostles*, 302.

24. At times the Way will be referred to as "the people of the Way." The addition of "people" is to distinguish between the Way as the Church and the Way as the Way of the Lord.

For Luke, the Way is both a description of the disciples and a description for following Jesus.[25] David Peterson suggests that Luke first identifies the Church as the Way in order to properly establish the significance of the Church, lest people misconstrue the meaning of the word "Church."[26] This suggestion is credible because it fits with the themes of Luke-Acts (e.g., vindicating Christians, see chapter six), and because early followers of Jesus would have been seen as a sect of Jews (Acts 24:14).[27] Early Christianity was thus at risk of being confused with Judaism, with magic, and other prevailing forms of religion.[28] Jesus' followers risked being confused with workers of magic and alternative religions because of their new and radical claims, alongside the performance of miracles.[29] Thus, the Way functions as a name for Christians, a group set apart from both Jews and pagans.

The context of Acts 9:3–30 provides satellite imagery (i.e., symbols that contribute to a fundamental symbol) of the way associated with Paul's travels on the Damascus Road. Images of the way arise also in the language of the narrative, as the Lord calls Ananias to a street called "straight." Furthermore, there is language that contrasts sight and blindness in conjunction with Ananias' vision, plus mention of the use of "hearing," and Paul receiving "instruction" from the Lord (Acts 9:6).

By Acts 9:31, Paul has not only become part of "the Way," now he is openly debating with the Jewish opposition and declaring to them that this emerging "Christian" movement is in fact the most biblical response to Jesus as Messiah, and thus it is now the Church that will carry forth YHWH's relationship with His people in perfect continuity with OT religion. Two references inform the reader about the Way metaphor: (1) the list of local churches and (2) how the churches walk in "the fear of the Lord." The long list of local churches shows that the Holy Spirit is present, and is growing the Church, which is evidence that the Father blesses Jesus's ministry.[30] While the people walk in the fear of the Lord, the Holy Spirit is multiplying and strengthening the Church.[31] This is a statement of

---

25. Peterson, *The Acts of the Apostles*, 94. This concept is discussed further in relation to Acts 18:5.
26. Peterson, *The Acts of the Apostles*, 93.
27. Schnabel, *Acts*, 289.
28. Witherington III, *The Acts of the Apostles*, 397.
29. Witherington III, *The Acts of the Apostles*, 397.
30. Bock, *Acts*, 372.
31. Marshall, *Acts*, 186.

the devotion of the followers and the devotion of God.[32] The phrase "the fear of the Lord" and the blessings associated with walking in fear of the Lord are connected to the Way metaphor. Marshall sees Luke's use of "the fear of the Lord" as an allusion to the book of Proverbs, writing, "By this usage Luke indicates that the Christian religion is in continuity with OT religion."[33] John Goldingay writing about Proverbs comments, "It is thus a feature [the fear of the Lord] of New Testament spirituality (e.g., Acts 9:31; 2 Cor 7:1; Eph 5:21; Phil 2:12; Heb 12:28; Rev 15:4) and not a side issue in the Scriptures but a central issue."[34]

Like Marshall, scholars have previously made observations about Luke's use of "the fear of the Lord." There has been no synthesis made of this work. However, a synthesis of scholars' observations would show that Luke is alluding to Proverbs' use of the way metaphor to describe the Christian Church as God's true community. Osborne writes that "the fear of the Lord" is a metaphor for "walking with Christ."[35] Drawing the same conclusion, Fitzmyer finds Luke uses "the fear of the Lord" with the same OT understanding as Proverbs "(Prov 1:7, 29; 2:5; 9:10; 19:23; Ps 19:9; Sir 9:16; 25:6), the beginning of knowledge."[36] All three scholars, Marshall, Osborne, and Fitzmyer, see Luke employing OT language to locate Christians in the family of God. Osborne's observation begins to connect OT wisdom directly to the Way metaphor: "Here the metaphor is walking with Christ, advancing on the road to 'the measure of the fullness of Christ' (Eph 4:13). Their church growth is in every area—not just in numbers but also in the spiritual and social arenas, and in their fellowship."[37] In similar vein, Keener suggests "the fear of the Lord" describes the Church's "spiritual or numerical growth."[38]

Moreover, Luke's audience would recognize the claim that Christians are the true people of God, an argument that opposes the claims of the Pharisees and Sadducees. Referring to Luke's use of "the church," Keener writes, "Luke's ideal audience, however, was steeped in the LXX (and, as Paul's letters indicate, by now conventional Christian usage); they would

---

32. Witherington III, *The Acts of the Apostles*, 326.
33. Marshall, "Acts," 576.
34. Goldingay, *Proverbs*, 26–32.
35. Osborne, *Acts*, 187.
36. Fitzmyer, *The Acts of the Apostles*, 441.
37. Osborne, *Acts*, 187.
38. Keener, *Acts: 3:1—14:28*, 1696.

recognize the traditional label for God's community."³⁹ Luke is making a polemical point by alluding to Proverbs. The allusion is that the people of the Way are God's people, because they "fear the Lord" as God's people did in the OT, and that the work of the Holy Spirit affirms Jesus's ministry.

Luke's use of the way metaphor to identify the Church as God's true people—supposedly the claim of the Jewish people—will be supported by further analysis of Acts. First, "the way" metaphor will be studied as a literary motif. Second, the metaphor is examined as an allusion to Proverbs.

Literary Analysis: Motif

Freedman's method identifies the presence of a motif in literature. Freedman's method necessitates the criteria of avoidability and frequency be met for the presence of a motif, while additional criteria show the strength of the motif. Within Acts 9, the model identifies the way metaphor as a motif and establishes its intentional role in promoting the themes of Acts.

Freedman's criterion of frequency confirms "the way" metaphor is a motif. The identification of frequency in Acts 9:1–31 informs of Luke's intentional use of the metaphor through the number of uses of ὁδός. The identification of frequency in Acts 9:1–31 primarily contributes data to establishing a pattern to the frequency in Acts 9–28. Therefore, the criterion of frequency will also be examined in the final section of this chapter, which will also include a summary and synthesis of each passage analysis. However, the criterion of frequency is also analyzed within the immediate context of the passage to show Luke's intentional use of "the Way" as a motif. Within the passage, the data for frequency is drawn from a limited number of occurrences of "the Way." However, there is no set number of occurrences required to be considered frequent in Freedman's analysis.⁴⁰ The first use of the Way provides a context for Luke's use of the term and establishes a boundary marker between Acts 1–8 and 9–28. If the way metaphor does have a high frequency throughout Acts, Luke will continue to use it as a descriptor for Christians or Christianity.

The criterion of avoidability validates Luke's use of ὁδός as a motif. By establishing that Luke could have avoided use of "the way" metaphor to describe the Church shows he is intentionally using the metaphor as a motif. Also, the criterion shows ὁδός functioning as a boundary marker (i.e.,

39. Keener, *Acts: 3:1—14:28*, 1696.
40. Keener, *Acts: 3:1—14:28*, 126.

between Acts 1–8 and Acts 9–31) to describe the Church, through which he continues establishing the significance of the metaphor throughout the book. The criterion of avoidability is met in Acts 9:1–31, because Luke uses ὁδός to describe the Church, incorporates satellite images of the Way (i.e., language associated with the way metaphor), and makes reference to the "fear of the Lord." Luke intentionally chooses "the Way" to describe the Church. Schnabel examines the Jerusalem Church's self-understanding,[41] by looking at eight words used to describe the Church and that church members used to address one another.[42] Luke had at his disposal these eight terms, plus "sect" and "crowd" (although the term "crowd" is ill-suited to serve Luke's purpose for the crowd generally represents a mixed group of people and is not specific enough to describe a Christian group). Even so, one of the nine alternative options might have been valid.[43] Based upon the multiple words available and used elsewhere by Luke, ὁδός was in fact avoidable. It appears that Luke purposefully chose "the Way" as his descriptor here. Freedman writes, "Clearly the more uncommon a reference is in a given context, the more likely it is to strike the reader, consciously or subconsciously, and the greater will be its effect."[44] Luke's use of the Way appears to create a "great effect" on the reader by heralding God's people through an association with "the fear of the Lord," and it also meets Freedman's criterion of avoidability.

Freedman's remaining three criteria provide a means of calculating the strength of a motif. Therefore, the remaining criteria bolster the claim that Luke is using the way metaphor as a motif. These criteria are the significance of the context, the coherence of the motif, and the symbolic appropriateness.[45] First, Acts 9:1–2 proves a significant context for the use of "the Way." Saul requests permission to persecute the Christian community in new regions. Already in Acts, Luke has introduced the Christian community as the Church (Acts 8:1, 3). Yet Luke has also described the Israelites as the Church, ἐκκλησία (Acts 5:11; 7:38). Two significant narrative events are occurring. The context provides an opportunity to differentiate between the Jews and Christians, plus the section begins to discuss the conversion

---

41. Schnabel, *Acts*, 288.
42. Schnabel, *Acts*, 288–90.
43. Of the remaining options some fit better than others, e.g., the "church" or "Nazarenes" appear to fit better than "brothers."
44. Freedman, "The Literary Motif," 126.
45. Freedman, "The Literary Motif," 126–27.

of Saul (Acts 9:1–19a).⁴⁶ Both contexts reflect a polemic between Christians and Jews, thereby strengthening the likely presence of a motif based on Freedman's criterion concerning the significance of context. Furthermore, concerning the significance of context, Acts 9:31 functions as a transition and a positive ending.⁴⁷ This additional literary feature suggests "the way" motif is critical to Luke's message about the Church. The upbeat conclusion is that the Church's newfound peace is affected by God granting salvation to their persecutor.⁴⁸ It seems that Acts 9:31 ends the section, as Keener states, and the passage has two references to Proverbs acting as bookends. Consequently, the Way motif describes Christians in 9:2 and the passage concludes by depicting the Church as living in "the fear of the Lord."

Second, Luke's use of satellite imagery (i.e., language in addition to ὁδός and images associated with the way metaphor) fulfills the criterion of coherence. The most important data here is the street called "straight" and the dichotomy between blindness and sight. The adjective εὐθύς (straight) is used four times in LXX Proverbs 2:13–21, in a section that teaches about the benefits of living by the way of wisdom.⁴⁹ Interestingly, Luke will use εὐθύς again in Acts 13:10 when describing "the paths of the Lord." The narrative does not require the name of the street, so it is probable that Luke adds the name to convey a message.

Further evidence of the intentionality of Luke's word choices can be identified in 9:3, where "suddenly" a "light from heaven" flashes down on Saul. Keener observes that "Luke uses 'suddenly' (Acts 9:3; 22:6) for another revelation (Luke 2:13; he only employs the word again in Luke 9:39); much more important is that though Luke describes light 'from heaven' only in the accounts of Paul's conversion (Acts 9:3; 22:6; 26:13), that shining light accompanies other divine revelations (such as the angelic appearance in 12:7; glory shining in Luke 2:9)."⁵⁰ Although Keener's observation refers to theophanies, his remarks highlight Luke's ability to avoid the light/dark dichotomy and his use of the root εὐθύς.⁵¹ Also, Keener notes that Luke

---

46. Bock, *Acts*, 353.

47. Keener, *Acts: 3:1—14:28*, 1695.

48. Keener, *Acts: 3:1—14:28*, 1695.

49. O'Dowd sees chapter two as a summary of the first nine chapters. O'Dowd, *Proverbs*, 76. Schipper titles the chapter "The 'Table of Contents' to the Instructions Text." Schipper, *Proverbs 1–15*, 101.

50. Keener, *Acts: 3:1—14:28*, 1633.

51. Keener, *Acts: 3:1—14:28*, 1633.

is conservative when using both "light from heaven" and εὐθύς.[52] Keener's observation suggests that the language Luke uses is avoidable and hence purposely chosen.

Further, Acts 9:31 contributes support for the coherence of Freedman's method. As mentioned in relation to the criterion of avoidability, Acts 9:31 uses language associated with the way metaphor, "the Fear of the Lord." Also, the verse is in a place of significance in terms of context, where it operates as an *inclusio*. Therefore, Acts 9:31 brings coherence through shared language with "the way" metaphor and by demonstrating Acts 9:1–31 is a cohesive unit.

Third, "the way" functioning as a motif is supported by its symbolic appropriateness. If the motif is designating the Christian Church as the people of the Way, then the symbol fits perfectly. Both Acts and Proverbs use the way motif and "two ways" theologies to contrast God's people with unbelievers. Also, both books present God as creating the Way, sustaining members on the Way, and both have "ways" that lead to life or destruction.

Luke's use of the Way in Acts 9:1–2, which speaks of those who "belong to the Way" thus establishes the probability of an allusion to Proverbs. The use of the Way is shared language within a shared context. Both Acts and Proverbs use the Way to describe following the Lord. In both contexts, the Way has two possible directions. In Proverbs, those on the Way follow the Lord, while those who are off the Way abandon the Lord. In Acts there is a polemical contrast between Christians following Jesus and the Jews who have condemned Jesus.

Theological Analysis: Allusion

Beale's method identifies OT allusions in the NT, and when it is met, it shows that in Acts 9 Luke is alluding to Proverbs' use of the way metaphor. In fact, several criteria of Beale's requirements for an allusion are met: availability, recurrence, and thematic coherence. Given Beale's method requires some of the criteria be met, and not all, meeting three of the four shows that Acts is indeed alluding to Proverbs. Furthermore, the criterion of thematic coherence is particularly strong in Acts 9.

Acts 9, and all of Acts, meets the criterion of availability. Chapter four showed how the Way motif/metaphor was familiar to Luke and his

---

52. Keener, *Acts: 3:1—14:28*, 1633.

audience. This is a "basic criterion"[53] that requires the referenced text (i.e., Proverbs) to be "available to the writer."[54] Questioning the usefulness of the criterion of availability, Stanley Porter suggests it isn't possible to determine if the referent text is unavailable to the audience or if the proposed audience for the NT text is incorrect.[55] However, as both Luke and his audience are familiar with "the Way," Porter's objection does not impact the effectiveness of the criterion. The criterion of availability is not only met, but is met while overcoming the weaknesses identified by scholars.

The criterion of volume is not met because of the absence of direct references to "the way" and limited repetition of other words in the allusion. While "the Way" occurs in v. 2 there is no verbatim language outside of ὁδός. Second, while use of "the fear of the Lord" in Acts 9:31 has a high degree of correlation to Proverbs, there is no direct reference to Proverbs. Because the high degree of correlation is not associated directly with use of ὁδός, the criterion of volume is not satisfied. However, recurrence and thematic coherence significantly make up for any lack of volume.

The requirement for recurrence is met within the context of Acts 9, which includes the phrase "the fear of the Lord" in v. 31 and Luke's placement of the way metaphor alongside Paul's conversion story. Therefore, although a specific passage is not explicitly referenced, here the Way is coupled with the satellite images (i.e., of the way metaphor and trademark saying from the book of Proverbs). In addition, Luke places the conversion story of Paul next, an account that incorporates both literal and figurative uses of the Way in a single passage. The supernatural event is cast in a bright light often associated with OT theophanies,[56] only here it is a Christophany.[57] When these events are considered along with Acts 9:1–2, 31, Luke portrays the revelation of divine knowledge in a manner that incorporates satellite imagery shared by both theophanies and "the way." Also, the section is bookended by the metaphor of the way. In many ways, the more literal use of the Way found in Acts 9 strengthens its metaphorical use, through a "correspondence between the literal and figurative meaning of

---

53. Beale, *Handbook*, 34.
54. Beale, *Handbook*, 33.
55. Beale, *Handbook*, 34; Porter, "Allusions and Echoes," 29–40.
56. Marshall, "Acts," 576.
57. Bock, *Acts*, 356.

the Way."⁵⁸ As noted above, Acts 9:31 represents a significant recurrence because it directly references Proverbs.

Marshall notes the saying "the fear of the Lord" is a Jewish expression and provides Job 28:28; Psalm 111:10; and Proverbs 1:7 as examples.⁵⁹ However, the examples are not equally probable as referents, and the ordering, if representing probability, is misleading. For example, the "fear of the Lord" occurs once in the book of Job and only three times in the book of Psalms, making these books less probable. From Marshall's examples both Job and Psalms better reflect Acts 9:31 linguistically. The LXX (i.e., the examples from Job and the Psalms) uses *kyrios* for "Lord," as does Acts 9:31. In comparison, Marshall's example from Proverbs has *theos* in the LXX, which is rendered "Lord." However, Marshall does not mention an additional thirteen instances of "the fear of the Lord" found in Proverbs (Prov 1:29; 2:5; 8:13; 9:10; 10:27; 14:26, 27; 15:16, 33; 16:6; 19:23; 22:4; 23:17). In fact, all the instances of "Lord" mentioned above have the tetragrammaton YHWH in the BHS and are only translated as *theos* twice in the LXX (Prov 1:7; 15:33). Interestingly, "Lord" is not represented by the tetragrammaton YHWH in Job 28:28, although the occurrences of "the fear of the Lord" found in the Psalms use YHWH in the BHS. Furthermore, Job uses a different word for "fear" from that found in Acts. Marshall does not mention the three occurrences in Isaiah or the four instances in 2 Chronicles (Isa 11:2, 3; 33:6; 2 Chron 14:4; 17:10; 19:7, 9). In sum, the frequency of occurrences and the linguistic similarities between "the fear of the Lord" in Proverbs suggests Proverbs is the likely referent.⁶⁰

There is thematic coherence between Acts and Proverbs with their use of "the fear of the Lord," to describe how to follow the Lord, and by

---

58. Of the Way metaphor, Bricker writes, "In order to comprehend the figurative level one must first be able to grasp the literal. If the correspondence between the two levels of meaning is not clear, the intended lesson of the proverb or saying will be lost. Interpreting a metaphor is dependent on transferring the meaning(s) from one level of meaning to another." Bricker, "The Doctrine of the 'Two Ways' in Proverbs," 511.

59. Marshall, "Acts," 576.

60. In Isaiah, all three occurrences of "the fear of the Lord" include the divine name YHWH in the Hebrew text, while a single occurrence is translated as *theos* by the LXX (Isa 11:3). Each passage uses the Hebrew term (יִרְאָה) for "fear," but the LXX only translates the term with φόβος, as Luke uses it in Acts 9:31 (Isa 11:3). In the other instances the LXX translates (יִרְאָה) with εὐσέβεια. In 2 Chronicles, three of the passages contain the Hebrew word (פַּחַד) for fear, while one uses (יִרְאָה). Of the four occurrences of "fear," the LXX translates two passages with ἔκστασις and the others with φόβος. Therefore, Proverbs not only has more occurrences but also more that match the use of φόβος for "fear" in Acts.

contrasting obedience to the Lord with disobedience. In the OT, in "most occurrences the 'fear of God' is a virtue that is encouraged and leads to right behavior and good results."[61] Within Proverbs, "the fear of the Lord" is a near-synonym of wisdom and is "connected to ethical behavior."[62] Longman writes, "Fear is a virtue that leads to piety, praise and humility, since one who fears God recognizes that God, not oneself, is the center of the cosmos."[63] It is noted above that Luke appears to be using the Way as it is used in Proverbs,[64] only now believers are walking with Christ as opposed to the Father (Acts 9:2; 19:23; 22:4).[65] Thus, use of the Way in Acts coheres thematically with its use in Proverbs.

Through the use of Freedman and Beale's methodology, it can be seen that Acts 9:1–31 presents the metaphor of the Way as a descriptor for Christians and Christian living. Freedman's method suggests the way the metaphor functions as a motif in Acts. While a further examination of frequency is still needed, Beale's method for identifying allusions reveals that Luke is using the Way to allude to Proverbs. Although Acts 9:31 does not mention ὁδός directly, it uses language found prominently in Proverbs, i.e., "the fear of the Lord." Additionally, the language of "the fear of the Lord" is directly related to the "two-way" theology or the Way motif (Prov 1:7; 2:5; 3:7; 14:2; 15:16; 16:6). Before Acts 9:31, the Way operates as a metaphor to describe Christians (Acts 9:1–2) while satellite words suggest the presence of "the way" motif.

Acts 13:4–12

Turning now from Acts 9 to Acts 13, the same analysis continues for Luke's next use of ὁδός. The ongoing analysis strengthens the conclusions surrounding Acts 9 that "the way" metaphor works as a literary motif and an allusion to Proverbs. Acts 13:4–12 contains a single use of ὁδός (Acts 13:10). In this verse, ὁδός is used in a similar manner to Acts 9:31. Although the passage has only a single occurrence of "the Way" and a limited context, it contributes to understanding how the way metaphor may be considered a motif or allusion.

61. Longman III, "Fear of the Lord," 201–05.
62. Longman III, "Fear of the Lord," 202.
63. Longman III, "Fear of the Lord," 205.
64. Fitzmyer, *The Acts of the Apostles*, 441.
65. Osborne, *Acts*, 187.

An Analysis of "the Way" in the Book of Acts

In this passage, Luke uses the way metaphor to contrast God's people to those living in darkness. The passage is about the mission work of Barnabas and Saul in Cyprus.[66] Paul, filled with the Spirit, is part of a scene that depicts the power of God against the power of the sorcerer.[67] There in Cyprus, Paul opposes a sorcerer.[68] The sorcerer is a "son of the devil."[69] The two parties stand in direct opposition: a Son of God against a son of the Devil, and the Apostle against the sorcerer. The contrast between God's way and others' way has been recognized by other scholars. Keener observes that John the Baptist prepared the way of the Lord, while Elymas made crooked the straight way.[70] However, Keener finds Luke uses similar language when depicting John the Baptist as "the true prophet," preparing the way in Luke 1:76; 3:4 (cf. Luke 7:27; Acts 9:2).[71] In contrast to Keener, Schnabel finds comparable uses of ὁδός in Prov 10:9; Hos 14:9 (LXX 14:10), and he finds merit in Pao's identification of Isaiah 40:3 as a source.[72] Although Schnabel is inconclusive, he allows for both the prophets and wisdom as examples for the contrast Luke portrays in Acts. For his actions, Elymas becomes blind from God's judgement.[73] Then, upon witnessing the judgment upon Elymas, the proconsul believed and was overwhelmed by the teaching of the Lord (v. 12).

Literary Analysis: Motif

Once again, Freedman's method is used to identify Luke's use of ὁδός as a motif in Acts 13. The continued success of ὁδός being confirmed as a motif reaffirms the conclusions concerning Acts 9. Freedman's method of identifying motifs begins with their frequency, which is assessed in the summary. The second criterion of avoidability is met, although with less confidence. Luke had available to him the cognate of ὁδός, τρίβος. In fact, Luke uses τρίβος in Luke 3:4 where he references Isaiah 40:3. For the remainder of Luke-Acts, Luke does not use τρίβος again. The change in vocabulary may

---

66. Bock, *Acts*, 441.
67. Keener, *Acts: 3:1—14:28*, 1996.
68. Keener, *Acts: 3:1—14:28*, 1995.
69. Keener, *Acts: 3:1—14:28*, 2017.
70. Keener, *Acts: 3:1—14:28*, 2023.
71. Keener, *Acts: 3:1—14:28*, 2023.
72. Schnabel, *Acts*, 559, fn. 27.
73. Keener, *Acts: 3:1—14:28*, 2023-24.

suggest Luke purposefully chose ὁδός, thus providing evidence that alternate vocabulary was available. Additionally, Freedman's remaining criteria supports the conclusion that the motif of the way is present.

The satellite language associated with "the Way" supports the criterion of coherence. As noted above, Acts 13:2–14 has similarities to Acts 9:1–31. First, the passages have a parallel in the narratives of Saul and Elymas. Second, both passages discuss the way and use the word εὐθύς.

Keener writes, "Paul recovered spiritual sight when struck blind; now Elymas, who also has opposed the faith, receives the same opportunity."[74] The parallels between Acts 9 and 13 show the consequences associated with following the Lord or not doing so (a two-ways theology). The parallels also introduce language associated with a "two-ways" theology and the way metaphor. Vocabulary associated with "the Way" motif in Acts includes δικαιοσύνη (righteous), εὐθύς (straight), and σκότος (darkness). The inclusion of the polemical-narrative with satellite imagery supports the Way functioning as a motif in Acts 13:2–14.

Acts 13:10 meets the criterion of symbolic appropriateness. Pao attempts to connect Acts 13:10 with Luke 3:4 and finds Elymas (Acts 13) in a role opposite that of John the Baptist (Luke 3).[75] Pao finds a more probable correlation perhaps between Acts 3:11 and Isaiah 42:16 LXX.[76] Yet, Pao's connections to both John the Baptist (Luke 3:4; Isa 40:3) and to Isaiah 42:16 LXX are flawed. First, the actions of the Baptist and Elymas are in opposition, but the opposition does not suggest Luke is referring to Isaiah 40:3. In fact, the divide between the contexts of the two passages is stark. John the Baptist declares the fulfillment of the coming Messiah, while Acts 13 discusses the work of the Spirit who was sent by the Messiah. Second, it is unusual that Luke does not use the term τρίβος for "path." Isaiah 42:16 LXX uses the term to describe the "path," and Luke uses τρίβος elsewhere (Acts 12:19; 14:3, 28; 15:35; 16:12; 20:6, 16; 25:6, 14). Hence, the use of ὁδός may better be understood as an intentional reference to the Way motif.

In brief, the occurrence of the Way in Acts 13:10 signals a higher frequency for the term (it's fourth use since Acts 9:2). Concerning the second criterion of avoidability, Luke's use of ὁδός appears to be intentional,

---

74. Keener, *Acts: 3:1—14:28*, 2024.

75. Pao, *Acts and the Isaianic New Exodus*, 202.

76. Pao, *Acts and the Isaianic New Exodus*, 202, fn.58. Isa 42:16 "And I will lead the blind in a way that they do not know, in paths that they have not known I will guide them. I will turn the darkness before them into light, the rough places into level ground. These are the things I do, and I do not forsake them."

strengthening the likelihood of the term being used as a motif. The passage has coherence, for the Way is surrounded by satellite language (e.g., the terms straight, righteous, darkness). The motif also has symbolic appropriateness as it is used in the way that Acts 9:1–31 uses the motif to describe Christian living, and which offers a better fit than Isaiah.

Theological Analysis: Allusion

As with Acts 9, Beale's method is used to determine if Luke uses ὁδός as an allusion to Proverbs. The continued confirmation of ὁδός as an allusion reaffirms the conclusions around Acts 9. The criterion of availability is met, see the analysis of Acts 9:2, above. Still, there remain three additional criteria to deal with. First, the volume is once again relatively low. Proverbs has multiple passages containing both "the way" and the word "straight" (Prov 2:13, 16; 20:11; 28:10; cognates 2:19; 3:6, 11:5) and "the way" and "crooked" (Prov 4:27; 8:13; 10:9; 11:20 cognates 2:15; 21:8; 22:5, 14; 28:18; 29:27). Nevertheless, Acts 13:10 has no significant parallel in Proverbs.

The criterion of recurrence is met, for "the way" metaphor is present alongside many satellite images. As discussed in relation to volume, many passages in Proverbs link "the way" with either "straight" or "crooked." Acts 13:10 discusses the "righteous." The term "righteous" is a satellite of the image of the way and is intimately associated with wisdom in Proverbs. Sun Myung Lyu considers the righteous and the wise in Proverbs has an "integrated conception" that he calls the "righteous-wise."[77] Acts 13:10 contains several references to "the way" as found in the book of Proverbs, thus meeting the requirement of recurrence.

The criterion of thematic coherence is also met. Luke is presenting the contrast between the power of God and the powerlessness of magic.[78] Bock observes the significance of the blinding of the magician, where the darkness of sight reflects the darkness of the mind.[79] Lack of wisdom is associated with a dark mind,[80] and a dark mind suggests the magician is "full of deceit and villainy as well as being opposed to righteousness."[81] While

---

77. Lyu, *Righteousness in the Book of Proverbs*, 75.

78. Bock, *Acts*, 441.

79. Bock, *Acts*, 445.

80. Bock mentions that the metaphor may relate to a rabbinic saying found in the Talmud. Bock, *Acts*, 445.

81. Bock, *Acts*, 446.

Acts 13:4–12 contrasts the faithful and the unfaithful, Luke goes even further and focuses on a specific contrast between two types of unfaithfulness: one "strenuously" objects to faith, and the other is "more neutral or open and needs to learn the first things about the faith."[82] This clearly reflects Proverbs' two types of unbelievers, the foolish (Prov 10:8, 10, 14) and the wicked (Prov 3:25, 33; 4:14, 19), who mirror the unbelievers of Acts. The Way is also represented by two contrasting figures (Lady Wisdom and Dame Folly). Van Leeuwen writes this about "the way" in Proverbs: "The sharp polarity of the two ways is a teaching tool parallel to the sharp contrast between 'righteous' and 'wicked.'"[83] Therefore, it appears that Luke is indeed appropriating the Way metaphor from Proverbs.

The analysis of Acts 13 contributes to the thesis of this work, as Freedman's method shows the way metaphor is used as a literary motif, and Beale's method shows "the way" metaphor alluding to Proverbs. Luke uses ὁδός to describe the ways of the Lord. Within the passage, ὁδός is used also in a polemical context that distinguishes God's people from not-God's people.

Acts 14:8–20

Moving from Acts 13 to Acts 14, the examination of Luke's use of ὁδός in light of Freeman and Beale's methods adds support for "the way" metaphor operatinging as a literary motif. Acts 14:16 uses the term "the way" as part of Luke's account of the missionary work in Lycaonia in Acts 14:1–20.[84] Here he uses ὁδός as a metaphor for a way of life. In this section, the passage is summarized, and the two methods of analysis then determine the literary and theological function of "the way" in this particular context.

The larger unit containing v. 16 is Acts 14:8–20.[85] The passage has five sections: (1) Healing a lame man (vv. 8–10), (2) reactions to this miracle (vv. 11–13), (3) the apostles' reaction to being idolized, (4) the townspeople's near sacrifice to the apostles (v. 18), and (5) Paul being stoned and left for dead (vv. 19–20).[86] The entire unit will be considered in the analysis of "the way" in Acts 14:8–20.

---

82. Bock, *Acts*, 447.
83. Van Leeuwen, "The Book of Proverbs," 63.
84. Pervo, *Acts*, 345.
85. Culy and Parsons, *Acts*, 275; Holladay, *Acts*, 286.
86. Bock, *Acts*, 473.

An Analysis of "the Way" in the Book of Acts

The healing account in Acts 14:8–10 mirrors Peter's healing in Acts 3:1–8,[87] although Richard Longenecker observes Luke uses more "local color" in this later miracle account.[88] Longenecker suggests the additional details provided in the account of Acts 14:8–20. In Acts 3:1–8, the lame man is pleading for money when Peter stops and blesses him. Following the blessing, the man is described as having been strengthened, jumping, and going on his way. In contrast, Acts 14:8–10 discusses the longevity of the man's disability (from birth), the man's actions in listening to Paul (only assumed in Acts 3), and also has Paul stating that the man is healed (saved) by faith. The linguistic differences are also noteworthy as they highlight connections to Proverbs.

First, the man is said to "listen" to Paul. In Proverbs, lessons are often introduced with an exhortation to "listen."[89] Proverbs uses the admonition in conjunction with "son" to "connote that the father considers his son as his spiritual heir."[90] The shared language between Acts and Proverbs continues.

Second, Paul asks the man to stand ὀρθός (straight), a word that is associated with the way in Proverbs (Prov 4:11, 25, 26, 27). In Proverbs 4:11, "straight" indicates the path is easy to walk and is an adjective for the paths of "uprightness." The word ὀρθός qualifys the imperative "to stand," has received little attention.[91] The adverbial use of the word is likely part of an idiomatic statement.[92] As discussed below, this idiomatic statement relates to Proverbs. The word may be understood literally as "stand erect,"[93] although the saying likely relates to metaphorical speech about faith. Pervo writes, "The one who had never walked now does so, with ease and vigor. A person who was 'powerless' (ἀδύνατος) had been transformed by power from on high."[94] Bruce writes, "in Acts, as in the Gospels, faith is regularly emphasized as a condition of receiving both physical and spiritual

---

87. Longenecker, "The Acts of the Apostles," 435.

88. Longenecker, "The Acts of the Apostles," 435.

89. Waltke, *The Book of Proverbs: Chapters 1–15*, 11; Fox, "Ideas of Wisdom in Proverbs 1–9," 46, fn. 52.

90. Waltke, *The Book of Proverbs: Chapters 1–15*, 186.

91. Keener addresses the man's "leaping" and suggests an allusion to Isaiah 35:6. Keener, *Acts: 3:1—14:28*, 2131. Bock considers the man's "leaping," but not the adjective "straight. Bock, *Acts*, 475.

92. Conzelmann, *Acts of the Apostles*, 111. See Kellum, *Acts*, 169.

93. Barrett, *Acts of the Apostles*, 675.

94. Pervo, *Acts: A Commentary on the Book of Acts*, 353.

healing."[95] Peterson also connects "standing straight" to the man's faith, for Paul "challenged the lame man to express his faith by doing what seemed impossible for him."[96] The connection to rising in faith seems correct. Thus, the connection between Acts and Proverbs may be further strengthened when considering the adjective ὀρθός is used in Proverbs 4:26, 12:15 LXX. Following, one more linguistic feature shows the similarities between Acts 14 and Proverbs.

Third, Luke states that by faith, the man has been "saved" (or healed). This salvation will be shown to directly relate to the destination of "the way" in Proverbs within the theological analysis of this section. Bock mentions that the man is "physically delivered" and the meaning of "saved" is "the common non-theological use of the term."[97] Nevertheless, Paul's use of salvation alongside sharing the Gospel and performing a miracle suggests this "non-theological" use of "salvation" has secondary theological undertones. Bock writes, "The picture of the miracle, however, moves in this more spiritual direction because the scene typifies the signs and wonders Paul and Barnabas have done."[98] Thus, the picture of the man healed by a miracle is both a literal depiction of events and a metaphorical depiction of a personal faith transformation.

Within the context of the passage, "the way" refers to man's choice to follow God or idols.[99] God has allowed people to follow whomever they choose throughout history.[100] Perhaps Acts is proposing that God refrains from executing justice in order for some to repent of following idols and receive salvation.[101] Although Luke is not specifically referring to Christians or any group of people as the Way, he is using the metaphor of the way. Luke's symbolic use of the way is similar in function. Keener notes that the language is similar to Paul (Rom 3:25) and Wisdom 11:23, "where God mercifully overlooks people's sins 'for repentance,' probably meaning that God allows them opportunity to repent."[102] Although the passage speaks of God's relationship with His people throughout time, Luke makes known

---

95. Bruce, *The Book of the Acts*, 274.
96. Peterson, *The Acts of the Apostles*, 407.
97. Bock, *Acts*, 475.
98. Bock, *Acts*, 475.
99. Schnabel, *Acts*, 610.
100. Keener, *Acts: 3:1—14:28*, 2168.
101. Keener, *Acts: 3:1—14:28*, 2168.
102. Keener, *Acts: 3:1—14:28*, 2168.

through the context that Jesus is the one who brings salvation now.[103] In v. 15, the men's actions are undesirable.[104] These actions are contrasted with actions becoming of God, the creator of all. Paul exhorts the people to *turn* from their previous actions[105] and adopt those of God. Bock mentions the contrast is also between idols and God.[106] Other contrasting imagery is used in v. 17, such as presumed unacceptable behavior contrasted with doing good and presumed fruitlessness contrasted with fruitfulness or blessing. Last, vv. 19–20 captures the sinful actions of the Jews who seek to bring about Paul's death, which contrasts with Paul's mission to bring eternal life to those who hear and believe the Good News.

Literary Analysis: Motif

As previously applied to Acts 9 and 13, Freedman's method for identifying a motif is now applied to Luke's use of ὁδός in Acts 14. The criterion of frequency is starting to be met as Luke introduces the fifth direct use of "the way" since Acts 9. Nevertheless, the criterion of frequency will only be fully addressed in the summary section below.

The criterion for avoidability is met, as discussed above in relation to Luke's choice of vocabulary to describe "the Way" (Acts 13:10). It is important to the analysis to remember that Luke is capturing Paul's speech.[107] Further, Paul is reminding the people of Lystra of their relationship with God by recounting history and using a metaphor.

The criterion of coherence is met, supporting arguments for the use of "the Way" as a motif. Alongside the direct use of the term itself, the surrounding context contains satellite imagery. Luke recounts the healing of a man in Lystra who is unable to walk. Paul recognizes the man's faith and instructs him to stand "upright." The context of Proverbs 4:26 is a metaphor of the way, and Proverbs 12:15 uses the way motif to contrast the foolish and the wise. Also, "straight/upright" is a satellite image of the way,

---

103. Keener, *Acts: 3:1—14:28*, 2168, fn.1825.

104. The ESV supplies vain, while the CSB supplies worthless. ESV cites Deut 32:21; 1 Sam 12:21; Jer 14:22; [1 Cor 8:4]. The CSB cites 1 Sam 12:21; 1 Cor 8:4; 1 Thes 1:9.

105. Haenchen suggests Paul's question, "Men, why are you doing these things?" is a command to stop doing them. Haenchen, *The Acts of the Apostles*, 428.

106. Bock, *Acts*, 477.

107. The selection of speech is important for continuing the narrative and conveying the message in Acts. See Witherington III, *The Acts of the Apostles*, 665.

indicating righteousness. In Bruce and Peterson's view, Paul is asking the man to stand straight, both physically and spiritually, with straightness in faith reflecting the Way motif.[108] The terminology and symbolism suggests words intentionally chosen to strengthen the Way motif.

As previously discussed, the Way motif is connected to the ministry of calling sinners to faith. The "two ways" of the motif provide a clear contrast between following idols and following the Lord. Within the passage, men may choose the way of God or idols. The two options directly oppose one another. Luke presents God as sovereign over both groups of people and exercising His judgment over them. Only those who choose the way of Jesus will receive salvation.

In brief, the Way motif appears repeatedly in Acts 14:8–20. First, the passage contains a reference to the way. Second, satellite imagery of the way is used, and third, the passage shares language with Proverbs.

Theological Analysis: Allusion

Here Beale's method showing Luke's use of ὁδός as an allusion to Proverbs is continued in relation to Acts 14. The following theological analysis will show that the four criteria of an allusion are met in the passage. (For information about meeting the requirement of availability, see the discussion on Acts 9). The remaining criteria are examined below.

The criterion of volume is partially met in Acts 14:16. The phrase "πορεύεσθαι ταῖς ὁδοῖς αὐτῶν" has parallels in the OT (e.g., 1 Sam 1:19; Ezek 11:21) plus three instances in Proverbs (Prov 1:15; 2:13; 6:12). There appears to be no context in the OT where the subjects who are "walking in their ways" are the nations (ἔθνο), however.[109] Although the language may not point directly to Proverbs verbatim, the phrases that parallel "πορεύεσθαι ταῖς ὁδοῖς αὐτῶν" often relate to walking in disobedience to or away from the Lord (1 Kgs 15:34; 16:19, 26 [walk in the sinful ways of Jeroboam]; 2 Kgs 21:21, 22 [Walk in sinful ways of their father]; Ruth 1:7 [Choosing to go back to gentile nation]; 1 Sam 1:19 [Moving spatially away from a place of worship]).[110] The survey of the OT parallels suggest that Proverbs is a

---

108. Bruce, *The Book of the Acts*, 274; Peterson, *The Acts of the Apostles*, 407.

109. Nations are associated with a "way" of living (Jer 10:2; Ezek 36:19).

110. There are numerous references to following in the Way of the Lord. The parallels above are primarily associated with someone other than God. At times individuals walk in the way of their fathers, who were obedient to the Lord (2 Kgs 22:2). The book of

plausible, if not probable, referent, with the concept of "walking in disobedience" surely the intended meaning.[111]

The criterion of recurrence is met. The passage opens with language common to the Wisdom literature. The vivid account of a miraculous healing may be the tool for introducing wisdom language. Acts 14:8–10 uses satellite language such as hearing, straightness, and salvation, which points to "the way" in Proverbs. A contextual dichotomy is presented between God and the Greek gods, alongside people's attempts to worship the apostles. The language and context, combined with reference to "the way" in Acts 14:16, appear to connect to "the way" found in Proverbs, thus meeting the criterion of recurrence.

Thematic coherence between the two books is also met, as the way metaphor from Proverbs suits the context of Acts 14:8–20 also. Shared thematic features include the use of a "two ways" theology where God is pitted against a false god, and the use of ὁδός as a metaphor for a way of living.

First, both Proverbs and Acts 14:8–20 use "two ways" theology. Proverbs presents a choice between Wisdom and Folly; Acts provides a choice between God and false gods. As discussed in chapter 3, Dame Folly represents false gods, and Lady Wisdom represents God.[112] In Acts 14:15, Paul pleads with the crowd to turn from vain things (worship of false gods) to the living God. Marshall recognizes that "vain things" describe also the false idols of the OT.[113]

Second, both Proverbs and Acts use ὁδός as a metaphor for living. In Proverbs, "the way" has an observable four-fold pattern: (1) God's people are those who travel the path (Prov 1:7; 2:1–22; 3:5–7; 9; 16); (2) God creates the path (3:5–7; 16); (3) God directs and sustains His people on the path (Prov 2:1–22; 3:5–7; 9; 14:1–32; 16); and (4) choosing to follow the path has consequences that lead to life or death (Prov 2:1–22; 4:14–18; 9; 14:1–32; 15). In Acts 14:8–20 Paul presents an alternative to walking in the sinful ways of the fathers. Paul's alternative way is the Gospel: Jesus is the Way (Acts 14:7, 15); God's people are the Way (Acts 14:9 "lame man"; 14–15 "Barnabas and Paul"); Jesus is the one who sustains God's people on

---

Isaiah does not offer a parallel of individuals or groups walking in their own ways against the Lord.

111. See Schnabel, *Acts*, 610; Keener, *Acts: 3:1—14:28*, 2168.
112. Longman, III, *Proverbs*, 59.
113. Marshall, "Acts," 588.

the Way (Acts 14:16 "God allows nations to walk in their own ways"); and Jesus is the one who provides salvation (Acts 14:9–10).

The analysis of Acts 14 endorses the previous findings in Acts 9 and 13 that Luke is—without exception—using the way metaphor as a literary motif and as an allusion to Proverbs. Luke is using metaphor to describe a way of life. Moreover, the way metaphor describes a way of life that is found in following the Lord.

Acts 16:11–40

Continuing the analysis of Luke's use of ὁδός, the focus moves from Acts 14 to 16. Acts 16:11–40 recounts the ministry of Paul and Silas in Philippi. Within the passage there is a single occurrence of ὁδός in the passage. The following analysis will capture the use of the way metaphor in Acts 16 and examine its use as a possible literary motif and allusion.

The passage is often subdivided into four events: (1) The conversion of Lydia, (2) the exorcism of the possessed woman, (3) the imprisonment of Paul and Silas, and (4) the release of Paul and Silas.[114] The "way" in Acts 16:17 does not appear to be used as a name for early Christians. From a linguistic standpoint, the anarthrous use of ὁδός suggests the "way" here stands for a way to salvation.[115] Nevertheless, the passage contributes to an understanding of Luke's use of the way metaphor. To narrow the examination, the primary focus is on Acts 16:16–24, which contains the singular use of ὁδός. It is important to notice that two conversion stories surround the focus-text, and two groups who oppose the Christians inhabit the greater context (i.e., pagans and Jews). The context contributes to understanding how Luke is using "the way" metaphor in Acts 16:16–24, because the surrounding text present a polemical situation that reflects a "two-ways" theology.

Keener recognizes the audience would associate "the way of salvation" of verse 17 with the truth.[116] Similarly, Keener notes Luke's audience also

---

114. Holladay, *Acts*, 318–30. Bock's divisions are also helpful because they draw attention to the conversion story of the jailer during Paul's imprisonment: (1) Lydia, (2) the possessed woman, (3) the jailer's conversion, and (4) Paul and the magistrates. Bock, *Acts*, 530.

115. Schnabel, *Acts*, 683. Schnabel suggests the pagan audience may have thought this "way" Paul proclaims is yet another way to salvation.

116. Keener, *Acts: 15:1—23:35*, 2458.

associates the people of the Way with truth.[117] In fact, verse 18 clarifies that the way here references Jesus and Christians.[118] "Paul's use of Jesus's name removes any ambiguity attached to 'the Most High God' or 'a salvific way' (Acts 16:17)."[119] Because the way of salvation is associated with Christians, the exorcism contrasts Jesus and Christians with pagan cult practices and false gods.[120] Thus, the context sets the two-ways before the reader, with Christians associated with the Messiah and salvation.

Literary Analysis: Motif

Here in Acts 16, once again use Freedman's method is useful for recognizing Luke's blatant use of ὁδός as a motif. Freedman's method begins with two criteria that must be met: Frequency and avoidability.[121] First, the frequency is increasing, which brings further affirmation that ὁδός is a motif. Acts 16:17 is the sixth direct use of "the way." Second, the criterion of avoidability is met. Luke did not need to include a metaphor when describing "salvation." The criterion of symbolism is also met, for it is appropriate to use the "two ways" metaphor to contrast pagan and Christian behavior, or pagan idols and God. The symbolism is also an appropriate description of how the disciples are living "in the way of" the Lord.

Theological Analysis: Allusion

Beale's method remains a helpful tool for classifying Luke's use of "the way" as an allusion to Proverbs. The first criteria—availability—for the presence of allusion is met. The criterion of volume is not well satisfied, if at all, for verbatim repetition is limited to a single instance of "the way." However, a complete analysis of all four of Beale's criteria will show Proverbs functions as an allusion in Acts 16.

The requirement for recurrence can be considered met in terms of the entire context of Acts 16:11–40. First, the pericope of the possessed girl is sandwiched between two conversion stories. Second, the account of Paul

---

117. Fitzmyer, *The Acts of the Apostles*, 705.
118. Keener, *Acts: 15:1—23:35*, 2464.
119. Keener, *Acts: 15:1—23:35*, 2464.
120. For further information about the contrast between Christianity and pagan use of "the Most High God," see Keener, *Acts: 15:1—23:35*, 2462–63.
121. Freedman, "The Literary Motif," 126.

and Silas' escape uses language reminiscent of the way. Both "light" and "harm" (evil) are satellite images of the way. Additional satellite language arises as the jailer falls before the apostles in "fear." Keener states that fear in this context causes trembling, such as "Moses's fear at Sinai."[122] Also, fear may recall the proverb about the fear of the Lord. The language is also reminiscent of a theophany or angelic appearance. However, the jailor does not respond as if to a divine intervention.[123] Lastly, no physical light appears before the jailor. Instead, Luke seems to use the words "light," "harm," and "fear" to signal a turning from one's own ways to those of the Lord.

The criterion of thematic coherence is met. The way of salvation is the Gospel. Thus, Jesus creates the Way for God's people, and the Way leads to salvation. Again, the pattern reflects the way of Proverbs in providing a path for God's people that leads to life.

Acts 16 contributes to an understanding of the use of the Way as both a motif and an allusion. First, Freedman's analysis leads towards the conclusion that the Way is a motif. The final summary analysis will provide a more definitive answer. Second, Beale's analysis shows "the way" is an allusion to Proverbs. Acts 16 portrays Jesus as the Way (Acts 16:17, 18, 31), God's people as the Way (Acts 16:17, 29), Jesus as the one who sustains God's people on the Way (Acts 16:18, 25, 26), and the Way as leading to salvation (Acts 16:17, 18, 30). This usage in Acts aligns with Proverbs, where : (1) God creates the way (Prov 3:5–7, 16); (2) the way is for God's people (Prov 1:7; 2:1–22; 3:5–7; 9; 16); (3) God sustains the people on the path (Prov 2:1–22; 3:5–7; 9; 14:1–32; 16); and (4) the way leads to the consequences of life or death (Prov 2:1–22; 4:14–18; 9; 14:1–32; 15).

Acts 18:24–28

Turning now from Acts 16 to Acts 18, the same method is used to examine Luke's next use of ὁδός. Luke uses ὁδός twice in Acts 18:25–26. Modern translations often leave the word uncapitalized.[124] Translating ὁδός uncapitalized as "the way," suggests that Luke is not referencing the Church. Yet, Acts 18:25 may be referring to the people of the Way. Regardless, Luke uses

---

122. Keener, *Acts: 15:1—23:35*, 2509.

123. Bock, *Acts*, 541.

124. The following translations leave the way uncapitalized: ESV, Christian Standard Bible, King James Version, New International Version (2011), and the New American Standard Bible (1995 and 2020). The New Revised Standard Version uses a capital.

the way metaphorically, and Acts 18:25–26 contributes to an understanding of the Way as a possible motif and allusion.

In Act 18:24–28, Luke writes of Apollos preaching the baptism of John, and Priscilla and Aquila correcting Apollos.[125] Acts 18:25 uses the way to refer to living as the Lord has instructed. The UBS5 gives "τὴν ὁδὸν τοῦ θεοῦ" a rating showing the Committee had difficulty determining if the text is original to the autographs.[126] However, both "τὴν ὁδὸν τοῦ κυρίου" and "τὴν ὁδὸν τοῦ θεοῦ" are "synonymous with τὴν ὁδὸν τοῦ κυρίου (see v. 25; 9:2)."[127] How one interprets ὁδός in v. 25 influences the interpretation of v. 26. For example, the NRSV translates both occurrences of ὁδός as "the Way," while translations such as the ESV and NIV translate both uses of ὁδός as "the way."[128] However, there are three possible meanings. First, the Way is a name for Christians. Second, the Way describes Christian living. Third, the Way may represent Jewish living. Barrett writes, "If *the way of God* and *the way of the Lord* (v. 25) were reversed in order we might guess that Apollos knew already the (Jewish) way of God . . . and now needed to be taught the (Christian) way of the Lord (Jesus)."[129]

Bock affirms that the Way in v. 25 is a short-form for "the way of the Lord," and that it is short for those following in God's will.[130] Schnabel equates the Way with the people of the Way, and says that the people of "*the Way*" is also short for "the Way of the Lord" and "the Way of God."[131] If Apollos is a believer, Schnabel's conclusion may be accurate.[132] Apollos, as a believer, is part of the Way, and as a member of the Way, will follow it as a natural outworking of his faith. Therefore, ὁδός may not be a demarcation for the Church, but it does mean Christianity.

---

125. Bock, *Acts*, 590.

126. K. Aland, B. Aland, J. Karavidopoulos, C. M. Martini, and Bruce M. Metzger, eds., *The Greek New Testament*, 5th rev. ed., Acts 18:26,fn.10.

127. Culy and Parsons, *Acts*, 357.

128. In each of these translations both occurrences are translated as "the way," uncapitalized: ESV, CSB, KJV, NIV (2011), and the NASB (1995 and 2020).

129. Barrett, *Acts of the Apostles*, 889; italics in the original.

130. Bock, *Acts*, 591.

131. Schnabel, *Acts*, 290; italics in the original.

132. Bock and Peterson conclude that because Apollos was instructed in the way of the Lord and is fervent in the Spirit, Apollos likely has a saving faith. Bock, *Acts*, 591–92; Peterson, *The Acts of the Apostles*, 525–26.

Bock understands the Way as a reference to "the way of God," and not to Christians.[133] Nonetheless, Bock finds that "Appolos has a more accurate understanding of the gospel than before."[134] Therefore, Appolos is a Christian, and the way references Christianity. Similarly, Schnabel translates ὁδός in v. 26 as the Way.[135] Schnabel writes, "They are eager and able to explain "the Way of God," the revelation of God's path to salvation for Israel and for the world through Jesus, in particular his death and resurrection."[136] As Schnabel depicts Priscilla and Aquila's actions in Acts 18:26, he defines the Way both as an abbreviated term for "the Way of God" and as a name for followers of Jesus. Last, Carl Holladay concurs the phrase is short for the expression "the Way of the Lord."[137] He suggests that the shorthand expression, "occurs only here in the NT in this precise form (with an article modifying both "way" and "Lord")."[138] Thus, the Way has several viable meanings as (1) the way of the Lord, (2) a word for Christians, (3) both "the way of the Lord," and a name for Christians.

Literary Analysis: Motif

Reaffirming Luke's use of ὁδός as a motif, Freedman's method is applied to Acts 18. Once again, Freedman's method begins with two criteria that must be met: frequency and avoidability.[139] The criterion of frequency can be considered met by this passage. Luke has now used ὁδός (the way) eight times since Acts 9, and a pattern, based on the context of the passages, is forming. A cursory observation shows Luke uses the Way motif to describe Christians and Christian teaching, and in contexts where Christianity is juxtaposed to other teaching. A full analysis will be reserved until after the remaining passages have been addressed.

Likewise, the criterion of avoidability is met. For a preliminary discussion on Greek vocabulary, see the earlier analysis of Acts 9. The analysis of ὁδός in Acts 9:2 is applicable if Luke is referring to the Church. However, if Luke is referencing instruction or education, he could have chosen from a

133. Bock, *Acts*, 593.
134. Bock, *Acts*, 593.
135. Schnabel, *Acts*, 785.
136. Schnabel, *Acts*, 785.
137. Holladay, *Acts*, 362.
138. Holladay, *Acts*, 362.
139. Freedman, "The Literary Motif," 126.

different vocabulary set.¹⁴⁰ Luke's use of the way is nevertheless intentionally chosen in order to speak metaphorically of the Church or Christian education. The short passage is discussing a man who is "able," "accurate," "knowing," and who is "teaching" the things of Jesus. These terms, although not paralleling Proverbs, are all related to wisdom.

The supporting criterion of symbolism is also met. Two dichotomies are displayed. Firstly, the baptism of John is compared to the baptism of Jesus. Although a great teacher, John does not know the baptism of Jesus. Secondly, the Jews' understanding of Scripture is contrasted with the Christian understanding of Scripture.

Theological Analysis: Allusion

In step with the previous passages, Beale's method of identifying allusions is used here to identify ὁδός as an allusion to Proverbs. Beale's four criteria are *availability, volume, recurrence,* and *thematic coherence*.¹⁴¹ The criterion of availability is again reached, with the remaining criteria for identifying an allusion examined below. First, the criterion for volume is possibly met. The saying, "the way of the Lord" (τὴν ὁδὸν τοῦ κυρίου) has parallels in the OT (LXX: Pss 1:6; 24:4, 10; 137:5; Gen 18:19; Judg 2:22; 2 Sam 22:22; 2 Kgs 21:22; 2 Chr 17:6). Marshall notes, "The 'way of the Lord' is OT language for the kind of conduct that the Lord requires of his people and hence for the teaching that describes it (Exod 32:8; Deut 5:33). Cf. 9:2; 13:10."¹⁴² Surprisingly, Proverbs does not make this direct association, but instead discusses "the way" without connecting it directly to the Lord (κύριος) or God (θεός).

Second, the criterion of recurrence is met within the immediate context of 18:24–28. The passage has two uses of ὁδός (vv. 25–26), in which the Way is associated with both κύριος and θεός, which may suggest Luke is making a more explicit connection to the OT, as θεός may refer to YHWH and κύριος to Jesus.¹⁴³ Furthermore, language characteristic of Proverbs is

---

140. For example: κατηχέω, teach or instruct, (Luke 1:4; Acts 18:25; 21:21), διδάσκω, teach or instruct (Luke 4:15, 31, 5:3, 17; 6:6; 20:21; 21:37; 23:5; Acts 1:1; 4:2, 18; 5:21, 25, 28, 42; 11:26; 15:1, 35; 18:11, 25; 20:20; 21:21, 28; 28:31).

141. Beale, *Handbook*, 35.

142. Marshall, "Acts," 596.

143. For further discussion about Luke's use of κύριος to identify Jesus as Lord and to distinguish between Jesus and God, see Fitzmyer, "The Semitic Background of the New Testament Kyrios Title;" Rowe, *Early Narrative Christology*, 199–202; Staples, "'Lord, Lord.'" Similarly, New Testament studies of Pauline literature also discuss the

used alongside this metaphor of the way, with reference to teaching and explaining (κατηχέω, διδάσκω, ἐκτίθημι),[144] and accuracy (ἀκριβῶς).

Third, the final criterion of thematic coherence is met, for in Acts 18:24–28, Luke is using "the way" to reference Jesus as the Way (18:25, 28), God's people as following the Way (18:24, 27), and Jesus bringing salvation in the Way (18:28). When Christians are pitted against Jews in v. 28, Luke appears to be drawing on the "two-ways" theology present in the way metaphor. Proverbs likewise presents the way as constructed by God for His people, and leading to either life or death. In Proverbs, the "two-ways" theology presents a choice between God and false idols, or between Wisdom and Folly. Such a theme applies to the narrative in Acts.

In sum, Acts 18:24–28 is using "the Way" to describe Christianity and not as a name for the Christian church. Further, the Way appears here as a motif, and alludes to Proverbs, with the metaphor here associated with Jesus' followers and salvation.

Acts 19:1–41

Moving from Acts 18 to Acts 19, the analysis of Luke's use of ὁδός with Freeman and Beale's methods continues. In Acts 19, Paul continues his ministry into Ephesus (19:1–41).[145] In this section of Acts, the Way is used twice as an alternative name for the Church (19:9, 23).[146] The two uses of the Way metaphor will be examined by Freedman and Beale's methods in turn, to determine if the Way is a literary motif and an allusion.

Both uses of the Way in this passage are found within a narrative about Paul's ministry. Fitzmyer suggests vv. 8–12 describe Paul's first months in Ephesus, a place he would spend two years.[147] Bock suggests vv. 23–41 occur near the end of Paul's time in Ephesus, and that the scene depicts the

---

phenomenon of using θεός and κύριος to distinguish respectfully between the Father and Jesus. See Fitzmyer, "New Testament *Kyrios* and *Maranatha* and Their Aramaic Background;" Hurtado, *Lord Jesus Christ*; Hurtado, *One God, One Lord*.

144. Marshall, "Acts," 596. Marshall writes, "the 'way of the Lord' is OT language for the kind of conduct that the Lord requires of his people and hence for the teaching that describes it (Exod. 32:8; Deut. 5:33), Cf. 9:2; 13:10."

145. Bock, *Acts*, 595.

146. Culy and Parsons determine both references are used to describe Christians, just as Luke does in Acts 9:2. Culy and Parsons, *Acts*, 362, 72.

147. Fitzmyer, *The Acts of the Apostles*, 646.

An Analysis of "the Way" in the Book of Acts

Ephesians voicing their concerns about the negative impact of the Way on their economy and religious life.[148]

In Acts 19:9, Luke writes of the reaction of the Jews as Paul preaches the good news of Jesus.[149] Keener notes that Paul is initially speaking on an invitation (18:20), yet his zeal for Jesus yields a "predictable hostility" from those in the synagogue.[150] Here Paul's message of Christ is opposed by the Jews. The hostility within the synagogue amounts to a conclusive rejection of the Way by the Jews.[151] Keener notes the "speaking evil" by the Jews amounts to a curse (Exod 21:17; 22:28; 1 Sam 3:13; Prov 20:20).[152] Barrett notes a slight ambiguity:

> It is not clear how πλῆθος is to be taken. It may refer to (a) the Christians in the synagogue; for πλῆθος as a local community of Christians cf. e.g. 15:30; the effect on them might be to cause them to give up the faith they had accepted; (b) the synagogue community as a whole, who might in consequence expel or punish the Christians; (c) the general public of the city, who would decide not to become Christians and perhaps to persecute those who were.[153]

He chooses the third option.[154] Two observations arise from the scholarly review: (1) The Way refers to the Christian Church, and (2) the Church and non-believers are in opposition.

Following the account of disciples casting out demons and showing God's power as supreme over the actions of Jews and magicians (Acts 19:13–16), Jesus' name is honored. Acts 19:7 concludes, ἐπέπεσεν φόβος ἐπὶ πάντας αὐτοὺς (fear fell upon them), the Jews, the magicians, and all of Ephesus. Continuing in the same verse, καὶ ἐμεγαλύνετο τὸ ὄνομα τοῦ κυρίου Ἰησοῦ (and the name of the Lord Jesus was extolled). Acts 19:18 then records many conversions to Christianity.[155] This scene first captures the power of Jesus' name against false idols.[156] Second, the scene captures the "fear" coming upon the unrepentant and an understanding of Jesus as

---

148. Bock, *Acts*, 595.
149. Keener, *Acts: 15:1—23:35*, 2825.
150. Keener, *Acts: 15:1—23:35*, 2825–26.
151. Keener, *Acts: 15:1—23:35*, 2826.
152. Keener, *Acts: 15:1—23:35*, 2826.
153. Barrett, *Acts of the Apostles*, 904.
154. Barrett, *Acts of the Apostles*, 904.
155. Keener, *Acts: 15:1—23:35*, 2853.
156. Barrett, *Acts of the Apostles*, 912.

Lord (God), which leads the unrepentant to faith. This formulaic statement reflects the foundation of wisdom, which is "the fear of the Lord." Luke uses the word "fear" to describe a reaction prior to conversion, having presented a similar three-fold approach to accepting Jesus earlier in Acts 2:37–41: "(1) repent, (2) be baptized each one of you in the name of Jesus Christ for the forgiveness of sins, and (3) you shall receive the gift of the Spirit."[157] There, in Acts 2:37–39, Luke describes people cut to the heart upon hearing the Gospel, and later, being baptized. Similarly. Acts 8:26–40 describes the convert "believing" and being baptized. Later in the book, Agrippa accuses Paul of "persuading" him to Christianity in Acts 26:28–32. Conversion with "fear" occurs with the jailor in Acts 16:29 also. Luke often uses "fear" to describe believers' awe and reverence for the Lord (Acts 5:5, 11; 9:31; 13:16, 26). In the context of the passage, use of the Way, illustrations of "two-ways" theology, imagery, and Luke's use of the word "fear" may all be a nod in the direction of "the fear of the Lord."

Acts 19:23 begins a new section, transitioning to a later time in Paul's ministry in Ephesus when a riot breaks out.[158] Keener suggests that Luke presents the historical conflict in Ephesus as dramatically as possible.[159] Moreover, Luke depicts the riot as started by business owners who make images of Artemis.[160] However, the riot does not concern Paul specifically.[161] Rather, the rioters take offense at the Way: "The movement [the Way] represents the power of God."[162] Conzelmann writes, "For the Christian reader, the charge against Paul is a testimony to the victorious advance of the mission."[163]

Literary Analysis: Motif

In this section, Freedman's method for identifying motifs is applied to Acts 19. The two necessary criteria of Freedman's model are again met (i.e., frequency and avoidability). Also, the criteria of significance and coherence are satisfied to establish that "the way" is a motif in Acts.

157. Bock, *Acts*, 141.
158. Keener, *Acts: 15:1—23:35*, 2879.
159. Keener, *Acts: 15:1—23:35*, 2866.
160. Fitzmyer, *The Acts of the Apostles*, 655.
161. Bock, *Acts*, 606.
162. Bock, *Acts*, 606.
163. Conzelmann, *Acts of the Apostles*, 165.

An Analysis of "the Way" in the Book of Acts

Luke's use of the Way meets Freedman's criteria for frequency in this passage. Chapter 19 has two occurrences of the Way. These passages will later be used again to determine the frequency of the way metaphor in Acts as a whole.

The second necessary criterion, avoidability, is also met. First, Luke's word choice to describe the Church is deliberate. In fact, Luke uses an alternative name for a congregation or multitude in verses 32, 39, and 40. He could have avoided the use of ὁδός to describe the church. Even within the same verse as ὁδός Luke uses a different word for a congregation. Barrett highlights uncertainty over who is the referent of the noun πλῆθος in Acts 19:19.[164] The uncertainty created by πλῆθος may be a reason why Luke uses "the Way" in place of other available words.

Two criteria are emerging with more clarity as the study progresses: significance and coherence. A context is forming; each occurrence contrasts the Church with an opposing force: Jews (v. 9), and idols (v. 23). A final review will synthesize the cumulative use of the Way in the book. Still, this passage suggests a significant context for finding the Way appears when Christians are presented in opposition to Judaism and paganism.

The criterion of coherence is also satisfied. The context of Acts 19 incorporates many elements of the Way motif. There is an emphasis on teaching the Way of Jesus, and the language connected with knowledge that is shared with Proverbs persists throughout the passage: (1) [v.8] διαλέγομαι (interchange of ideas), πείθω (persuade), (2) [v. 9] σκληρύνω (stubborn), διαλέγομαι, [v. 15] ἐπίσταμαι (recognize), [v. 17] γνωστός (known), "φόβος ἐπὶ πάντας αὐτοὺς καὶ ἐμεγαλύνετο τὸ ὄνομα τοῦ κυρίου Ἰησοῦ," and fear fell upon them all, and the name of the Lord Jesus was extolled, [v. 25] ἐπίσταμαι (caused to recognize), [v. 26] πείθω (persuade). While the concentration of vocabulary relating to the Way motif cannot be seen as directly referencing Proverbs—for several words occur with some regularity throughout the NT—yet the cumulative effect of the shared vocabulary increases the probability Luke is highlighting the Way motif. Christians (the Way) are represented by reason, knowledge, goodness,[165] and above all, are identified as God's chosen people. Jews and idol worshipers are portrayed as speaking evil, standing against God, and foolish. Speaking about their portrayal as

---

164. Barrett, *Acts of the Apostles*, 904.

165. "Good" is implied by the contrast with the evil being spoken against the Way (v. 9). Also, Acts 19:11–20 contrast Christians to those who are ill, to Jews, and to magicians. These passages highlight God's power and blessing in contrast.

foolish, Conzelmann writes, "Demetrius naively identifies the temple replicas with the gods (is Luke intentionally portraying him as stupid?)."[166] The Jews are unable to cast out demons and look foolish, while the idol makers attribute divinity to man-made inanimate objects.

Theological Analysis: Allusion

Beale's criteria for determining the presence of allusion continues to elucidate the Way as an allusion to Proverbs. First, the criteria of availability is affirmed, with more information found in relation to the earlier discussion about Acts 9:2. The criterion of volume is not met, however, for the passage does not have significant repeat wording. The only direct instance of repetition is in the use of the Way (the article and the noun ὁδός).

The criterion of recurrence is met, for Acts 19 is filled with vocabulary reminiscent of Proverbs, as noted in the literary analysis above. Also, the Way is used twice over fifteen verses. The combination of two direct references with other vocabulary shared between Acts 19:1–41 and Proverbs, meets the criterion of recurrence.

The criterion of thematic coherence is also met. Both Acts and Proverbs use the Way and a "two-ways" theology to contrast believers (i.e., Christians and Jews) against non-believers (i.e., idol worshipers of false gods). Luke portrays the Way centered around Jesus (i.e., Jesus creates the Way [vv. 4, 5]; Christians are followers of the Way [vv. 9, 23]; Jesus sustains the Way [vv. 10, 11], and the Way is a means of salvation [vv. 5, 6 Baptism and the Holy Spirit]). Luke's use of the Way is thematically similar to Proverbs, which presents the Way as created by God (e.g., 3:5–7; 16) for His people (e.g., Prov 1:7; 2:1–22); is sustained by God (e.g., Prov 2:1–22); and leads to life (e.g., Prov 4:18).

Acts 19 uses the Way metaphor to describe the Church. The way metaphor has four components in this passage: Jesus creates the Way, believers follow the Way, Jesus sustains followers on the Way, and the Way leads to salvation. Further, the Way functions as a literary motif, and also alludes to Proverbs' use of the way.

---

166. Conzelmann, *Acts of the Apostles*, 165.

An Analysis of "the Way" in the Book of Acts

Acts 22:1–22

Now, moving to Acts 22, the same methods are applied to Luke's use of ὁδός to re-enforce previous conclusions since Acts 9. Acts 22:1–22 contains a single use of ὁδός (v. 4). Like previous conversion stories discussed above (see Acts 9), Acts 22:1–22 contains satellite images of the way metaphor. Below is a summary of Acts 22:1–22 with the two-fold analysis of the way metaphor.

Witherington labels Acts 21:37–22:29 as "the First Defense."[167] The passage may be broken down into three sections "Paul's Conversation with the Tribune (21:37–40);" "Paul's Defense (22:1–22);" and his sequential conversation with the tribune (22:22–29).[168] Acts 22:1–22 contains Paul's defense speech.[169] In defending himself, Paul describes his Jewish background and ambitions as a Pharisee.[170] In Paul's testimony of his life as a zealous Pharisee, he tells of his persecution of the Way.[171]

The primary focus here is on Acts 22:1–22. This passage contains the first use within the chapter of ὁδός as well as satellite imagery of the way metaphor: walking (πορεύομαι), light (φῶς), blinded (οὐκ ἐνέβλεπον v. 11), and the Righteous One (δίκαιον v. 14). Second, two contexts are established in the passage: Paul's previous life and his current life. Interestingly, the two contexts are very similar, and both reflect a conflict between Christians and Jews. However, Paul's current situation is also in opposition to the Roman authorities. Witherington finds that Luke uses speeches to capture how the Way is spreading God's Word.[172] Moreover, Witherington suggests that the multiple accounts of Paul's conversion story have a cumulative effect on the audience.[173] It is near the beginning of Paul's speech that he mentions the Way. Dean Pinter observes that in v. 3, Paul's speech may read, "I continue to be zealous for God."[174] Paul then continues his account by mentioning his persecution of the Way (Christians). Seemingly Paul never stopped being

---

167. Witherington III, *The Acts of the Apostles*, 659.

168. Dean Pinter, *Acts*, The Story of God Bible Commentary, ed. Scot McKnight (Grand Rapids, MI: Zondervan, 2019), 501–10; Osborne suggests the same divisions. Osborne, *Acts*, 391–400.

169. Osborne, *Acts*, 392.

170. Fitzmyer, *The Acts of the Apostles*, 703.

171. Fitzmyer comments that Paul validates Luke's account in Galatians 1:13. Fitzmyer, *The Acts of the Apostles*, 705.

172. Witherington III, *The Acts of the Apostles*, 663.

173. Witherington III, *The Acts of the Apostles*, 666.

174. Pinter, *Acts*, 503.

zealous for the Lord. Immediately following v. 4, Paul gives his account of meeting Jesus and becoming a dedicated, perhaps zealous, follower of Christ. He speaks of his blindness, a sign of disobedience.[175] It is the light of God's glory that blinds Paul.[176] The moment Jesus meets Paul is the end of Paul's previous life without the Messiah. Bock states that Paul's response to the voice of Jesus is one of respect.[177] It may be that Luke is using the speeches recounting the conversion stories in order to illuminate the Church.

Acts 22:12–16 tells of Paul's calling. Ananias recognizes Paul as a brother, or fellow believer, and tells him to see again (v.13). Ananias proceeds to commission Paul. Bock writes, "God had appointed (προεχειρίσατο, *proecheirisato*) Saul to know God's will, see the Just one, and hear from him . . . The reference to Jesus as the Just One (τὸν δίκαιον, *ton dikaion*) points to his exalted position and to the vindication of his innocence that Luke 23 highlighted."[178] Paul was a zealous Jew, thereby losing his vision. Nevertheless, after meeting Jesus and responding in faith, Paul's sight was restored. In this one conversion story, all Christians are vindicated.

Literary Analysis: Motif

Coming now to the analysis, Freedman's analysis of ὁδός finds the way metaphor is a motif in Luke's writing. Acts 22:4 meets Freedman's literary criteria for a motif: frequency and avoidability. The frequency is beginning to mount up, although in this chapter "the way" appears only once. Luke intentionally selects Paul's speech to discuss the Church and the spread of the Gospel. Thus, the criterion of avoidability is met. (For the discussion on the words available to describe the Church, see the discussion about Acts 9:2.)

Also, the criteria of significance and coherence are both fulfilled. Luke uses "the way" metaphor when recounting a critical moment in Paul's life. This moment is as he faces opposition. In both his past and now in his present, Christianity is held up against Jewish beliefs. Within the passage, Christian belief is vindicated and shown to be true to the God of the OT. Last, the criterion of coherence is met as the Way metaphor is supported with satellite imagery throughout the passage. Of particular note is the association between blindness and Paul's pre-conversion life, and Paul's

---

175. Bock, *Acts*, 660.
176. Bock, *Acts*, 661.
177. Bock, *Acts*, 660.
178. Bock, *Acts*, 661.

regained sight after being commissioned by God. This punishment and reward picture echoes the wicked walking in darkness and the wise walking in light in the book of Proverbs (Prov 2:13; 4:18–19; 6:23; 13:19; 20:20).

Theological Analysis: Allusion

Now Beale's method is applied to Acts 22 to show again that ὁδός is an allusion to Proverbs. As previously noted, the criterion of availability is met in terms of the book as a whole, because of widespread familiarity with the Wisdom literature. However, the criterion of volume is not satisfied in this passage, for the Way is mentioned verbatim with only the noun and its article. τὴν ὁδὸν.

However, Acts 22:1–22 meets the remaining two criteria. The criterion of recurrence is satisfied because of the several occurrences of satellite imagery: light, implied darkness, and righteousness. It is plausible to suggest that Luke was selecting vocabulary in keeping with Proverbs.

There is abundant thematic coherence also. In Acts 22:1–22, Luke employs the way metaphor for two purposes: (1) as a "two-ways" theology and (2) to describe the Way of Jesus. First, he stresses the "two-ways" theology. In his past Paul persecuted the Church. Then, when he is "on his way,"[179] Jesus meets him. Christ is righteous while Paul is not. Jesus is light, and Paul is left blind (in darkness). Paul is leading people to death, and Jesus is leading people to live. The Way is later pitted against the Roman court and the Jewish people. Further, the Way is shown to be the true faith of God, against the religious claims of the Jews.

Also, Luke uses the metaphor to present the Way as something established by Jesus (Acts 22:10, 21), as intended for Christians (Acts 22:4) who are sustained by Jesus (Acts 22:21), and as the path to salvation (Acts 22:13, 16). Theologically, Proverbs conveys the same notions about the way: God creates the way (e.g., Prov 3:5–7; 16), the way is for believers (e.g., Prov 1:7; 2:1–22; 3:5–7; 9; 16), God directs and sustains His people on the way (e.g., Prov 2:1–22; 3:5–7; 9; 14:1–32; 16), and the way leads to life (e.g., Prov 14:18).

---

179. It is difficult not to translate Acts 22:6 "As I was on my way" as the ESV does despite seeing this is incorrect (see Culy and Parsons, *Acts*, 424–425; and Kellum, *Acts*, 253). Within the context of the passage Paul has chosen to persecute the church and his route is to Jerusalem. In verse 6 Jesus comes to Paul as he is walking that literal and metaphorical path.

The True Identity of the People of the Way

Acts 24:1–27

Now, continuing the analysis of Luke's use of ὁδός, the focus moves from Acts 22 to 24. Within this section, there are two occurrences of the Way (Acts 24:14, 22). In both, the Way is used as a designation for Christians. The passage gives the third account of Paul's conversion and contributes to an understanding of the metaphor of the Way in the book of Acts.

In Acts 24:1–27, Luke recounts Paul's initial defense before the governor Felix.[180] Bock writes that Paul claims no proof exists that the charges against him are true, and the Way "is merely the completion of Judaism (vv. 9–21)."[181] Then in Acts 24:22–23, Felix delays his verdict over Paul.[182]

The passage continues to identify the early Church as God's people. Paul declares that the people of the Way are not a sect. Further, the people of the Way are the ones who worship "the God of our fathers." Peterson writes, "Paul served the God of the OT 'according to the way' . . . of Jesus and his followers."[183] Schnabel agrees, "For Paul, as for the other followers of Jesus, the worship . . . of God is now fundamentally and irrevocably connected with Jesus, Israel's Messiah, whose life, death, resurrection, and exaltation constitute the only 'way' to salvation, and who is thus Savior and Lord."[184] Paul demonstrates that he is righteous because he is following Jesus, which is in accordance with the Law, the Prophets, and historically aligned with the God of the OT. Acts 24:15 offers satellite language of the Way, with Paul speaking of the judgement of the righteous, δικαιοσύνη, and the unjust, ἄδικος. These two words capture the "two-ways" theology of the Way motif. In Proverbs 4:24, "unrighteous" lips are paralleled with "crooked." Throughout Proverbs, the righteous are often opposed to the unrighteous (Prov 10:31; 11:18; 12:17, 21). The passage employs law-court language (e.g., Felix, the seasoned judge, Paul's defense, and the criminal allegations), yet the portrayal of the Law goes beyond the courtroom. A shift of perspective begins when Paul confesses his faith and proclaims the way of salvation.

Moreover, Bock writes, "The Law here is seen in terms of redemption, salvation, and promise, that is, in terms of eschatological deliverance."[185]

---

180. Bock, *Acts*, 687.
181. Bock, *Acts*, 687.
182. Bock, *Acts*, 687.
183. Peterson, *The Acts of the Apostles*, 635.
184. Schnabel, *Acts*, 958.
185. Bock, *Acts*, 693.

Such Good News "provides an incentive for the moral life. Living with a sense of ultimate accountability before God fosters having a good conscience before God and the world (24:16)."[186] Holladay concludes that Paul's good conscience refers to how a person conducts their life.[187] For Holladay, Paul's "claim has two elements: (1) full consciousness and (2) moral conviction."[188]

In Acts 24:22, Luke discusses Felix's knowledge of the Way. Keener states that Felix's familiarity with the Christian movement helps justify Felix's handling of Paul's case.[189] Keener adds that Felix knows the Way belongs "to the minority sect of Nazarenes" and that the conflict between the Jews and the Way is a religious debate, not a political threat.[190] In the end, Felix defers the case, hoping not to offend "a minority of significant size" or the high priests.[191]

Barrett comments on Luke's use of "a sect" and "the Way." His description of Luke's use of the terms suggests distinct differences between the two groups the terms represent. First, Barrett proposes the phrase "κατὰ τὴν ὁδὸν . . . τῷ πατρῴῳ θεῷ," establishes bookends to highlight continuity with the God of the Old Testament, yet the phrase states Paul "worships the old God in the new way."[192] Further, Barrett stipulates Paul welcomes the title the Way, which implies the designation of "sect" is undesirable.[193] Moreover, Barrett writes, "Christianity regards itself not as a sect or group within the people of God; it is the people of God, and its way is the halakah for all Israel."[194] Likewise, Holladay suggests Luke's use of the Way is "insider's language," while "'a sect' is outsider' language."[195] Schnabel concludes that Paul still believes the Way "does not lead him outside of Judaism," but he worships God in a new way, one that results in salvation through Christ.[196]

---

186. Holladay, *Acts*, 451.
187. Holladay, *Acts*, 431.
188. Holladay, *Acts*, 431.
189. Craig S. Keener, *Acts: 24:1—28:31*, 3422.
190. Keener, *Acts: 24:1—28:31*, 3422.
191. Keener, *Acts: 24:1—28:31*, 3423.
192. Barrett, *Acts of the Apostles*, 1104.
193. Barrett, *Acts of the Apostles*, 1104.
194. Barrett, *Acts of the Apostles*, 1104.
195. Holladay, *Acts*, 450.
196. Schnabel, *Acts*, 959.

Thus, Christianity is the faith of the OT, but distinct from all of Judaism. Now, Jesus is the only way to salvation.

Literary Analysis: Motif

For a final time, Freedman's method for recognizing a motif in literature is applied. Freedman's analysis reveals that the Way functions as a motif in Acts 24. The criterion of frequency is met by two occurrences in the passage. With an additional two uses of the Way, Luke has now used the metaphor eleven times in Acts, all after Paul's conversion in Acts 9. Moreover, the criteria of avoidability and coherence are also met.

Use of the term "sect" in Acts 24:14 shows Luke is making (avoidable) decisions about how to label the Church. The criterion of coherence is also met. The passage presents a unified message through Luke's use of the Way and of satellite imagery. Although the context is a court, the Way and its satellite imagery create unity and are of benefit for understanding Acts 24. As scholars suggest, the court scene contains language that connects to morality, faith, and eschatology.[197] That is, each element of the Way and its satellite imagery contribute to revealing Paul's faith, moral compass, and eschatological beliefs.

Theological Analysis: Allusion

For the last time, Beale's method is used to identify "the way" as an allusion to Proverbs in Acts 24. Beale's method reveals the way metaphor is functioning as an allusion to Proverbs. The criterion of availability in Acts 24 is met, as previously discussed in relation to Acts 9:2. The criterion of volume is not satisfied, as each verse where ὁδός occurs in Acts only mirrors the text verbatim in Proverbs with the noun and the article for "the way."

The criterion of recurrence is possibly achieved, for Acts 24:1–27 contains several satellite images and some vocabulary characteristic of Proverbs. Satellite language includes judgment of the righteous, δικαιοσύνη, and the unjust, ἄδικος. Language in Proverbs includes "accurate," "knowledge," and "fathers." However, the satellite images and vocabulary in connection with Proverbs overlap with images and language associated with the law-court. Nevertheless, such language may still be referencing Proverbs exclusively,

---

[197]. Keener, *Acts: 24:1—28:31*, 3387. Holladay recognizes the passage "maintains the mood of a formal court proceeding." Holladay, *Acts*, 449.

although more likely serving a dual function, where at times Proverbs is accentuated more, and at others, the Law. The fact that term "the Way" is used multiple times, increases the likelihood that Proverbs is being referenced in some of the satellite images and proverbial language also.

Finally, the criterion of thematic coherence is met in two ways: (1) use of a "two-ways" theology, and (2) the depiction of the Way. Thus Luke uses "two-ways" theology to highlight the difference between Christians and Jews and other Jewish offshoots (e.g., Acts 22:14). The naming separates the two religions. This distinction may best be observed in Acts' portrayal of the Way. In Acts, the Way is linked to Jesus (e.g., Acts 24:5 "the sect of the Nazarenes"); to Jesus sustaining His people (e.g., Acts 24:17–18 "Paul's faith journey"); and to salvation (e.g., Acts 24:21, "resurrection").

THE WAY AS A LITERARY MOTIF: SUMMARY

The employment of Freedman's method to identify a motif reveals that Luke is indeed using the way metaphor as a motif in Acts. Moreover, Luke is using the Way as a motif in a manner much like its usage in Proverbs. An overview of the results of the analysis with Freeman's method follows.

Freedman's criterion of frequency is met. This work proposes a minimum of eleven occurrences of ὁδός that function metaphorically following Acts 9. However, Luke employs the term "the way" an additional nine times, which may contribute to the overall strength of the motif, especially Acts 8:6 and 9:17. These passages are conversion stories with symbolism that relates to the way metaphor, yet because here "the way" also has a literal sense, these occurrences were not incorporated in the analysis. Last, it should be noted that "the way" motif is found throughout Luke-Acts, but has a different literary function in Acts, particularly from Acts 9 onwards.

The second criterion necessary for establishing the existence of a motif, i.e., avoidability, is also satisfied. As shown throughout the analysis, Luke had many alternative words available he could have used to describe the Christian Church or living as a Christian. Furthermore, Luke intentionally selected speeches that contained the way motif.

A pattern emerges about the way Luke uses "the way" metaphor in Acts. Luke tends to employ the metaphor in three related areas that have significant overlap. The overlap occurs through shared language or concepts when talking about each category (e.g., Acts 24:14 uses court language "confess" in a court setting and talks about the coming Messiah, which is the Good News about salvation). This pattern suggests the criterion of significance is also met: He tends to refer to "the Way" when Christianity is in opposition to Jewish or pagan people (Acts 9:2; 13:10; 14:16; 19:9, 23; 22:4; 24:14, 22). Similarly, the metaphor is used in contexts depicting the proclamation of the Good News (Acts 19:9, 23; 24:14, 22) and salvation (Acts 14:16; 16:7).[198] Although lacking the same degree of overlap, "the way" is also used in court settings (Acts 22:4; 24:14, 23).

The Way motif meets the criterion of coherence in several passages (Acts 9:1–31; 13:4–12; 14:8–20; 22:1–22; 24:1–27). Within most contexts, the metaphor and its satellite imagery contribute to a better understanding of Luke's message. In some cases, the way motif elaborates on moral living, salvation, and Jesus. In every case, Christianity became easier to understand as a result of the way motif.

Freedman's final supportive criterion is "symbolic appropriateness." Luke uses the Way to describe Christian living; it is closely related to following Jesus, and it may also mean being a member of a group of Christians. Traveling along a path or a way is an appropriate metaphor for life, or as a designation for a group of people bound by their commitments in life. The metaphor of the way was already employed by Israel, as seen in chapter three. Using the metaphor of a way or path appears to have a universal appeal, one that goes beyond the Judeo Christian heritage. Kees Waaijman writes, "Who thinks about the question 'What is spirituality?' inevitably comes across the root word 'way'. The reason for this is that spirituality is not a static phenomenon but a process, or, more precisely: a divine-human relational process."[199] He notes how Buddhism, Chinese spirituality, Hellenistic spirituality, and Islamic spirituality all use a metaphor of a path or way.[200]

In both Proverbs and Acts, God generates the Way and God sustains His people in the Way. The comparison shows that the symbolic appropriateness between connecting Proverbs and the path, and Acts and the Way. Longenecker's conclusion about the origins of "the Way" speaks to both the book of Proverbs and Acts when he writes, "it surely had something to do with their consciousness of walking in the true path of God's salvation

---

198 The significant context appears to be "opposition to Jewish and pagan people." Underneath that banner, the Way is used to further declare a way of life, the Good News of Jesus, and salvation.

199. Waaijman, "The Way, Root Metaphor for Spirituality," 63, See Waaijman, *Spirituality*.

200. Waaijman, "The Way, Root Metaphor for Spirituality," 63–65.

and moving forward to accomplish his purposes."[201] Outside of religion, the metaphor of a way or a road finds a place in the twenty-first century to describe a life journey.

In sum, using Freedman's analysis shows the way metaphor functions as a motif in Acts, much as it does in Proverbs. The criterion of frequency, avoidability, significance, coherence, and symbolic appropriateness are met throughout Luke's use of the Way metaphor in Acts. Further, the summary below may provide increased certainty through an accumulation of data supporting the use of the way as a motif. Last, for the Way to operate as a motif, it must support the overall themes of Acts. The final chapter will discuss this matter, by looking at how "the way" motif functions in the book of Acts.

SUMMARY OF "THE WAY" AS AN ALLUSION TO PROVERBS

The criteria for determining use of the Way in Acts as an allusion to Proverbs have been met. Three of the criteria— availability, recurrence, and thematic coherence—were met regularly and overwhelmingly. Although the requirement for volume was less conclusively attained, the four criteria together still "point to the presence of an allusion." Therefore, by fully meeting three of the four criteria, it is possible to confidently assert that "the Way" in Acts alludes to "the way" in Proverbs.

The criterion of availability was uniformly met in every passage discussed. Chapter four looked at how the metaphor of the way was familiar to first-century people through several texts (e.g., the LXX). Thus, Luke and his audience had access to the metaphor, making it possible for them to use and understand it.

As predicted in chapter one, the criterion of volume was met only infrequently. There were few verbatim parallels between the metaphor and the LXX. Generally, the only text repeated verbatim was "the way" (ὁδός).

The criterion of recurrence was met with each passage discussed. This recurrence was in some passages part of the immediate verses under discussion, and in others it formed part of the greater pericope (10–20 verses). Thus Luke frequently uses satellite imagery and the phrase "the fear of the Lord" in conjunction with reference to "the Way." Hence the combination

---

201. Longenecker, *Acts*, 292.

of multiple occurrences of ὁδός together with satellite imagery within an immediate context satisfies the criterion of recurrence.

The Way as it is used in the book of Proverbs "is suitable and satisfying in that its meaning in the OT not only thematically fits into the NT writer's argument but also illuminates it."[202] In Proverbs, the metaphor of the "way" has four observable features. First, God's people are those who travel the way (Prov 1:7; 2:1–22; 3:5–7; 9; 16). Second, God creates the way (3:5–7; 16). Third, God directs and sustains His people on the way (Prov 2:1–22; 3:5–7; 9; 14:1–32; 16). Fourth, choosing to follow the way has consequences that lead to life or death (Prov 2:1–22; 4:14–18; 9; 14:1–32; 15).

The Way functions similarly in Acts. First, Luke shows Jesus as the Way or the creator of the Way (Acts 9:2; 16:17, 18, 31; 18:25, 28; 19:4, 5; 22:10, 21; 24:5). Second, the Way is for Christ followers (Acts 9:31; 16:17, 29; 18:24, 27; 19:9, 23; 22:4). Third, Acts shows Jesus sustains His people on the Way (Acts 9:2; 16:18, 25, 26; 19:10, 11; 22:21; 24:17–18). Fourth, Jesus' Way leads to salvation (Acts 13:4–12; 16:17, 18, 30; 18:28; 19:5, 6; 22:13, 16; 24:21).

In summary, the way metaphor alludes to Proverbs. Beale's study reveals a strong thematic fit and consistent fulfillment of three of the four criteria for identifying allusions. Beale's nine-fold analysis will shed further light on Luke's use of the allusion. This analysis will be conducted in the final chapter.

CONCLUSION

Following from this thorough examination of the use of the Way in Acts, two observations arise: (1) Luke uses the metaphor as a motif in Acts, and (2) Luke alludes to Proverbs. The foregoing examination covered the relevant passages containing ὁδός using two methods: Freedman's method for identifying motifs and Beale's criteria for identifying allusions. In chapter six, how "the way" motif functions or relates to the theme(s) of Acts and how the allusion operates within the book will be studied, and a summary and conclusion presented.

---

202. Beale, *Handbook*, 33.

6

Conclusion

INTRODUCTION

THE PREVIOUS CHAPTER PRESENTED data on Luke's use of "the way" metaphor in Acts, which led to the conclusion "the way" is used as a literary motif and that it also alludes to the book of Proverbs. This chapter draws the final conclusions about (1) how "the way" motif functions or relates to the themes of Acts, and (2) how the allusion operates within Acts.

First, a summary of the analysis of "the way" from chapters 1–5 is provided. After that, the themes of Luke-Acts are presented. The themes of Luke-Acts provide the information needed for analyzing the relationship of the literary motif to the themes and also for Step Two of Beale's nine-fold analysis. Third, the relationship between "the way" motif and the themes of Luke-Acts will be examined. Fourth, Beale's nine-fold approach interpreting the use of the OT in the NT (i.e., Luke's use of the metaphor of the way found in Proverbs) will be applied.[1] The conclusion is then presented, followed by brief suggestions for future research of "the way" in Acts.

SUMMARY

This study has examined in detail Luke's use of "the Way" in Acts. Specifically, this research has proposed that Luke uses "the Way" as a literary motif

---

1. Beale, *Handbook*, 42–43.

that alludes to "the path" of Proverbs. Chapter one identified the observable similarities between this usage in Acts and Proverbs. Also, that chapter identified a gap in the research concerning Luke's use of "the Way" as a name for Christians. As a result, the chapter suggested a fresh approach to researching the way in Acts. Namely, it suggested using Freedman's method for identifying motifs, plus Beale's method for identifying allusions, along with a discussion of how the NT uses the allusion.

Chapter two reviewed the literature about the use of "the Way" in Acts: (1) as a name for Christians, and (2) as a literary or theological device. Regarding "the people of the Way," a literature review revealed that scholars emphasize two aspects: (1) the source or background of the Way, and (2) the exact referent or meaning of the term.[2] Previously, scholars suggested the Qumran texts, Isaiah, or the "two-ways" tradition were the source or background for "the Way" as a people group. Alternatively, Pao has suggested looking for a literary function[3] of the Way, which he concludes marks a polemical narrative that identifies the "true" people of God.[4] Besides the literary or theological use of the Way within Luke-Acts, the chapter discussed "the way" as a contribution to the travel narrative of Acts and as a topos (i.e., of the New Moses the New Exodus). Last, the chapter concluded there was both a lack of consistency in understanding, and limited research into the Way as a designation for Christians, which created the need for the present research.

Chapter three described the literary and theological use of the way in Proverbs. Also, vocabulary associated with "the way" in Proverbs was discussed. The chapter concluded "the way" is a literary motif within Proverbs, and listed four features of the motif: (1) the Lord creates the way (Prov 3:5–7; 16), (2) it is for His people (Prov 1:7; 2:1–22; 3:5–7; 9; 16), (3) God sustains His people on the way (Prov 2:1–22; 3:5–7; 9; 14:1–32; 16), and (4) the way leads to life (Prov 2:1–22; 4:14–18; 9; 14:1–32; 15).

---

2. Pao, *Acts and the Isaianic New Exodus*, 60.

3. Since Pao, Huffman has proposed an organization of function classifications for the NT use of the OT, which includes "five broad usage clusters" (declaration, fulfillment, story, analogy, and ideas), and "ten specific function classifications" (ultimate truth, ethical wisdom, prophecy fulfillment, promising patterns, typological correlation, historical backdrop, cultural background, instructive examplars, illustrations and imagery, and vocabulary and style). Huffman, *Understanding the New Testament Use of the Old Testament*, 101–31 (107, 113).

4. Pao, *Acts and the Isaianic New Exodus*, 60.

Conclusion

Chapter four had two objectives: First, it sought to show how the Wisdom literature influenced the cognitive environment of the first-century authors, and second, it surveyed use of the way metaphor in other OT books and relevant first-century writings. Walton's "cognitive environment criticism," the discipline that discusses the OT's relationship (here the NT) with its cultural milieu, is used to analyze the cognitive environment of Acts.[5] More narrowly, chapter three proposed using the "echoes" model for analyzing Acts' cognitive environment.[6] Echoes are commonalities between texts through allusion, citation, or reference.[7] In brief, the chapter sought to determine if it is plausible to say the Wisdom literature influenced the NT authors.[8] The long history of metaphor in the Wisdom literature shows it plausibly influenced the first-century authors. The influence of "the way" metaphor continued through the intertestamental period into the first century. With little variation or development, the metaphor remained prevalent in Luke's day. Luke and the audience of Acts were familiar with the book of Proverbs. Moreover, teachers had taught Wisdom throughout Israel's history. Wisdom was how YHWH acted, and Israel was called to act similarly.[9] Therefore, it is plausible that Luke draws from "the way" metaphor found within the OT, as did his contemporaries.

Chapter five studied Luke's use of the way in the book of Acts. First, it carefully examined the literary and theological use of the metaphor. Second, it studied relevant passages containing ὁδός in light of two methods: Freedman's method for identifying motifs, and Beale's criteria for identifying allusions. Following the examination of "the way" passages, two conclusions were drawn: (1) Luke uses the Way as a motif in Acts, and (2) Luke alludes to Proverbs. However, two questions remain: (1) How does the Way motif support the themes of Acts, and (2) how is Luke using the allusions to Proverbs? To address these two questions, the themes of Acts will need to be studied, and Beale's nine-fold approach to understanding a NT use of the OT will be applied.[10]

---

5. Walton, "Interactions in the Ancient Cognitive Environment," 333.

6. Note that the echoes model is not the same as the technical term that denotes a weak allusion.

7. Walton, "Interactions in the Ancient Cognitive Environment," 334.

8. Walton, "Abductive, Presumptive and Plausible Arguments," 152.

9. Wright, *The New Testament and the People of God*, 264–65.

10. Beale, *Handbook*, 42–43.

THEMES OF LUKE-ACTS

This work uses the following definition for a theme: "A theme is an idea or point of view used by an author throughout their work to discuss the topic or central idea of the work."[11] As one proceeds, it is crucial to remember that a standard definition—or even language—is used to describe themes or central ideas. Therefore, the following scholarly review incorporates themes/theology/purpose in the construction of the themes of Luke-Acts.[12]

To obtain a complete view of the theological use of "the way" metaphor in Acts, the Gospel of Luke and the book of Acts should be viewed as two parts of a single writing.[13] The Gospel of Luke and the book of Acts were written to Theophilus. Hence, both the meta-narrative themes of Luke-Acts and the themes specific to Acts will be examined. First, the purpose of Luke-Acts will be discussed. Second, two overarching meta-narrative themes will be discussed, which are salvation and vindication of the Church. Third, within Acts, these two themes are reaffirmed.

Luke writes to give "an orderly account" to Theophilus that he "may have certainty concerning the things" taught to him (Luke 1:3-4). This purpose statement has two major components: to (1) "Review how God worked to legitimize Jesus and how Jesus proclaimed hope," and (2) "to defend God's faithfulness to Israel and his promises, despite the rejection of the promise by many in the nation."[14] Similarly, Joel Green writes that Luke-Acts is concerned with "legitimation and apologetic."[15] Further, Green proposes Luke's purpose is to "strengthen the Christian movement in the face of opposition."[16] He finds Luke focuses on ecclesiology and is "concerned with the practices that define the criteria for legitimating the

---

11. Harmon, *A Handbook to Literature*; *A Dictionary of Literary Terms and Literary Theory*, rev ed., s.v. "Theme;" *Webster's Basic Dictionary*, s.v. "Theme;" and *American Heritage Dictionary*, 2nd ed., s.v. "Theme." Alter, *The Art of Biblical Narrative*, 120.

12. These overarching categories of theme/theology/purpose have nuances that differentiate them, but which are nevertheless intimately connected if the writing is effective.

13. Bock, *A Theology of Luke and Acts*, 28. Peterson, *The Acts of the Apostles*, 64; Keener lists "Jesus as God's Agent of Salvation" and "Salvation" (or salvation history) as two themes. Keener, *Acts: 1:1—2:47*, 500-04.

14. Bock, *Luke: Volume 1*, 15.

15. Green, *The Gospel of Luke*, 21.

16. Green finds the Church strengthened in two ways: "by (1) ensuring them in their interpretation and experience of the redemptive purpose and faithfulness of God and by (2) calling them to continued faithfulness and witness in God's salvific project." Green, *The Gospel of Luke*, 21-22.

Conclusion

community of God's people, and centered on the invitation to participate in God's project."[17] Both the legitimacy of Jesus and the Church are intimately related to the themes of the salvation and vindication of the Church.

First, and foremost, scholars find the theme of salvation is central to Luke-Acts.[18] James Edwards writes, "Luke is the first Evangelist to present the gospel of Jesus Christ as a two-part story of salvation, beginning with the story of Jesus as the fulfillment of the OT messianic expectation, and concluding with the expansion of the gospel into the Gentile world of the Roman Empire."[19] Green writes, "Luke 1:5–2:52 initiates a narrative centered above all on God whose aim it is to bring salvation in all its fullness to all."[20] Moreover, salvation for all includes Israel. Bock writes, "throughout Acts, Israel's role remains central to the hope of salvation, including the expectation of national restoration."[21] Luke witnesses to Israel's chief role with the use of the word "redemption." David Ravens writes, "What is particularly significant is that on the four occasions when Luke uses these words they always refer to 'Israel', never to Christians or Gentiles (Luke 1:68; 2:38; 24:21; Acts 7:35)."[22] Rather, Jesus' arrival is for the spiritual and political deliverance of God's people.[23] Within Luke-Acts, the disciples are still concerned with "nationalistic"[24] vindication and "thinking in terms of Israel's story."[25] Thus, the hope in Luke-Acts is the hope found within the OT.[26]

Barrett nicely summarizes the theme of salvation in Luke-Acts:

---

17. Green, *The Gospel of Luke*, 21–22.

18. Liefeld, "Luke," 800, 11; Morris, *Luke*, 43. Morris lists both "Salvation History" and "Universality of Salvation" as facets of the theology of Luke-Acts. Bock, *A Theology of Luke and Acts*, 121.

19. Edwards, *The Gospel According to Luke*, 13.

20. Green, *The Gospel of Luke*, 52. Green specifically states this theme also applies to Acts. Green, "'Salvation to the End of the Earth.'" This article was originally published in *Witness to the Gospel* (1988).

21. Bock, "The Restoration of Israel in Luke-Acts," 175.

22. Ravens, *Luke and the Restoration of Israel*, 38. Bock cites Ravens in support of Israel as the recipient of "redemption" speech in Luke-Acts. Bock, "The Restoration of Israel in Luke-Acts," 171.

23. Bock, "The Restoration of Israel in Luke-Acts," 171.

24. Bock, "The Restoration of Israel in Luke-Acts," 174.

25. Bock, "The Restoration of Israel in Luke-Acts," 175.

26. Bock, "The Restoration of Israel in Luke-Acts," 176.

The gospel is not about a new God; it is about the God of Abraham, Isaac, and Jacob (3:13). The striking events of the gift of the Holy Spirit and the healing of a lame man are the fulfilment of purposes that this God had already declared in days of old: the prophecy of Joel of what should come in the last days (2:17–21) and the glorification of the servant of God (3:13; Isa 52:13). This leads to Christology, which is focused on the resurrection, which had been foretold by David (2:25–8; Ps 16:8–11). Jesus was not only alive but exalted as κύριος (2:34f; Ps 110:1). He was the promised Mosaic prophet (3:22; Deut 18:15–20). God's fulfilment of his prophecies meant the offer of salvation to all, as had been promised to Abraham (3:25; Gen 22:18; 26:4) and foretold by Joel (2:21; cf. 2:39).[27]

Second, first-century Christians were seeking vindication. Jewish rejection of the Gospel and the persecution of the church caused Theophilus to question the legitimacy of the early Church and of Jesus.[28] Therefore, a major concern for Luke was vindicating the early Church, and vindication for the early Church can be seen as one of the major purposes of Luke-Acts. Keener writes, "Luke probably has more than one agenda in Luke-Acts. One of them appears to be vindication for the mission of uncircumcised Gentiles."[29] Two major themes support Luke's desire to vindicate the early Church: The identity of the church as God's people and presenting the mission of the church as witnesses of Jesus.[30] Likewise, Walter Liefeld has the theme "Israel and the people of God," which focuses on those who follow God and those who do not (He pays particular attention to the impact the Gospel had on the Jewish people).[31] Last, François Bovon writes, "The Christians, troubled by the polemics of the Jews, yearn for an objective verification and theological justification of the facts."[32]

Bock lists nine themes specific to the Book of Acts.[33] Similarly, Jacob Jervell specifically analyzes the book of Acts to determine its themes.[34] A major theological theme in Acts is "The Plan and Work of the Mighty

---

27. Barrett, "Luke/Acts," 243.
28. Bock, *Luke: Volume 1*, 15.
29. Keener, *Acts: 1:1—2:47*, 458.
30. Schnabel, *Acts*, 38.
31. Liefeld, "Luke," 812–13.
32. Bovon and Koester, *Luke 1*, 6.
33. Bock, *Acts*, 32–42. It should be noted that these themes are necessarily exclusive to Acts. Bock is surveying Acts independently of Luke.
34. Jervell, *The Theology of the Acts of the Apostles*.

Conclusion

God."[35] The last theme concerns God's foreknowledge and promises, and is about the work of God through Jesus.[36] Bock states that Luke uses echoes of Scripture to affirm the new community of God as His people.[37]

Jervell identifies two similar themes in the theology of Acts: (1) "God and His People,"[38] and "Crisis: The Divided People of God."[39] Both themes relate to salvation history and the inclusion of the Gentiles. With the coming of the Messiah two groups form and both claim the same God.[40] Interestingly, Luke only mentions the history of Israel, while the history of the others is unimportant and they are left to their own devices (Acts 14:16).[41] Jervell claims that Jewish Christians were conflicted about the idea of salvation being offered to Gentiles because salvation was "reserved for Israel, the people of the law of God."[42] Also, the Gentiles didn't appear to be part of God's promises to Israel.[43] Jervell suggests that Luke proposed a solution to the Jewish Christians, that only Gentiles that are God-fearers join God's family.[44] Also, these new family members are part of the nation of God, despite the exclusive nomenclature of the "God of Israel."[45] Jervell writes:

> God has one people of his own. Luke has no interest in any other people; that is shown in his terminology, as he uses *laos*, a word reserved for Israel. The word is used in the New Testament 142 times; by Luke alone 84 times, that is 60 per cent of the total. When he uses the word in an unqualified way, he always has in mind Israel as a nation. Sometimes it means "crowd," a synonym for *ochlos*, but signifying a crowd of Jews.[46]

Yet Jervell notes that the faithlessness of Israel should have resulted in God's denunciation of his people.[47] Also, the Gentiles would not be brought into

---

35. Bock, *Acts*, 33.
36. Bock, *Acts*, 33.
37. Bock, *Acts*, 33.
38. Jervell, *The Theology of the Acts of the Apostles*, 18.
39. Jervell, *The Theology of the Acts of the Apostles*, 34.
40. Jervell, *The Theology of the Acts of the Apostles*, 18.
41. Jervell, *The Theology of the Acts of the Apostles*, 19.
42. Jervell, *The Theology of the Acts of the Apostles*, 22.
43. Jervell, *The Theology of the Acts of the Apostles*, 22.
44. Jervell, *The Theology of the Acts of the Apostles*, 22.
45. Jervell, *The Theology of the Acts of the Apostles*, 23.
46. Jervell, *The Theology of the Acts of the Apostles*, 23; italics in the original.
47. Jervell, *The Theology of the Acts of the Apostles*, 35.

the family because belonging to Israel is hereditary.[48] However, God's faithfulness and grace gave birth to the Church, made up of both Jews and Gentiles of faith (Acts 13:17–25).[49]

Luke-Acts has salvation and the vindication of the Church as themes. Scholars observe these themes when looking at the meta-narrative of Luke-Acts and at Acts in isolation, which confirms and validates each theme in Acts.

THE WAY MOTIF AND THE THEMES OF LUKE-ACTS

Again, a motif is a recurrent thematic element, idea, symbol, or image, used at selected moments to support a theme of the work.[50] A motif has no meaning without the context of its controlling theme.[51] Chapter five proposed "the way" motif is present and fits within the immediate context. However, for "the way" to be a motif in Acts, it must support the themes of Luke-Acts.

As discussed above, the central theme of Luke-Acts is salvation. Also, the theme of the vindication of the Church is also present within Luke-Acts. Freedman's criterion of symbolic appropriateness shows similarities in how God creates the Way, God's people travel the Way, God sustains people on the Way, and the Way leads to salvation. The final point shows that within the Way motif, salvation plays a significant role. Freedman's analysis also shows a pattern to the contexts in which Luke uses the motif in Acts. The motif is deployed in contexts where Christians oppose Jews or pagans. The symbolic appropriateness and the contexts reveal continuity between God's people in the OT and God's people in the NT. The continuity is displayed by showcasing that Jesus is God and the people of the Way are followers of God.

THE USE OF THE WAY AS AN ALLUSION (BEALE'S NINE-FOLD APPROACH)

Beale's nine-fold approach will be used with a slight modification, based on the previous analysis in chapter five. Thus, some steps will be a brief recap

   48. Jervell, *The Theology of the Acts of the Apostles*, 35.
   49. The Scripture reference is Jervell's. Jervell, *The Theology of the Acts of the Apostles*, 35.
   50. This definition is determined from *A Dictionary of Literary Terms and Literary Theory*, rev ed., s.v. "Motif;" *American Heritage Dictionary*, 2nd ed., s.v. "Motif;" Urban, "Imagery," 319–21; Fullmer, *Resurrection in Mark's Literary-Historical Perspective*, 34; Daemmrich, *Themes & Motifs in Western Literature*.
   51. Alter, *The Art of Biblical Narrative*, 120.

Conclusion

of material from chapters three to five, while others are eliminated. The nine-fold approach is as follows:

1. Identify the OT reference. Is it a quotation or allusion? If it is an allusion, then there must be validation that it is an allusion, judging by the criteria discussed in the preceding chapter.
2. Analyze the broad NT context where the OT reference occurs.
3. Analyze the OT context both broadly and immediately, especially thoroughly interpreting the paragraph in which the quotation or allusion occurs.
4. Survey the use of the OT text in early and late Judaism that might be of relevance to the NT appropriation of the OT text.
5. Compare the texts (including their textual variants): NT, LXX, MT, and targums, early Jewish citations (DSS, the Pseudepigrapha, Josephus, Philo). Underline or color-code the various differences.
6. Analyze the author's textual use of the OT. (Which text does the author rely on, or is the author making his own rendering, and how does this bear on the interpretation of the OT text?)
7. Analyze the author's interpretative (hermeneutical) use of the OT.
8. Analyze the author's theological use of the OT.
9. Analyze the author's rhetorical use of the OT.[52]

From the nine-fold approach, step one was completed in chapter five. In fact, nearly every step was discussed in some detail. Thus, the emphasis in this chapter will be on steps two, eight, and nine. Beale subdivides step two into: (1) "Overview of the broad NT context," and (2) "Overview of the immediate NT context."[53] This chapter provides an analysis of major themes in Acts to address the former subpoint, but the latter subpoint (2) is summarized below. Next, focused attention is given to the final two criteria, Luke's use of the way, and its contribution to understanding Acts.

Step One: Identify the OT Reference and Determine if an Allusion[54]

Chapter five concluded that Proverbs is the OT referent for "the Way" metaphor in Acts, and that Proverbs is alluded to in Acts in light of Beale's four criteria for identifying allusions: "*availability, volume, recurrence*, and

---

52. Beale, *Handbook*, 42–43.
53. Beale, *Handbook*, 43.
54. Full Title: "Identify the OT reference. Is it a quotation or allusion? If it is an allusion, then there must be validation that it is an allusion, judging by the criteria discussed in the preceding chapter." Beale, *Handbook*, 43.

Step Two: Analyze the Broad NT Context where the OT Reference Occurs.[56]

Proverbs' use of "the way" directly relates to the themes of Luke-Acts. The broad context of Luke-Acts is covered above. Further, the purpose of Luke-Acts is to give legitimacy to Jesus and the Church. The major theme of Luke-Acts is salvation. Also, Luke-Acts has a theme of the vindication of the Church.

The immediate context for the use of the Way metaphor in Acts was provided in chapter five. First, Luke uses the Way in situations where Christianity opposes Jewish and pagan people (Acts 9:2; 13:10; 14:16; 19:9, 23; 22:4; 24:14, 22). Second, the local context of the way passages show Jesus creates the Way (Acts 9:2; 16:17, 18, 31; 18:25, 28; 19:4, 5; 22:10, 21; 24:5), God's people are the Way (Acts 9:31; 16:17, 29; 18:24, 27; 19:9, 23; 22:4), Jesus is the one who sustains God's people on the Way (Acts 9:2; 9:31; 16:18, 25, 26; 19:10, 11; 22:21; 24:17–18), and Jesus' Way leads to salvation (Acts 13:4–12; 16:17, 18, 30; 18:28; 19:5, 6; 22:13, 16; 24:21).

Step Three: Analyze the OT Context[57]

Proverbs is the OT referent of the Way in Acts. With its broad context of teaching, the theme of Proverbs is to teach wisdom, its ethical and practical characteristics, and show that wisdom requires "right relation to God" while living in His will.[58] Limiting the context to passages in Proverbs about the Way: (1) it is God's people who traverse the Way (Prov 1:7; 2:1–22; 3:5–7; 9; 16), (2) God creates the Way (3:5–7; 16), (3) God guides and keeps His people on the Way (Prov 2:1–22; 3:5–7; 9; 14:1–32; 16), and (4) the

---

55. Beale suggests the first four criteria of Hays' method are the best. Beale, *Handbook,*, 35.

56. Beale, *Handbook*, 43.

57. Full Title: "Analyze the OT context both broadly and immediately, especially thoroughly interpreting the paragraph in which the quotation or allusion occurs." Beale, *Handbook*, 44.

58. Berry, *The Book of Proverbs*, xii–xiii.

Conclusion

consequence of life or death comes from following or abandoning the Way (Prov 2:1–22; 4:14–18; 9; 14:1–32; 15).

Step Four: Survey the Use of the OT Text in Early and Late Judaism[59]

The use of "the way" in Proverbs and from early to late Judaism is relevant to Acts because various texts relate wisdom to Israel's history (e.g., Wisdom of Solomon), wisdom to the Law (e.g., Ben Sira), use a two-ways theology to instruct on Christian living (e.g., *Didache*), and use the Way as nomenclature for a people group (e.g., the Qumran community). The survey of texts was conducted in chapters two, three, and four. Chapter two surveyed uses of the "way" metaphor in different contexts and determined Proverbs as the probable referent. Chapter three examined the metaphor in Proverbs. Chapter four examined the use of the way metaphor across multiple books of both early and late Judaism. The conclusion was that "the way" metaphor was still known and used much as it is in Proverbs.

Step Five: Compare the NT, LXX, and the MT.[60]

Although a comparative analysis of the texts is not given, the fruits from step five are outlined in chapters 3–5. First, step five is manifest in the word studies: beginning with Proverbs, the vocabulary of "the way" was determined, both the term and its cognates as well as satellite vocabulary. Word usage was traced from the Hebrew Text to the LXX, and the LXX vocabulary was compared to the NT text. Second, sentence structure and word order were considered when comparing the Greek NT text and the LXX text. Third, the contexts of the primary texts were considered (e.g., the use of the Way in the Dead Sea Scrolls etc.). The textual comparison confirmed that the language of the Way metaphor used by Luke in Acts reflects the language used in Proverbs.

---

59. Full Title: "Survey the use of the OT text in early and late Judaism that might be of relevance to the NT appropriation of the OT text." Beale, *Handbook*, 46.

60. Full Title: "Compare the texts (including their textual variants): NT, LXX, MT and targums, early Jewish citations (DSS, the Pseudepigrapha, Josephus, Philo). Underline or color-code the various differences." Beale, *Handbook*, 49.

Step Seven: Analyze the Author's Interpretive Use of the OT."[61]

The seventh step is to understand the immediate context of Luke's uses of the Way metaphor in Acts. This step was conducted in chapter 5, but here the observation of the Way as a motif is helpful. Generally, Luke uses the Way to differentiate believers (Christians) and unbelievers (Jews and Gentiles), often in polemical situations. Alongside ὁδός (the way), Luke's use of satellite images and "the fear of the Lord" communicates a consistent message that Christians are God's chosen people, while unrepentant Jews and Gentiles are not. Chapter four showed how Paul uses the metaphor of the way to communicate Jesus as the Way,[62] and how James may understand the Way as representing following God.[63]

Step Eight: Luke's Theological Use of the Way of Proverbs[64]

In this step, Beale asks: "To what part of theology does this use of the OT passage contribute?"[65] He lists Christology, ecclesiology, and pneumatology as examples.[66] Luke's use of the Way contributes to the soteriology and ecclesiology of Luke-Acts. It does so by aligning the use in the immediate context with the theology of Luke-Acts. The immediate context shows the Way was used to differentiate the followers of Jesus from unbelievers (Jews and Gentiles). Specifically, Jesus creates the Way, Christians are the people on the Way, Jesus is the one who sustains God's people on the Way, and the Way leads to salvation.

The theology of the way metaphor displays continuity between God's people of the OT and those of the Way. In both Proverbs and Acts the One true God is sovereign and is the head of the Way. However, Luke Christologically applies the "way" metaphor as used in Proverbs. Where once God the Father (by His Wisdom) stood as the foundation of the Way, it is Jesus who does so in Acts. Similarly, Luke is redefining the followers of God from those of Jewish nationality to the Church (Jews and Gentiles).

---

61. Beale, *Handbook*, 50.
62. Steinmann and Eschelbach, "Walk This Way," 61.
63. Davids, *The Epistle of James*, 198.
64. Full Title: "Analyze the author's theological use of the OT." Beale, *Handbook*, 52.
65. Beale, *Handbook*, 52.
66. Beale, *Handbook*, 52.

Conclusion

Beale writes that NT authors will often interpret OT texts Christologically, writing, "Thus with respect to Christology, there are some cases where an OT passage describing God is applied to Christ (e.g., see Matt 3:3; John 1:23); with regard to ecclesiology, many NT passages take OT prophecies about Israel and apply them to the church (e.g., Rom 9:26; 10:13)."[67] This is precisely what Luke does in Acts with the Way metaphor, as used in Proverbs. Thus, unredeemed Jews are no longer following the Way of God. Rather, Christians are now following the Way of Jesus. Where in the OT, God's people hoped to receive immediate salvation (e.g., healing, prosperity), Jesus exceeds the immediate and temporary salvation of Proverbs by offering eternal salvation. Also, the ecclesiology of the Way in Proverbs and Acts is similar. Just as the way metaphor of the OT once characterized the lives of faithful Jews, the Way in Acts shows the characteristics of faithful Christians. Green writes, "The purpose of Luke-Acts, then, would be primarily ecclesiological concerned with the practices that define and the criteria for legitimating the community of God's people, and centered on the invitation to participate in God's project."[68] Therefore, the use of the Way in Acts supports the ecclesiology of Luke-Acts.

Step Nine: Luke's Rhetorical Use of the Way[69]

The final step seeks to show how allusion moves "the readers in a particular direction theologically or ethically."[70] In the introduction, "Luke 1:1–4 reflects Luke's rhetorical interests."[71] As stated above, this purpose statement translates into two components; (1) to "review how God worked to legitimize Jesus and how Jesus proclaimed hope," and (2) "to defend God's faithfulness to Israel and his promises, despite the rejection of the promise by many in the nation."[72] Therefore, Proverbs' use of "the way" metaphor guides readers to the theological and moral ends of the book of Acts.

---

67. Beale, *Handbook*, 52, fn.20.
68. Green, *The Gospel of Luke*, 22.
69. Full Title: "Analyze the author's rhetorical use of the OT." Beale, *Handbook*, 53.
70. Beale, *Handbook*, 52.
71. Bock, *Luke: Volume 1*, 15.
72. Bock, *Luke: Volume 1*, 15.

Summary of Nine-Fold Analysis

Beale's nine-fold analysis investigates how the Book of Acts uses the Way as an allusion to "the path" in Proverbs. Luke uses the Way metaphor to support the theology of the immediate context of passages containing ὁδός (the way) and the themes of Luke-Acts. Specifically, the book of Acts uses the Way to support the main theological themes of Acts: which are soteriology and ecclesiology. In the local context, the Way differentiates between Christians and unbelievers, and the Way shows that God has created a Way for His people, sustains His people on the Way, and that the Way leads to salvation.

CONCLUSION

This study sought to identify the literary function and theological referent of the Way in Acts. Previous scholarship reached only inconclusive results in identifying a referent for the way in Acts as it describes Christians. Despite the difficulty in identifying a source, referent, or function of the Way in Acts, scholars were accurately able to translate and understand Luke's name for Christians (See Table 4). Scholars have proposed multiple options when seeking to identify "the source and background of the term," "the exact referent of and meaning embedded in the term," and the function of the term within Acts.[73] This study builds upon the work of several scholars, both their conclusions and questions.

The study reached two primary conclusions. First, the referent of the Way is probably the Way as it is used in the book of Proverbs. Second, the function of the Way in Acts is to provide instruction for Christian living under Christ, but also to serve as a polemical tool in the contrast between believers of Jesus and unbelievers. First-century Christians were vindicated by use of the Way in Luke-Acts, for it demonstrates, particularly to unrepentant Jews, that Christians are God's true people. Thus, both Jewish and Gentile Christians had confidence in their faith in Jesus.

The use of two corroborating methods, those of Freedman and Beale, substantiate the argument that the book of Proverbs is the referent. Freedman's study shows that the book of Acts uses the motif of the Way much like the book of Proverbs. Similarly, Beale's method confirms that the Way contributes to an understanding of the relationships between God and His people.

---

73. Pao, *Acts and the Isaianic New Exodus*, 60.

Conclusion

Both Freedman and Beale's methods affirm that the Way is used to vindicate the Church. First, Freedman's analysis identifies that the Way is used in contexts where Christians are in opposition to unbelievers. This conclusion is derived from Freedman's step of identifying the significance of the context in which the motif occurs. Upon examining its uses in Acts it became apparent that Luke uses the Way in polemical contexts. Second, Beale's method of identifying allusions requires the immediate NT context be examined and the context to be compared to the OT passage. This analysis revealed that the Way and its "two-ways" theology is employed in both Proverbs and Acts to differentiate between God's people and those who are not God's people. In Proverbs the contrast is between those who follow Wisdom and those who follow Folly. In Acts, the contrast is between Christians and unrepentant Jews, magicians, and those who have false idols or false gods.

As the last point accentuated, the path in Proverbs and the Way in Acts are not an exact one-to-one correlation. For in the NT, Jesus the Messiah has come, shifting the focus or use of the path in three areas: (1) the Person of the Godhead, (2) the people groups mentioned, and (3) the salvation offered. (1) Jesus the Messiah stands in place of the Father (represented by Wisdom). Thus, Jesus creates or is the Way. Similarly, where the Father sustains His people through wisdom, the NT places living in Christ. Jesus also plays a role in sustaining God's people in the Way. (2) As previously mentioned, the people of Proverbs (e.g., the righteous, wise, fools, and wicked) are supplanted with Christ-followers and non-believers (e.g., pagans and unrepentant Jews). Although this shift may appear drastic, the people of Proverbs represent groups like Israel and the nations during the time the book was written. Therefore, God's people shift from Israel or the Jewish people to a remnant of Israel and Gentiles. (3) The salvation given by the Way shifts significantly from the OT to the NT. Where salvation in Proverbs was associated with prosperity and health, the salvation of Acts includes eternal salvation. However, within the scope of Scripture this shift is readily understood.

RECONSIDERING ISAIAH AS THE FOUNDATION FOR "THE WAY"

Having examined Luke's reference to Proverbs when discussing believers as the Way, a preliminary challenge to the leading alternate view is prudent.

David Pao and his New Exodus paradigm provided the most robust and probable understanding of the Way as a people group in Acts. This brief examination does not explore the New Exodus paradigm in its totality but only Pao's view of the Way.[74] There are three objections to Pao's argument: (1) Pao's ill-defined theme(s) of Luke-Acts, (2) the misappropriation of John the Baptist as a type, and (3) the study's lack of consideration of the role of genre in the NT use of the OT.

First, Pao does not define a theme or how it functions. Pao begins his study by analyzing the book of Acts's direct citations and allusions to Isaiah.[75] His approach correctly starts with reviewing the literature of Acts (i.e., examining the texts of Acts first). However, Pao associates the high frequency of citations and allusions as dictating the theme for Luke.[76] Further, he finds the theme of Isaiah also captures the Exodus story.[77] Pao's understanding of Acts' theme(s) has two critical faults: The themes of Isaiah and Acts conflate into one, and the literary and theological categories conflate.

As this study has done, careful consideration should first be given to understand the theme of Acts. Pao does not examine the book of Acts as a literary unit to determine the theme. Without an analysis of Acts's literary theme, it becomes unclear how Luke's citations or allusions fit into the narrative of Acts. Besides this inaccuracy, Pao conflates the theme and theology of the book of Acts. This study has found a significant overlap between a book's theme and theology, but a theme is directly tied to a work-oriented or objective approach. Subsequently, the conflation of theme and theology can lead to misunderstanding symbols or literary techniques, such as metaphor. Consequently, as Pao conflates the two categories (i.e., theme and theology) and the books, the unique authorial intent in Exodus, Isaiah, and Acts becomes whitewashed.

Second, within Pao's proposal of the Isaianic New Exodus program, he suggests the way-terminology in Acts evokes Isaiah 40:3–5 and "the wider Isaianic program."[78] This claim fits within Pao's claim that Isaiah 40:3–5,

---

74. Pao is only one proponent of the New Exodus Paradigm. See Estelle, *Echoes of Exodus*, 2018; Morales, *Exodus Old and New: A Biblical Theology of Redemption*, 2020.

75. Pao, *Acts and the Isaianic New Exodus*, 18–19.

76. Pao notes here that Luke is referencing Isaiah not simply as proof texts to state John the Baptist has fulfilled prophecy, but that Isaiah should be used throughout Luke-Acts. Pao, *Acts and the Isaianic New Exodus*, 40.

77. Pao, *Acts and the Isaianic New Exodus*, 5.

78. Pao, *Acts and the Isaianic New Exodus*, 37.

Conclusion

quoted in Luke 3:4–6, is the "hermeneutical key for the Lukan program."[79] Yet, as this study has shown, it is more probable that Proverbs is the referent. Also, implications associated with Pao's claim are difficult to accept. Both John the Baptist and his preparing the way for the Lord have two meanings (i.e., literal and topological).

Certainly, Pao's conclusion is correct that Isaiah speaks directly about John the Baptist in Luke 3 (i.e., John the Baptist is a literal fulfillment of the prophecy). However, in Acts, John the Baptist must be a type when considering Elymas and the people of the Way. In the analysis of Acts 13 above, John the Baptist as a type does not fit well within the passage's context. That comparison discussed how the actions of John the Baptist are in opposition to those of Elymas, and where the Baptist proclaims the coming Messiah, Elymas talks about the Spirit's work.[80] Further, there are difficulties understanding the people of the Way with Isaiah and John the Baptist, i.e., it is difficult to see how Christians today are preparing the way for Jesus' second return (Matt 24:36; Mark 13:32; 2 Cor 1:22; Eph 1:13–14; 4:30). Goldingay recognizes that the way in Isaiah 40:3–5 does need not be for God, but a victory procession, writing, "There are connotations of a road from Babylon to Jerusalem along which Yahweh leads the returning exiles, as also in the parallel passages ([Isa] 35:10; 49:11–12)."[81] However, this possibility does not align with the New Exodus or Pao's position. This alternative reading only bears witness to the difficulty in uniformly applying a metaphor across texts.

Pao notes that the Qumran community uses the Way as an "identity marker."[82] However, the Qumran community is in a categorically different context. The group existed before Jesus and before John the Baptist. As a result, Luke is not likely to interpret Isaiah in the same way as the Qumran community does. Pao suggests that belonging to the Way was "to study the law" and fulfill the prophecy of preparing the way to the wilderness. Because of the Qumran's understanding of the Way, Pao suggests that the Qumran need not be a source of Luke's, but Isaiah alone captures Luke's use of the Way. Yet, Pao's dismissal of the Qumran community does not

---

79. Pao, *Acts and the Isaianic New Exodus*, 38.

80. The discussion of Acts 13 also discussed that it seems the Greek terms do not align well because Luke does not use the term τρίβος for "path."

81. Goldingay continued his comments on Isaiah 40:3–5 writing, "The image is rooted in this [i.e., the victory procession] but need not be restricted to it. The central point is that Yahweh comes to take up his rule in Zion." Goldingay, *Isaiah*, 448.

82. Pao, *Acts and the Isaianic New Exodus*, 66.

address how applying Isaiah 40:3 is entirely different than the Qumran's use of the Way.

Concerning Acts, Pao discusses how John the Baptist is a type for Christians. Pao writes, "in both Acts and the Qumran literature, the way-terminology functions as an identity marker, and in the Qumran literature the term's use is also derived from Isa 40:3."[83] Where John prepares the way for the Lord, Pao suggests the people themselves are becoming prepared.[84] He goes on to write, "'The Way' functions as a symbol evoking the transformed foundation story of Israel found in Isaiah 40–55 in the construction of the identity of the community. The symbol signifies the movement's continuity with the past as well as its distinctiveness."[85] Pao continues, "In Isa 40:3, the call for the preparation of the Way of the Lord is also the call for the preparation of the people (cf. Luke 1:76–77)."[86] These quotes capture the typological use of Isaiah 40:3 to Christians. Therefore, Christians are a type of John the Baptist who still function as one who prepares for the Lord.

However, Pao does not address two difficulties within his argument. First, Pao does not adequately address how both Christians and the Qumran community can apply Isaiah similarly yet differently. Above, Pao recognizes that the Qumran community identifies itself as a John the Baptist type who is preparing the way for the Lord. Similarly, the Christian community is a John the Baptist type that is preparing the way of the Lord. It appears plausible that a Christian may be considered one who also studies the Law, like the Qumran community's understanding of the Way. Additionally, it seems impossible for both the Qumran community and Luke to be correct in understanding Isaiah's prophecy after the coming of John the Baptist and Jesus. Second, Pao's suggestion that Isaiah supports the Way in Acts, John the Baptist is fulfilling the prophecy of Isaiah 40:3 in Luke 3, but in Acts, the people of the Way are now only preparing themselves. Even if Luke only uses Isaiah 40:3 as a hermeneutical lens (i.e., Luke is not stating the people of the Way are functioning as a fulfillment of Isaiah's prophecy), there is a shift in understanding the metaphor associated with the Way that makes the typology unclear.

Third, Pao does not thoroughly examine the role genre may play within Luke's use of the Old Testament. This is somewhat surprising

---

83. Pao, *Acts and the Isaianic New Exodus*, 66.
84. Pao, *Acts and the Isaianic New Exodus*, 68, fn.113.
85. Pao, *Acts and the Isaianic New Exodus*, 68.
86. Pao, *Acts and the Isaianic New Exodus*, 68, fn.113.

Conclusion

because Pao sought to highlight the "limitations of the narrow scheme of 'prediction-fulfillment.'"[87] For Pao, the statement "limited narrow scheme" refers to viewing the NT as completing prophesy without influencing the "organization and construction" of Luke-Acts.[88] This study argues that the "limited narrow scheme" of prediction-fulfillment blinds the interpreters's eyes to other oral or written sources that plausibly influence the organization and construction of Luke-Acts.

Pao's work in *Acts and the Isaianic New Exodus* contains a superb examination of Luke-Acts. However, this section identifies three critiques: (1) The study did not consider the role of genre in Luke's choice of OT referent; (2) the study did not examine the repercussions to a typological John the Baptist and his role; and (3) the study did not carefully handle the use of theme(s). This section naturally segues into areas of future research.

AREAS OF FUTURE RESEARCH

The current emphasis on the Way metaphor has shown that many uses of ὁδός in Acts likely allude to Proverbs and are used as a motif to support the themes of Acts. The examination of three areas will solidify the conclusions. First, previous proposals of Isaiah as a referent should be re-examined. Specifically, Luke's use of the Way with Isaiah as a universal referent for all of Luke-Acts should be reconsidered, with Proverbs functioning as an alternative referent, and the Way seen as a motif in Acts. This leads into the second area of prospective research. This study has understood the connection between Acts and Proverbs is founded on the Way as a literary motif and an allusion to Proverbs, a wisdom text. Thus, the genre of the OT text may have influenced Luke's selection of referent texts. For example, when Luke references John the Baptist fulfilling prophecy, Isaiah 40:3 is fitting as a prophetic text, while Proverbs may have been selected for portraying an ethical way of life, because the text has to do with morals and right living. Andrew Judd has recently asked a similar question in his article, "Do the Speakers in Acts Use Different Hermeneutics for Different Old Testament Genres?"[89] His conclusion, in part, is that "modern genre theory is really quite ancient: for the first-century Christian readers of the OT, the genre

---

87. Pao, *Acts and the Isaianic New Exodus*, 37.
88. Pao, *Acts and the Isaianic New Exodus*, 37, fn.1.
89. Judd, "Do the Speakers in Acts Use Different Hermeneutics for Different Old Testament Genres?"

of the source text determines the hermeneutical strategy they employ."[90] Perhaps, Luke is applying different genres of texts, the Prophets and the Writings, in accordance with the context he is writing about. Thus, future research could examine if Luke is considering the genre of the referent text when discussing the prophetic fulfillment of John the Baptist making "a way" for the Lord, and when describing the Church as the Way. Further research in these areas, and a re-examination of the role of genre in Luke-Acts, would bring further clarity in understanding Luke-Acts.

---

90. Judd, "Do the Speakers in Acts Use Different Hermeneutics for Different Old Testament Genres?," 127.

Appendix

Table 1: Scholarly Understanding of "the Way" in Acts
1800s

Scholar	Date	Work	Usage
Abiel Abbot Livermore	1853	*The Acts of the Apostles: With a Commentary*	**Metaphor**: Christians[1]
Rev. Bradford K. Peirce	1854	*Notes on the Acts of the Apostles*	**Metaphor**: A way of thinking, or a sect, namely Christians.[2]
William Gilson Humphry	1854	*A Commentary on the book of the Acts of the Apostles*	**Metaphor**: The Christian life.[3]
Joseph Addison Alexander	1857	*The Acts of the Apostles*	**Metaphor**: New Way of Life and Salvation[4]
Paton J. Gloag	1870	*A Critical and Exegetical Commentary on the Acts of the Apostles*	**Metaphor**: A way of life or a Jewish sect who believes Jesus is messiah.[5]
Rev. W. Denton	1874	*A Commentary on the Acts of the Apostles*	**Metaphor**: Used similarly to Hebrew usage, "The way of the Lord," and as a way of living in Christ.[6]

1. Livermore, *The Acts of the Apostles*.
2. Peirce, *Notes on the Acts of the Apostles*.
3. Humphry, *A Commentary on the Book of the Acts of the Apostles*.
4. Alexander, *The Acts of the Apostles Explained*.
5. Gloag, *A Critical and Exegetical Commentary on the Acts of the Apostles*.
6. Denton, *A Commentary on the Acts of the Apostles*.

Appendix

Lyman Abbot	1876	*The Acts of the Apostles with Notes, Comments, Maps, and Introduction*	**Metaphor**: The way of salvation in Jesus.[7]
	1879	*Short Notes on the Greek Text of the Acts of the Apostles*	**Metaphor**: The way that leads to salvation.[8]
Horatio B. Hackett	1882	*A Commentary on the Acts of the Apostles*	**Metaphor**: Christians, regarding faith and living.[9]
Thomas M. Lindsay	1884	*The Acts of the Apostles with Introduction, Notes, and Maps*	**Metaphor**: Christian discipleship.[10]

7. Abbott, *The Acts of the Apostles with Notes, Comments, Maps, and Illustrations*.
8. Smith, *Short Notes on the Greek Text of the Acts of the Apostles*.
9. Hackett, *A Commentary on the Acts of the Apostles*.
10. Lindsay, *The Acts of the Apostles with Introduction, Notes, and Maps*.

Appendix

Table 2: Scholarly Understanding of "the Way" in Acts 1900–1949 AD

Scholar	Date	Work	Usage
Richard Francis Weymouth	1903	The New Testament in Modern Speech: An Idiomatic Translation into Everyday English from the Text of "The Resultant Greek Testament": Commentary	**Metaphor**: Christians[11]
Rev H.T. Andrews	1908	The Acts of the Apostles	**Metaphor**: Christians[12]
George Holley Gilbert	1908	Acts: The Second Volume of Luke's Work on the Beginnings of Christianity with Interpretative Comment	**Metaphor**: Christians, (Evidence: Psalms)[13]
William Owen Carver	1916	The Acts of the Apostles	**Metaphor**: Disciples[14]
Charles Cutler Torrey	1916		**Semitic Locution**: Gentile Christians (Evidenced from Talmud and Arabic)[15]
F.J. Foakes Jackson and Kirsopp Lake	1931	The Acts of the Apostles	**Metaphor**: Name for Christians and associated with the Way of God.[16]
Henry J. Cadbury	1933	The Beginnings of Christianity, Part I: The Acts of the Apostles: Additional Notes to the Commentary	**Metaphor**: Christian, Way of the Lord or God, Not Aramaic, Likely from OT. Similar in use with Tao, and Methodist[17]

11. Weymouth, *The New Testament in Modern Speech*.
12. Andrews, *The Acts of the Apostles*.
13. Gilbert, *Acts*.
14. Carver, *The Acts of the Apostles*.
15. Torrey, *The Composition and Date of Acts*.
16. *The Beginnings of Christianity, Part I: The Acts of the Apostles*.
17. Cadbury, "Names for Christians and Christianity in Acts."

Appendix

Table 3: Survey of Scholarship in Acts concerning designation of "the Way" 1950–1999 AD

Scholar	Date	Work	Usage
Gustaf Wingren	1951	"'Weg', 'Wanderung', und verwandte Begriffe"	**Metaphor:** Christian living or Christian ethic. OT & NT: The Path, Traveling, and related terms.[18]
Vernon McCasland	1958	"The Way"	**OT Referent:** Isaiah[19]
Paul S. Minear	1960	*Images of the Church in the New Testament*	**Metaphor:** Disciple of Jesus **Function:** Differentiate between true believers (Jesus' followers) and the Jewish Community[20]
Eero Repo	1964	Der' Weg' als Selbstbezeichnung des Urchristentums: Eine traditionsgeschichtliche und semasiologische Untersuchung	**OT Referent:** Isaiah[21]
F.F. Bruce	1970[22]	*The Book of the Acts*	**Metaphor:** Christian life similar to use in Rabbinical Hebrew, Syriac, Arabic, Indian, and Chinese usages.[23]
Christoph Burchard[24]	1970	Der dreizehnte Zeuge	**Metaphor:** Christianity; Qumran is not source of use.[25]

18. Wingren, "'Weg', 'Wanderung', Und Verwandte Begriffe."
19. McCasland, "The Way."
20. Minear, *Images of the Church in the New Testament*, 148–49.
21. Repo, Der "Weg."
22. First printing 1954.
23. Bruce, *The Book of Acts*.
24. Lüdeman *Early Christianity According to the Traditions in Acts*, 216. Lüdeman cites Burchard's work as a possibility.
25. Burchard, 43, fn. 10. Burchard, "Der Dreizehnte Zeuge."

Appendix

Ernst Haenchen	1971	*The Acts of the Apostles: A Commentary*	**Metaphor:** Christian Community; Dismisses equivalence with "way of life" and narrowly defining as 'teaching'; Repo's Proposal of Isaiah.[26]
I. Howard Marshall	1980	*Acts: An Introduction and Commentary*	**Metaphor:** Christian. Interesting connection to Qumran.[27]
Francois Bovon	1987	*Luke the Theologian: Thirty-Three Years of Research (1950–1983)*	**Metaphor:** Christian. Ecclesiological not Christological[28]
L.T. Johnson	1992	*The Acts of the Apostles*	**Metaphor:** Christians. A *way* of life derived from the OT and used in the NT (LXX Ps 1:1, 6; 2:2; 118:29; Rom 3:17; 1 Cor 12:31; Jude 11).[29]
Ben Witherington III	1998	*Acts of the Apostle*	**Metaphor:** Christians. Notes similarity to Qumran.[30]

26. Haenchen, *The Acts of the Apostles: A Commentary*.
27. Marshall, *Acts*, 178.
28. Bovon, *Luke the Theologian*.
29. Johnson, *The Acts of the Apostles*.
30. Witherington III, *The Acts of the Apostles*, 316.

Appendix

Table 4: Survey of Scholarship in Acts concerning designation of "the Way" 2000 AD–Present

Scholar	Date	Work	Usage
David W. Pao	2002[31]	*Acts and the Isaianic New Exodus*	**OT Referent:** Isaiah 40. **Function:** Serves polemically, casting "the church as the true heir of the ancient traditions of Israel."[32]
C.K. Barrett	2004	*A Critical and Exegetical Commentary on the Acts of the Apostles*	**Metaphor:** Parallel Qumran: (1QS 9:17, 18) (1QS 10:21) (CD 1:13), (CD 2:6) 1QS 11:13 See Fitzmyer[33]
William Larkin	2006	*Acts*	**Metaphor:** Christians. Way of salvation and life. Related to "Jesus who said, 'I am the Way.'"[34]
Darrel L. Bock	2007	*Acts*	**Metaphor:** Christians. Way of salvation and life.
Joseph A. Fitzmyer	2008	*The Acts of the Apostles: A New Translation with Introduction and Commentary*	**Metaphor:** Christians.[35]
Richard I. Pervo	2008	*Acts: A Commentary on the Book of Acts*	**Metaphor:** Christians. Self-designation similar to Qumran (Isa 40:3).[36]
David G. Peterson	2009	*The Acts of the Apostles*	**Metaphor:** Christians. May be ellipsis for 'the way of the Lord' and 'the way of salvation.'[37]
Craig S. Keener	2013	*Acts: An Exegetical Commentary: 3:1—14:28*	**Metaphor:** Christian. Likely Semitic context. Origin of "absolute use" became known with DSS.[38]

31. Original dissertation in 1998. Pao, *Acts and the Isaianic New Exodus* (2002).
32. Pao, *Acts and the Isaianic New Exodus*, 60–61 (61).
33. Barrett, *A Critical and Exegetical Commentary on the Acts of the Apostles*.
34. Larkin, "Acts," 459.
35. Fitzmyer, *The Acts of the Apostles*, 423–24.
36. Pervo, *Acts*.
37. Peterson, *The Acts of the Apostles*, 302.
38. Keener, *Acts: 3:1—14:28*. Keener maintains his position in his abridged commentary on Acts. Keener, *Acts, The New Cambridge Bible Commentary*, 276.

Appendix

James D. Dunn	2016	*The Acts of the Apostles*		**Metaphor**: Derived from tradition, see Qumran. (1QS 9.17–18; 10.21; CD 1.13; 2.6).[39]
Grant R. Osborne	2019	*Acts: Verse by Verse*		**Metaphor**: Christians. Christians are proclaiming *the way* for the Messiah as in Isa 40:3.[40]

---

39. Dunn, *The Acts of the Apostles*.
40. Osborne, *Acts*, 174.

Appendix

Table 5: Designations for Christians, Religious and People Groups

Word	Translation(s)	People Represented	Frequency in Luke-Acts
ὁδός	The Way	Christians	6x: Acts 5:17; 15:5; 24:5, 14; 26:5; 28:22
αἵρεσις	Sect/Faction/Party	Sadducees, Pharisees, Nazarenes, Christians (Group Paul Represents)	22x: Acts 5:11; 7:38; 8:1, 3; 9:31; 11:22,26; 12:1, 5; 13:1; 14:23, 27; 15:3, 4, 22; 16:5; 18:22; 19:32, 39, 40; 20:17, 28
ἐκκλησία	Church/Assembly	Congregation (Jewish), Church (Christian)	Luke 8:21; Acts 1:16; 6:3
οἱ ἀδελφοί	The brothers	Christians	Luke 8:21; Acts 1:16; 6:3
οἱ πιστεύοντες	The believers	Christians	Acts 2:44; 4:32; 5:14
τὸ πλῆθος	The Congregation/Multitude	Believers, Both Jews and Gentiles (Coming to faith), Pharisees and Sadducees	21x: Acts 2:6; 14:1, 4; 19:9; 21; 25:24
οἱ μαθηταί	The disciples	Jesus's followers	Acts 6:1, 2, 7; 9:1, 25, 26; 11:26; 15:10
οἱ ἅγιοι	The saints	Christians	Acts 9:13, 32, 41; 26:10
οἱ Ναζωραῖοι	The Nazarenes	Christians	Acts 24:5
ὄχλος	crowds	Non-specific: Christians, Gentiles (non-Christians), Sadducees, Pharisees	83x

Appendix

Table 6: Greek Vocab for Wisdom/Knowledge Words derived from Proverbs

BHS	Gloss	Proverbs	Rahlf's LXX
בִּינָה/ מְזִמָּה	Understanding	1:2; 2:3; 3:5; 4:1, 5, 7; 9:6, 10; 16:16	φρόνησις
בִּינָה/ חָכְמָה/ דַעַת	Understanding	1:2; 2:3; 3:5; 4:1, 5, 7; 9:6, 10; 16:16	Σοφία νοέω
דֶּרֶךְ	Way, Path	1:15, 31; 2:8, 12, 13, 20; 3:6, 17, 23, 31; 4:11, 14, 19, 26; 9:6, 15; 14:2, 8, 12, 14; 15:9, 19; 16:2, 7, 9, 17, 25, 29, 31	Τρίβος πυθμήν
עָרְמָה	Cleverness	1:4	πανουργία
מְזִמָּה	Plan, Scheme, Prudence	1:4; 3:21; 14:17	ἔννοια
תּוּשִׁיָּה/ עֹשֶׂה	Insight	3:27; 6:23; 13:16; 14:17	Βουλή Πράσσω ποιέω
דַעַת	Knowledge	1:4, 7, 22, 29; 3:20; 9:10; 13:16; 14:6, 7, 18; 15:2, 7, 14	αἴσθησις

Appendix

Table 7: Greek Vocab for Satellite Images from Proverbs

BHS	Gloss	Proverbs	Rahlf's LXX
יָשָׁר	Straight/Smooth	e.g., 3:6, 32; 4:11, 25; 9:15; 14:2, 9, 11, 12; 15:8, 19, 21; 16:13, 17, 25	ὀρθός/ὀρθοτομέω νεύω κατευθύνω εὐθύς δίκαιος ἀνδρεῖος
סֶלֶף / עָוֺת	Bend/Twist	e.g., 3:32, 15:4	
הלך	Walk	e.g., 1:11, 15; 3:23, 28; 4:12, 18; 9:5; 14:2, 7; 15:12, 21; 16:29	ἔρχομαι Πορεύομαι/προπορεύομαι ἐπανέρχομαι
רֶשַׁע	Wicked	e.g., 3:25, 33; 4:14, 17, 19; 9:7; 14:11, 19, 32; 15:6, 8, 9, 28, 29; 16:4, 12	ἀσεβής κακός
צַדִּיק	Righteous	e.g., 3:33; 4:18; 9:9; 14:19, 32; 15:6, 28, 29	Δίκαιος/δικαιοσύνη
צְדָקָה	Loyalty, Justice	e.g., 14:34; 15:9, 16:8, 12, 31	Διώκω/δικαιοσύνη
	Unrighteous	e.g., 15:29	ἀδικία
יָרֵא		e.g., 14:2	φοβέω
כְּסִיל	Fool	e.g., 3:35; 14:7, 8, 16, 24; 15:7	ἄφρων
חשׁך	Darkness	e.g., 2:3; 4:19	σκότος
אור	Light	e.g., 4:18; 16:15	φῶς/ φωτίζω
יָשָׁר	Straight/Smooth	e.g., 3:6, 32; 4:11, 25; 9:15; 14:2, 9, 11, 12; 15:8, 19, 21; 16:13, 17, 25	ὀρθός/ὀρθοτομέω νεύω κατευθύνω εὐθύς, δίκαιος ἀνδρεῖος
סֶלֶף / עָוֺת	Bend/Twist	e.g., 3:32, 15:4	
הלך	Walk	e.g., 1:11, 15; 3:23, 28; 4:12, 18; 9:5; 14:2, 7; 15:12, 21; 16:29	ἔρχομαι Πορεύομαι/προπορεύομαι ἐπανέρχομαι
רֶשַׁע	Wicked	e.g., 3:25, 33; 4:14, 17, 19; 9:7; 14:11, 19, 32; 15:6, 8, 9, 28, 29; 16:4, 12	ἀσεβής κακός

Appendix

צַדִּיק	Righteous	e.g., 3:33; 4:18; 9:9; 14:19, 32; 15:6, 28, 29	Δίκαιος/δικαιοσύνη
צְדָקָה	Loyalty, Justice	e.g., 14:34; 15:9, 16:8, 12, 31	Διώκω/δικαιοσύνη
	Unrighteous	e.g., 15:29	ἀδικία

Appendix

Table 8: Hellenistic Source Summary of "the Way" Usage

Author/Motif	Date	Work	Usage
Euripides	5th Century	Hecuba	ὁδός describes the thoughts or feelings of another.[41]
Euripides	5th Century	Hippolytus	ὁδός describes the path one's thoughts take.[42]
Sophocles	5th Century	Oedipus Tyrannus and Oedipus at Colonus.[43]	ὁδός is a metaphor to describe how one accomplishes a task, e.g., divining.
Aristophanes	5th Century	Knights	Uses ὁδός as a metaphor for meaning, i.e., "the way" of words.[44]
Motif of the Honored, Journeying Hero[45]	~8th Century BC – 3rd Century BC	(e.g., Homer and Pindar,[46] and Paremindes[47])	ὁδός used for divine knowledge.

Event	Date		Usage
"Solemn Procession" (Eleusinian Celebrations)[48]	~2nd Century BC[49] – 1st Century AD[50]		Uses ὁδός for sacred traveling.[51]

41. E.Hec.744. 424 BC.
42. Id.Hipp.290. 428 BC.
43. Soph. OT 311; Soph. OC 1314. 441 BC 401 BC.
44. Aristoph. Kn. 1015. 424 BC.
45. Baban, *On the Road Encounters*, 52.
46. Baban, *On the Road Encounters*, 52–54. Homer, *Odyssey*, 13.112. Pindar, *Pythian Ode*, 3.103.
47. Jaeger, *The Theology of the Early Greek Philosophers*, 91–108, 134–35. Cornford, "Parmenides' Two Ways," 97–111.
48. Baban, *On the Road Encounters*, 50–51.
49. James, "The Religions of Antiquity," 145–46.
50. James, "The Religions of Antiquity," 146.
51. Baban, *On the Road Encounters*, 51.

Bibliography

Abrams, M. H. *The Mirror and the Lamp: Romantic Theory and the Critical Tradition.* The Norton Library. New York: Norton, 1958.
Aland, Barbra et al. eds. *The Greek New Testament.* 5th Rev. ed. Stuttgart, DE: Deutsche Bibelgesellschaft, 2014.
———. *Novum Testamentum Graece.* 28th Rev. ed. Stuttgart: Deutsche Bibelgesellschaft, 2012.
———. *Novum Testamentum Graece (Greek New Testament) Apparatus (NA28 Apparatus).* 5th Corrected ed., Accordance ed.Stuttgart, DE: Deutsche Bibelgesellschaft, Stuttgart, 2016.
Alexander, Loveday. *The Preface to Luke's Gospel: Literary Convention and Social Context in Luke 1.1-4 and Acts 1.1.* Vol. 78, Society for New Testament Studies Monograph Series. Cambridge: Cambridge University Press, 1993.
Alouf-Aboody, Hilla N. *Through the Prism of Wisdom: Elijah the Prophet as a Bearer of Wisdom in Rabbinic Literature.* Vol. 23, Judaism in Context, edited by Rivka Ulmer et al. Piscataway, NJ: Gorgias Press, 2020.
Alter, Robert. *The Art of Biblical Narrative.* Rev. ed. New York: Basic Books, 2011.
Andersen, Francis I. *Job: An Introduction and Commentary.* Vol. 14, Tyndale Old Testament Commentaries. Downers Grove, IL: InterVarsity, 1976.
Andrews, H. T. *The Acts of the Apostles.* London: Andrew Melrose, 1908.
Athas, George. *Bridging the Testaments: The History and Theology of God's People in the Second Temple Period.* Grand Rapids, MI: Zondervan Academic, 2023.
———. *Ecclesiastes, Song of Songs.* Story of God Bible Commentary. Grand Rapids, MI: Zondervan, 2020.
Baban, Octavian D. *On the Road Encounters in Luke-Acts: Hellenistic Mimesis and Luke's Theology of the Way,* edited by Paternoster Biblical Monographs. Waynesboro, VA: Paternoster, 2006.
Bakker, Arjen. "Wisdom in the Dead Sea Scrolls and Early Jewish Interpretation." In *The Oxford Handbook of Wisdom and the Bible,* edited by Will Kynes, 141–54. New York: Oxford University Press, 2021.
Balentine, Samuel E. "Proverbs." In *The Oxford Handbook of Wisdom and the Bible,* edited by Will Kynes, 495–514. Oxford, UK: Oxford, 2021.
Barrett, C. K. *A Critical and Exegetical Commentary on the Acts of the Apostles.* International Critical Commentary. Edinburgh, UK: T&T Clark, 2004.
———. "Luke/Acts." In *It Is Written: Scripture Citing Scripture,* edited by D. A. Carson and H.G.M. Williamson, 231–44. Cambridge, UK: Cambridge University Press, 1988.

Bibliography

Bartholomew, Craig G., and Ryan P. O'Dowd. *Old Testament Wisdom Literature: A Theological Introduction*. Downers Grove, IL: IVP Academic, 2011.
Bauckham, Richard. *James*. New Testament Readings. London, UK: Routledge, 1999.
Beale, G. K. *Handbook on the New Testament Use of the Old Testament: Exegesis and Interpretation*. Grand Rapids, MI: Baker Academic, 2012.
Beetham, Christopher A. *Echoes of Scripture in the Letter of Paul to the Colossians*. Vol. 96, Biblical Interpretation Series. Leiden, UK: Brill, 2008.
———. "Quotation, Allusion, and Echo." In *Dictionary of the New Testament Use of the Old Testament*, edited by G. K. Beale et al., 684–92. Grand Rapids, MI: Baker Academic, 2023.
Berry, George R. *The Book of Proverbs*. Philadelphia, PA: American Baptist Publication Society, 1904.
Bird, M.F. et al. eds. *Rethinking the Unity and Reception of Luke and Acts*. Columbia: University of South Carolina Press, 2010.
Bihler, Johannes. *Die Stephanusgeschichte im Zusammenhang der Apostelgeschichte*. Munich, DE: Max Hueber, 1963.
Black, Max. "Metaphor." *Proceedings of the Aristotelian Society* 55 (1954) 273–94.
———. "More About Metaphor." *Dialectica* 31, no. 3/4 (1977) 431–57.
Bock, Darrell L. *Acts*. Baker Exegetical Commentary on the New Testament. Grand Rapids, MI: Baker Academic, 2007.
———. *Luke: Volume 2: 9:51—24:53*. Vol. 3B, Baker Exegetical Commentary on the New Testament, edited by Moisés Silva. Grand Rapids, MI: Baker Academic, 1996.
Bovon, François. *Luke the Theologian: Thirty-Three Years of Research (1950–1983)*. Translated by Ken McKinney. Allison Park, PA: Pickwick Publications, 1987.
———. *Luke the Theologian Fifty-Five Years of Research (1950–2005)*. 2nd rev. ed. Waco, TX: Baylor University Press, 2006.
Bovon, François, and Helmut Koester. *Luke 1: A Commentary on the Gospel of Luke 1:1–9:50*. Minneapolis, MN: Fortress, 2002.
Boyarin, Daniel. *Dying for God: Martyrdom and the Making of Christianity and Judaism*. Stanford, CA: Stanford University Press, 1999.
Brettler, Marc Z. "Identifying Torah Sources in the Historical Psalms." In *Subtle Citation, Allusion, and Translation in the Hebrew Bible*, edited by Ziony Zevit, 73–90. Sheffield, UK: Equinox, 2017.
Bricker, Daniel P. "The Doctrine of the 'Two Ways' in Proverbs." *Journal of the Evangelical Theological Society* 38, no. 4 (1995) 501–17.
Bruce, F. F. *The Book of Acts*. The New International Commentary on the New Testament, edited by F. F. Bruce. Grand Rapids: Eerdmans, 1970.
———. *The Book of the Acts*. Rev. ed. Grand Rapids, MI: Eerdmans, 1988.
Burchard, Christoph. "Der Dreizehnte Zeuge. Traditions- U. Kompositionsgeschichtl. Untersuchungen Zu Lukas' Darstellung D. Frühzeit D. Paulus." Habilitationsschrift, Göttingen, 1970.
Buth, Randall. "Language, Linguistics." *Dictionary for Theological Interpretation of the Bible*, 431–35. Grand Rapids, MI: Baker Academic, 2005.
Cadbury, Henry J. "Names for Christians and Christianity in Acts." In *The Beginnings of Christianity, Part I: The Acts of the Apostles: Additional Notes to the Commentary*. Vol. V, edited by Kirsopp Lake et al., 375–92. London: Macmillan and Co., Limited, 1933.
Calvin, John, and H. Beveridge. *Commentary Upon the Acts of the Apostles*. Vol. 1. Bellingham, WA: Logos Bible Software, 2010.

Bibliography

Calvin, John, and John King. *Calvin's Commentaries (Complete)*. Accordance electronic ed. Edinburgh, UK: Calvin Translation Society, 1847.

Cancik, Hubert. "The History of Culture, Religion, and Institutions in Ancient Historiography: Philological Observations Concerning Luke's History." *Journal of Biblical Literature* 116, no. 4 (Wint 1997) 673–95.

Carr, David McLain. "Method in Determination of Direction of Dependence: An Empirical Test of Criteria Applied to Exodus 34,11–26 and Its Parallels." In *In Gottes Volk Am Sinai: Untersuchungen Zu Ex 32-34 Und Dtn 9-10*, edited by Matthias Kockert and Erhard Blum. Giitersloh, DE: Kaiser, Gutersloher Verlagshous, 2001.

Carver, William Owen. *The Acts of the Apostles*. Nashville, TN: Sunday School Board of the Southern Baptist Convention, 1916.

Clements, Ronald E. *Commentary on the Bible: Proverbs*. Grand Rapids, MI: Eerdmans, 2019.

Clifford, Richard J. *Proverbs: A Commentary*. Louisville, KY: Westminster John Knox, 1999.

Clines, David J. A. *Job 21–37*. Vol. 18A, Word Biblical Commentary. Nashville, TN: Thomas Nelson, 2006.

Collins, John J. *Jewish Wisdom in the Hellenistic Age*. The Old Testament Library. Louisville, KY: Westminster John Knox, 1997.

Conzelmann, Hans. *Acts of the Apostles: A Commentary on the Acts of the Apostles*, edited by Eldon Jay Epp and Christopher R. Matthews. Philadelphia, PA: Fortress, 1987.

———. *The Theology of St. Luke*. Translated by Geoffrey Buswell. New York: Harper & Row, 1961.

Cornford, F. M. "Parmenides' Two Ways." *The Classical Quarterly* 27, no. 2 (1933) 97–111.

Craigie, Peter C. *Psalms 1–50*. Vol. 19, Word Biblical Commentary. Nashville, TN: Thomas Nelson, 2004.

Crawford, Sidnie White. "Lady Wisdom and Dame Folly at Qumran." *Dead Sea Discoveries* 5, no. 3 (1998) 355–66.

Crenshaw, James L. "Method in Determining Wisdom Influence Upon 'Historical' Literature." *Journal of Biblical Literature* 88, no. 2 (1969) 129–42.

———. *Old Testament Wisdom: An Introduction*. 3rd ed. Louisville, KY: Westminster John Knox, 2010.

Culy, Martin M., and Mikeal C. Parsons. *Acts: A Handbook on the Greek Text*. Waco, TX: Baylor University Press, 2003.

Daemmrich, Horst S. *Themes & Motifs in Western Literature: A Handbook*, edited by Ingrid Daemmrich. Tübingen, DE: Francke, 1987.

David, Ravens. *Luke and the Restoration of Israel*. Journal for the Study of the New Testament. Supplement Series. Sheffield, UK: Sheffield Academic, 1995.

Davids, Peter H. *The Epistle of James: A Commentary on the Greek Text*. Accordance electronic ed. New International Greek Testament Commentary. Grand Rapids, MI: Eerdmans, 1982.

Dell, Katharine J. *The Lord by Wisdom Founded the Earth: Creation and Covenant in Old Testament Theology*. Waco, TX: Baylor University Press, 2023.

Denaux, Adelbert., Rita Corsjens. *The Vocabulary of Luke: An Alphabetical Presentation and a Survey of Characteristic and Noteworthy Words and Word Groups in Luke's Gospel*. Vol. 10, Biblical Tools and Studies, edited by Hellen Mardaga. Leuven, Belgium: Peeters, 2009.

Denton, W. *A Commentary on the Acts of the Apostles*. Vol. 1. London, UK: George Bell and Sons, 1874.

Bibliography

Di Lella, Alexander A., and Patrick W. Skehan. *The Wisdom of Ben Sira: A New Translation, with Notes*. Vol. 39, The Anchor Bible. Garden City, NY: Doubleday & Company Inc., 1987.

Dibelius, Martin, and Heinrich Greeven. *James: A Commentary on the Epistle of James*. Philadelphia, PA: Fortress, 1976.

Dinkler, Michal Beth. *Literary Theory and the New Testament*. The Anchor Yale Bible Reference Library. New Haven: Yale University Press, 2019.

Dunn, James, D. G. *The Acts of the Apostles*. Grand Rapids, MI: Eerdmans, 2016.

Du Plessis, I. J. "Reading Luke 12:35–48 as Part of the Travel Narrative." *Neotestamentica* 22, no. 2 (1988) 217–34.

Eaton, Michael A. *Ecclesiastes: An Introduction and Commentary*. Vol. 18, Tyndale Old Testament Commentaries. Downers Grove, IL: InterVarsity, 1983.

Edwards, James R. *The Gospel According to Luke*. Accordance electronic ed. Pillar New Testament Commentary. Grand Rapids, MI: Eerdmans, 2015.

Errington, Andrew. *Every Good Path: Wisdom and Practical Reason in Christian Ethics and the Book of Proverbs*. T&T Clark Enquiries in Theological Ethics, edited by Brian Brock and Susan F. Parsons. London, UK: T&T Clark, 2020.

Eubanks, Philip. *Metaphor and Writing: Figurative Thought in the Discourse of Written Communication*. Cambridge, UK: Cambridge University Press, 2011.

Evans, Craig A. "The Synoptic Gospels and the Dead Sea Scrolls." In *The Bible and the Dead Sea Scrolls, Volume Three: The Scrolls and Christian Origins: The Second Princeton Symposium on Judaism and Christian Origins*, edited by James H. Charlesworth, 75–96. Waco, TX: Baylor University Press, 2006.

Evans, Nancy A. "Sanctuaries, Sacrifices, and the Eleusinian Mysteries." *Numen* 49, no. 3 (2002): 227–54.

Fauconnier, Gilles, and Mark Turner. *The Way We Think: Conceptual Blending and the Mind's Hidden Complexities*. New York: NY: Basic Books, 2002.

Fishbane, Michael A. *Biblical Interpretation in Ancient Israel*. Oxford, UK: Oxford University Press, 1985.

Fitzmyer, Joseph A. *The Acts of the Apostles: A New Translation with Introduction and Commentary*. Vol. 31. New Haven, CT: Yale University Press, 2008.

———. "New Testament *Kyrios* and *Maranatha* and Their Aramaic Background." In *To Advance the Gospel*, 218–235. Grand Rapids, MI: Eerdmans, 1998.

———. "The Semitic Background of the New Testament Kyrios Title." In *A Wandering Aramean*. Sblms. Vol. 25, 115–42. Chico, CA: Scholars, 1979.

———. "The Use of the Old Testament in Luke-Acts." *Society of Biblical Literature Seminar Papers* 31 (1992) 524–38.

Fox, Michael V. "Ideas of Wisdom in Proverbs 1–9." *Journal of Biblical Literature* 116, no. 4 (1997) 613–33.

———. *Proverbs 1–9: A New Translation with Introduction and Commentary*. Vol. 18A, The Anchor Yale Bible. New York: Doubleday, 2000.

———. *Proverbs 10–31: A New Translation with Introduction and Commentary*. Vol. 18B, The Anchor Yale Bible, edited by John J. Collins. New Haven, CT: Yale University Press, 2009.

———. "Words for Wisdom: 'Tevunah' and 'Binah'; 'Ormah' and 'Mezimah'; 'Ezah' and 'Tushiyah.'" *Zeitschrift für Althebraistik* 6, no. 2 (1993) 149–69.

Fox, Nickolas A. *The Hermeneutics of Social Identity in Luke-Acts*. Eugene, OR: Pickwick, 2021.

Bibliography

Frank, Robert W. *Poetics of Biblical Narrative*. Sonoma, CA: Polebridge Press, 1998.

Freedman, William. "The Literary Motif: A Definition and Evaluation." *Novel: A Forum on Fiction* 4, no. 2 (1971) 123–31.

Frey, Jörg. "The Impact of the Dead Sea Scrolls on New Testament Interpretation: Proposals, Problems, and Further Perspectives." In *The Bible and the Dead Sea Scrolls, Volume Three: The Scrolls and Christian Origins: The Second Princeton Symposium on Judaism and Christian Origins*, edited by James H. Charlesworth, 153–85. Waco, TX: Baylor University Press, 2006.

Fullmer, Paul. *Resurrection in Mark's Literary-Historical Perspective*. Vol. 360, Library of New Testament Studies. New York: T&T Clark, 2007.

Gaventa, Beverly Roberts. *The Acts of the Apostles*. Abingdon New Testament Commentaries. Nashville: Abingdon, 2003.

Gilbert, George Holley. *Acts: The Second Volume of Luke's Work on the Beginnings of Christianity with Interpretative Comment*. New York: The Macmillan Company, 1908.

Giszczak, Mark. *Wisdom of Solomon*. Catholic Commentary on Sacred Scripture, edited by Mark Giszczak et al. Grand Rapids, MI: Baker Academic, 2024.

Goldingay, John. *Biblical Theology: The God of the Christian Scriptures*. Downers Grove, IL: IVP Academic, 2016.

———. *Isaiah*. Baker Commentary on the Old Testament Prophetic Books, edited by Mark J. Boda and J. Gordon McConville. Grand Rapids, MI: Baker Academic, 2023.

———. "The Arrangement of Sayings in Proverbs 10–15." *Journal for the Study of the Old Testament* 19, no. 61 (1994) 75–83.

———. *Proverbs*. Commentaries for Christian Formation, edited by Stephen E. Fowl et al. Grand Rapids, MI: Eerdmans, 2023.

———. *Psalms 1–41*. Vol. 1, Baker Commentary on the Old Testament Wisdom and Psalms. Grand Rapids, MI: Baker Academic, 2006.

Green, Joel B. *The Gospel of Luke*. New International Commentary on the New Testament, edited by Gordon D. Fee. Grand Rapids, MI: Eerdmans, 1997.

———. "'Salvation to the End of the Earth': God as Savior in the Acts of the Apostles." In *Luke as Narrative Theologian*. Wissenschaftliche Untersuchungen Zum Neuen Testament. Vol. 446, 261–82. Tübingen, DE: Mohr Siebeck, 2020.

Greenstein, Edward L. "Method in the Study of Textual Source Dependence: The Covenant Code." In *Subtle Citation, Allusion, and Translation in the Hebrew Bible*, edited by Ziony Zevit, 143–58. Sheffield, UK: Equinox, 2017.

Greenstone, Julius H. *The Holy Scriptures: Proverbs with Commentary*. Philadelphia: The Jewish Publication Society of America, 1950.

Habel, N. C. "The Symbolism of Wisdom in Proverbs 1–9." *Interpretation: A Journal of Bible and Theology* 26, no. 2 (1972) 131–57.

Hackett, Horatio B. *A Commentary on the Acts of the Apostles*, edited by Alvah Hovey and Ezra Abbot. Philadelphia, PA: American Baptist Publication Society, 1882.

Haenchen, Ernst. *The Acts of the Apostles: A Commentary*. Philadelphia, PA: The Westminster, 1971.

Hartley, John E. *The Book of Job*. New International Commentary on the Old Testament. Grand Rapids, MI: Eerdmans, 1988.

Hastings, Adrian. *Prophet and Witness in Jerusalem: A Study of the Teaching of Saint Luke*. Baltimore, MD: Helicon Press, 1958.

Hays, Richard B. *Echoes of Scripture in the Gospels*. Waco, TX: Baylor University Press, 2016.

Bibliography

Heim, Knut Martin. *Like Grapes of Gold Set in Silver: An Interpretation of Proverbial Clusters in Proverbs 10:1—22:16. Beihefte Zur Zeitschrift FüR Die Alttestamentliche Wissenschaft*. Berlin: De Gruyter, 2001.

———. "Structure and Context in Proverbs 10:1—22:16." PhD diss., University of Liverpool, 1996.

Hemer, Colin J. *The Book of Acts in the Setting of Hellenistic History*, edited by Conrad H. Gempf. Winona Lake, IN: Eisenbrauns, 1990.

Holladay, Carl R. *Acts: A Commentary*. Louisville, KY: Westminster John Knox, 2016.

Horton, Dennis J. *Death and Resurrection: The Shape and Function of a Literary Motif in the Book of Acts*. Cambridge: James Clarke & Co., 2011.

Huffman, Douglas S. *Understanding the New Testament Use of the Old Testament: Forms, Features, Framings, and Functions*. Grand Rapids, MI: Baker Academic, forthcoming.

Hurtado, Larry W. *Lord Jesus Christ: Devotion to Jesus in Earliest Christianity*. Grand Rapids, MI: Eerdmans, 2003.

———. *One God, One Lord: Early Christian Devotion and Ancient Jewish Monotheism*. 3rd ed. London, UK: Bloomsbury T&T Clark, 2015.

Jackson-McCabe, Matt. *Jewish Christianity: The Making of the Christianity-Judaism Divide*. London, UK: Yale University Press, 2020.

Jacobson, Rolf A., and Beth Tanner. "Book One of the Psalter: Psalms 1–41." In *The Book of Psalms*, edited by R. K. Harrison E. J. Young, and Robert L. Hubard Jr., 55–391. Grand Rapids, MI: Eerdmans, 2014.

Jaeger, Werner. *The Theology of the Early Greek Philosophers: The Gifford Lectures 1936*, translated by Edward Schouten Robinson. London, UK: Oxford University Press, 1947.

James, E. O. "The Religions of Antiquity." *Numen* 7, no. 2 (1960) 137–47.

Jefford, Clayton N. "The Wisdom of Sirach and the Glue of the Matthew-Didache Tradition." In *Intertextuality in the Second Century*. Vol 11, Bible in Ancient Christianity, edited by D. Jeffery and Clayton N. Jefford Bringham, 8–23. Leiden, Netherlands: Brill, 2016.

Jefford, Clayton N., and Jonathan A. Draper. *The Didache: A Missing Piece of the Puzzle in Early Christianity. Early Christianity and Its Literature*. Atlanta, GA: SBL Press, 2015.

Jervell, Jacob. *The Theology of the Acts of the Apostles. New Testament Theology*. Cambridge, UK: Cambridge University Press, 1996.

Johnson, Luke Timothy. *The Acts of the Apostles*. Vol. 5, Sacra Pagina Series, edited by Daniel J. Harrington. Collegeville, PA: The Liturgical Press, 1992.

———. "Literary Criticism of Luke-Acts: Is Reception History Pertinent?" In *Rethinking the Unity and Reception of Luke and Acts*, edited by Andrew F. Gregory and C. Kavin Rowe, 66–69. Columbia, SC: The University of South Carolina Press, 2010.

Judd, Andrew. "Do the Speakers in Acts Use Different Hermeneutics for Different Old Testament Genres?" *Journal of Evangelical Theological Society* 64, no. 1 (2021) 109–27.

———. *Modern Genre Theory: An Introduction for Biblical Studies*. Grand Rapids, MI: Zondervan Academic, 2024.

Kampen, John. *Wisdom Literature*. Eerdman's Commentaries on the Dead Sea Scrolls. Grand Rapids, MI: Eerdmans, 2011.

Keefer, Arthur Jan. *Proverbs 1–9 as an Introduction to the Book of Proverbs*. Vol. 701, Library of Hebrew Bible/Old Testament Studies, edited by Claudia V. Camp and Andrew Mein. New York: T&T Clark, 2020.

Keener, Craig S. *Acts: An Exegetical Commentary: 1:1—2:47*. Vol. 1. Grand Rapids, MI: Baker Academic, 2012.

Bibliography

———. *Acts: An Exegetical Commentary: 3:1—14:28*. Vol. 2. Grand Rapids, MI: Baker Academic, 2013.

———. *Acts. The New Cambridge Bible Commentary*, edited by Ben Witherington III. Cambridge, UK Cambridge University Press, 2020.

———. *Christobiography: Memory, History, and the Reliability of the Gospels*. Grand Rapids, MI: Eerdmans, 2019.

Kellum, L. Scott. *Acts. Exegetical Guide to the Greek New Testament*, edited by Andreas J. Köstenberger and Robert W. Yarbrough. Nashville, TN: B&H Academic, 2020.

Kelly, Joseph Ryan. "Identifying Literary Allusions: Theory and the Criterion of Shared Language." In *Subtle Citation, Allusion, and Translation in the Hebrew Bible*, edited by Ziony Zevit, 22–40. Sheffield, UK: Equinox, 2017.

Kidner, Derek. *Proverbs: An Introduction and Commentary*. IVP/Accordance electronic ed. Vol. 17, Tyndale Old Testament Commentaries. Downers Grove, IL: InterVarsity, 1964.

Kitchen, John A. *Proverbs*. A Mentor Commentary. Berker, DE: Mentor, 2006.

Klink III, Edward W., and Darian R. Lockett. *Understanding Biblical Theology: A Comparison of Theory and Practice*. Grand Rapids, MI: Zondervan, 2012.

Kloppenborg, John S. "The Transformation of Moral Exhortation in Didache 1–5." In *The Didache in Context: Essays on Its Text, History and Transmission*, edited by Clayton N. Jefford, 88–109. New York: Brill, 1995.

Koptak, Paul E. "Personification." *Dictionary of the Old Testament: Wisdom, Poetry & Writings*, 516–19. Downers Grove, IL: InterVarsity, 2008.

Kovalishyn, Mariam Kamell. "Wisdom in the New Testament." In *The Oxford Handbook of Wisdom and the Bible*, edited by Will Kynes, 173–86. New York: Oxford University Press, 2021.

Kynes, Will. *An Obituary for "Wisdom Literature": The Birth, Death, and Intertextual Reintegration of a Biblical Corpus*. New York: Oxford University Press, 2019.

———. "'Wisdom' as Mask and Mirror: Methodological Questions for 'Wisdom's' Dialogue with the Canon." In *Riddles and Revelations: Explorations into the Relationship between Wisdom and Prophecy in the Hebrew*. Vol. 634, Library of Hebrew Bible/Old Testament Studies, edited by Russell L. Meek et al., 19–29. London, UK: T&T Clark, 2018.

Lake, Kirsopp, and Henry J. Cadbury. *The Beginnings of Christianity, Part I: The Acts of the Apostles: Commentary*, edited by F. J. Foakes Jackson and Kirsopp Lake. Vol. IV. London, UK: Macmillan and Co., Limited, 1933.

Lakoff, George, and Mark Johnson. "The Metaphorical Structure of the Human Conceptual System." In *Perspectives on Cognitive Science*, edited by Donald A. Norman, 193–206. Norwood, NJ: Albex, 1981.

Lanfer, Peter. "Anti-Language." In *Encyclopedia of Hebrew Language and Linguistics*, edited by Geoffrey Khan. Vol. 1. Leiden: Brill, 2013.

Lanier, Gregory R. *Old Testament Conceptual Metaphors and the Christology of Luke's Gospel*. Vol. 591, Library of New Testament Studies, edited by Chris Keith. London, UK: T&T Clark, 2018.

Larkin, William J. "Acts." In *The Gospel of Luke & Acts*. Vol. 12, Cornerstone Biblical Commentary, edited by Philip W. Comfort, 349–652. Carol Stream, IL: Tyndale House, 2006.

Leonard, Jeffery M. "Identifying Inner-Biblical Allusions: Psalm 78 as a Test Case." *Journal of Biblical Literature* 127, no. 2 (2008) 241–65.

Liefeld, Walter L. "Luke." In *Matthew, Mark, Luke*. Vol 8, The Expositor's Bible Commentary, edited by Frank E. Gæbelein, 795–1059. Grand Rapids, MI: Zondervan, 1984.

Bibliography

———. "The Acts of the Apostles." In *John and Acts: Commentary with the New International Version.* Vol 9, The Expositor's Bible Commentary, edited by Frank E. Gæbelein, 205–573. Grand Rapids, MI: Zondervan, 1981.

Litke, Andrew W. "Journey." In *Lexham Theological Wordbook*, edited by Douglas Mangum. Lexham Bible Reference Series. Bellingham, WA: Lexham, 2014.

Longenecker, Richard N. *Acts*. Expositor's Bible Commentary. Grand Rapids, MI: Zondervan, 2017.

Longman III, Tremper, "Book of Proverbs 1." *Dictionary of the Old Testament: Wisdom, Poetry & Writings*, 531–52. Downers Grove, IL: InterVarsity, 2008.

———. *The Fear of the Lord Is Wisdom: A Theological Introduction to Wisdom in Israel.* Grand Rapids, MI: Baker, 2017.

———. *Job*. Baker Commentary on the Old Testament Wisdom and Psalms. Grand Rapids, MI: Baker Academic, 2012.

———. *Proverbs*. Baker Commentary on the Old Testament Wisdom and Psalms. Grand Rapids, MI: Baker Academic, 2006.

———. "Prophecy and Wisdom: Connections, Influences, Relationships." In *Riddles and Revelations: Explorations into the Relationship between Wisdom and Prophecy in the Hebrew Bible*, edited by Russell L. Meek et al., 259–268. Vol. 634. Library of Hebrew Bible/Old Testament Studies. London: T&T Clark, 2018.

Lucas, Ernest C. "Wisdom Theology." *Dictionary of Old Testament: Wisdom, Poetry & Writings*, 901–12. Downers Grove, IL: InterVarsity, 2008.

Lyu, Sun Myung. "Righteousness in the Book of Proverbs." University of Wisconsin-Madison, 2006.

Mánek, Jindr[set hacek over r]ich. "The New Exodus in the Books of Luke." *Novum Testamentum* 2, no.1 (1957) 8–23.

Marguerat, Daniel. *The First Christian Historian: Writing the "Acts of the Apostle."* Society for New Testament Studies Monograph Series, 121. Cambridge, UK: Cambridge University Press, 2002.

Marshall, I. Howard. "Acts." In *Commentary on the New Testament Use of the Old Testament*, edited by G. K. Beale and D. A. Carson, 513–606. Grand Rapids, MI: Baker Academic, 2007.

———. *Acts: An Introduction and Commentary*. Vol. 5, Tyndale New Testament Commentaries. Downers Grove, IL: InterVarsity, 1980.

Mazzinghi, Luca. *Wisdom*, trans. Michael Tait, International Exegetical Commentary on the Old Testament. Stuttgart, GE: W. Kohlhammer GmbH, 2019.

McCartney, Dan. *James*. Baker Exegetical Commentary on the New Testament. Grand Rapids, MI: Baker Academic, 2009.

McCasland, Vernon. "The Way." *Journal of Biblical Literature* 77, no. 3 (1958) 9.

McKane, William. *Proverbs: A New Approach*. Old Testament Library. Philadelphia, PA: Westminster, 1970.

Meade, James K. *Biblical Theology: Issues, Methods, and Themes*. Louisville, KY: Westminster John Knox, 2007.

Meek, James A. *The Gentile Mission in Old Testament Citations in Acts: Text, Hermeneutic, and Purpose*. T&T Clark Library of Biblical Studies. London, UK: T&T Clark, 2008.

Meek, Russell. "Intertextuality, Inner-Biblical Exegesis, and Inner-Biblical Allusion: The Ethics of a Methodology." *Biblica* 95, no. 2 (2014) 280–91.

Minear, Paul S. *Images of the Church in the New Testament*. Philadelphia, PA: Westminster, 1960.

Bibliography

Moo, Douglas J. *The Letter of James: An Introduction and Commentary*. The Pillar New Testament Commentary. Grand Rapids, MI: Eerdmans, 2000.

Morris, Leon. *Luke: An Introduction and Commentary*. Vol. 3, Tyndale New Testament Commentaries. Downers Grove, IL: InterVarsity, 1988.

Murphy, Roland E. *Ecclesiastes*. Accordance electronic ed. IVP/Accordance electronic ed. Vol. 23A, Word Biblical Commentary. Grand Rapids, MI: Zondervan, 1992.

———. *Proverbs*. Word Biblical Commentary. Grand Rapids, MI: Zondervan, 2018.

———. *The Tree of Life: An Exploration of Biblical Wisdom Literature*. 2nd ed. Grand Rapids, MI: Eerdmans, 1996.

Nicholls, Benjamin Elliott. *The Book of Proverbs, Explained and Illustrated*. London, UK: J. G. F. & J. Rivington, 1842.

Niederwimmer, Kurt, and Harold W. Attridge. *The Didache: A Commentary*. Minneapolis, MN: Fortress, 1998.

O'Dowd, Ryan P. *Proverbs*. The Story of God Bible Commentary, edited by Tremper Longman III & Scot McKnight. Grand Rapids, MI: Zondervan, 2017.

Oden, Thomas C., and Francis Martin. *Acts*. Vol. 5, Ancient Christian Commentary on Scripture. New Testament. Downers Grove: IVP Books, 2006.

Oesterley, W. O. E. *The Book of Proverbs*. New York: E. P. Dutton, 1929.

Olbricht, T.H. "Apostolic Fathers." *Dictionary of New Testament Background*, 81–85. Downers Grove, IL: InterVarsity, 2000.

Osborne, Grant R. *Acts: Verse by Verse*. Bellingham, WA: Lexham, 2019.

Pao, David W. *Acts and the Isaianic New Exodus. Biblical Studies Library*. Grand Rapids, MI: Baker Academic, 2002.

Parsons, Mikeal C. *Acts*. Paideia. Grand Rapids, MI: Baker Academic, 2008.

Parsons, Mikeal C., and Richard I. Pervo. *Rethinking the Unity of Luke and Acts*. Minneapolis: Augsburg Fortress, 1993.

Pathrapankal, Joseph. "Christianity as a 'Way' According to the Acts of the Apostles." In *Les Actes Des Apotres: Traditions, Redactino, Theologie*, edited by J. Duculot, 533–39. Vol. 48, Bibliotheca Ephemeridum Theologicarum Lovaniensium. Louvain: Leuven University Press, 1979.

———. "Way, The." *Oxford Companion to the Bible*, edited by Bruce M. Metzger and Michael D. Coogan. Oxford University Press, UK, 1993, 793–94.

Perdue, Leo G. *Proverbs*. Interpretation, a Bible Commentary for Teaching and Preaching. Louisville, KY: John Knox, 2000.

———. *The Sword and the Stylus: An Introduction to Wisdom in the Age of Empires*. Grand Rapids, MI: Eerdmans, 2008.

Pervo, Richard I. *Acts: A Commentary on the Book of Acts*, edited by Harold W. Attridge. Minneapolis, MN: Fortress, 2009.

Peterson, David. *The Acts of the Apostles*. Pillar New Testament Commentary: Eerdmans, 2009.

Pinter, Dean. *Acts*. The Story of God Bible Commentary, edited by Scot McKnight. Grand Rapids, MI: Zondervan, 2019.

Porter, Stanley E. "Allusions and Echoes." in *As it is Written: Studying Paul's Use of Scripture*. SBL Symposium Series 50, edited by Stanley Porter and Christopher D. Stanley, 29–40. Atlanta: Society of Biblical Literature.

Repo, Eero. *Der "We" als Selbstbezeichnung des Urchristentums: Eine traditionsgeschichtliche und semasiologische Untersuchung*. Annales Academic Scientiarum Fennicae, Ser. B, Tom 132.2. Helsinki, FI: Sumalainen Tiedeakatemia, 1964.

Bibliography

Rhodes, James N. "The Two Ways Tradition in the "Epistle of Barnabas": Revisiting an Old Question." *The Catholic Biblical Quarterly* 73, no. 4 (2011) 797–816.

Robinson, J. Armitage. "The Problem of the Didache." *The Journal of Theological Studies* 13, no. 51 (1912) 339–56.

Ross, Allen P. "Proverbs." In *Proverbs-Isaiah*. Rev. ed. Vol. 6, Expositor's Bible Commentary, edited by Tremper Longman III and David E. Garland, 21–252. Grand Rapids: Zondervan, 2008.

Rotasperti, Sergio. *Metaphors in Proverbs: Decoding the Language of Metaphor in the Book of Proverbs*. Vol. 188, Vetus Testamentum, Supplements. Leiden: Brill, 2021.

Rowe, C. Kavin. *Death and Resurrection: The Shape and Function of a Literary Motif in the Book of Acts*, by Dennis J. Horton. *The Catholic Biblical Quarterly* 72 (2010) 829–30.

———. *Early Narrative Christology: The Lord in the Gospel of Luke*. Berlin: Walter de Gruyter, 2006.

———. "History, Hermeneutics, Adn the Unity of Luke-Acts." In *Rethinking the Unity and Reception of Luke and Acts*, edited by Andrew F. Gregory and C. Kavin Rowe, 43–65. Columbia, SC: The University of South Carolina Press, 2010.

Schipper, Bernd U. *Proverbs 1–15: A Commentary on the Book of Proverbs 1:1—15:33*, edited by Thomas Krüger, translated by Stephen Germany. Hermeneia—a Critical and Historical Commentary on the Bible. Minneapolis, MN: Fortress, 2019.

Schnabel, Eckhard J. *Acts*. Vol. 5, Zondervan Exegetical Commentary on the New Testament, edited by Clinton E. Arnold. Grand Rapids, MI: Zondervan, 2012.

Schultz, Richard L. *The Search for Quotation Verbal Parallels in the Prophets*. Sheffield, UK: Sheffield Academic, 1999.

Schwab, George M. "The Book of Proverbs." In *The Book of Psalms, the Book of Proverbs*. Vol. 7, Cornerstone Biblical Commentary, edited by Philip W. Comfort, 451–661. Carol Steam, IL: Tyndale House, Inc., 2009.

Scott, R. B. Y. *Proverbs Ecclesiastes*. 2nd ed. Vol. 18, The Anchor Bible, edited by William Foxwell Albright and David Noel Freedman. Garden City, NY: Doubleday & Company, Inc., 1965.

———. *The Way of Wisdom in the Old Testament*. New York: The Macmillan Company, 1971.

Seely, David Rolph. "Barki Nafshi." *Dictionary of Early Judaism*, 416–17. Grand Rapids, MI: Eerdmans, 2010.

Shauf, Scott. *Theology as History, History as Theology: Paul in Ephesus in Acts 19*. Beihefte Zur Zeitschrift Für Die Neutestamentliche Wissenschaft Und Die Kunde Der Älteren Kirche: Bd. 133. New York: Walter de Gruyter, 2005.

Sigvartsen, Jan Age. *Afterlife and Resurrection Beliefs in the Apocrypha and Apocalyptic Literature*. Vol. 29, Jewish and Christian Texts in Contexts and Related Studies, edited by James H. Charlesworth. London, UK: Bloomsbury T&T Clark, 2019.

———. *Afterlife and Resurrection Beliefs in the Pseudepigrapha*. Vol. 30, Jewish and Christian Texts in Contexts and Related Studies, edited by James H. Charlesworth. London, UK: Bloomsbury T&T Clark, 2019.

Slingerland, Edward G. "Conceptual Metaphor Theory as Methodology for Comparative Religion." *Journal of the American Academy of Religion* 72, no. 1 (2004) 1–31.

Steinmann, Andrew E. *Proverbs: A Theological Exposition of Sacred Scripture*. Concordia Commentary. St. Louis, MO: Concordia Pub. House, 2009.

Steinmann, Andrew E., and Michael A. Eschelbach. "Walk This Way: A Theme from Proverbs Reflected and Extended in Paul's Letters." *Concordia Theological Quarterly* 70, no. 1 (2006) 43–62.

Bibliography

Sterling, Gregory E. *Historiography and Self-Definition: Josephos, Luke-Acts and Apologetic Historiography.* Vol. 64. Supplements to Novum Testamentum. Leiden: Brill, 1992.

———. *Shaping the Past to Define the Present: Luke-Acts and Apologetic Historiography.* Grand Rapids, MI: Eerdmans, 2023.

Stevens, Gerald L. *Acts: A New Vision of the People of God.* 2nd ed. Eugene, OR: Pickwick Publications, 2019.

Stöckl, Hartmut. "Metaphor Revisited Cognitive-Conceptual Versus Traditional Linguistic Perspectives." *AAA: Arbeiten aus Anglistik und Amerikanistik* 35, no. 2 (2010) 189–208.

Strauss, Mark L. *The Davidic Messiah in Luke-Acts: The Promise and Its Fulfilment in Lukan Christology.* Journal for the Study of the New Testament. Supplement Series. Sheffield, UK: Sheffield Academic, 1995.

Strecker, George. *Theology of the New Testament*, edited by Friedrich Wilhelm Horn. Translated by M. Eugene Boring. German ed. Louisville, KY: Westminster John Knox, 2000.

Talbert, Charles H. *Reading Acts: A Literary and Theological Commentary on the Acts of the Apostles.* Reading the New Testament Series. New York: Crossroad, 1997.

Tannehill, Robert C. *Luke.* Abingdon New Testament Commentaries. Nashville, TN: Abingdon, 1996.

Taylor, John B. *Ezekiel: An Introduction and Commentary.* Vol. 22. IVP/Accordance electronic ed. Tyndale Old Testament Commentaries. Downers Grove, IL: InterVarsity, 1969.

Thompson, Alan J. *Luke.* Exegetical Guide to the Greek New Testament, edited by Andreas J. Köstenberger and Robert W. Yarbrough. Nashville, TN: B&H Academic, 2016.

Torrey, Charles Cutler. *The Composition and Date of Acts.* London, UK: Humphrey Milford Oxford University Press, 1916.

Urban, David V. "Imagery." *Dictionary for Theological Interpretation of the Bible*, 319–21. Grand Rapids, MI: Baker Academic, 2005.

Uytanlet, Samson. *Luke-Acts and Jewish Historiography: A Study on the Theology, Literature, and Ideology of Luke-Acts.* Wissenschaftliche Untersuchungen Zum Neuen Testament. 2. Reihe: 366. Tübingen, DE: Mohr Siebeck, 2014.

Van Leeuwen, Raymond C. "Liminality and Worldview in Proverbs 1–9." *Semeia* 50 (1990) 111–44.

———. "The Book of Proverbs: Introduction, Commentary, and Reflections." In *Introduction to Wisdom Literature: Proverbs, Ecclesiastes, Song of Songs, Wisdom, Sirach.* Vol. 5. 17–264. The New Interpreter's Bible. Nashville: Abingdon, 1997.

———. "Theology: Creation, Wisdom, and Covenant." In *The Oxford Handbook of Wisdom and the Bible*, edited by Will Kynes, 65–82. New York: Oxford University Press, 2021.

Von Rad, Gerhard. *Old Testament Theology.* Translated by D. M. G. Stalker. Vol. 2 of 2. New York: Harper & Row, 1965.

———. *Wisdom in Israel.* Translated by James D. Martin. Harrisburg, NJ: Trinity Press International, 1993. Originally published in 1972.

Waaijman, Kees. "The Way, Root Metaphor for Spirituality: A Biblical Exploration." *Studies in Spirituality* 13 (2003): 63–79.

Wall, R. W. "Intertextuality, Biblical." *Dictionary of New Testament Background*, 541–51. Downers Grove, IL: InterVarsity, 2000.

Waltke, Bruce K. "Biblical Studies: Righteousness in Proverbs." *Westminster Theological Journal* 70 (2008) 225–37.

Bibliography

———. *The Book of Proverbs 1–15*. New International Commentary on the Old Testament. Grand Rapids, MI: Eerdmans, 2004.

———. *The Book of Proverbs Chapters 15–31*. New International Commentary on the Old Testament. Grand Rapids, MI: Eerdmans, 2005.

Waltke, Bruce K., and Fred G. Zaspel. *How to Read and Understand the Psalms*. Wheaton, IL: Crossway, 2023.

Walton, Douglas N. "Abductive, Presumptive and Plausible Arguments." *Informed Logic* 21, no. 2 (2001) 141–69.

Walton, John. "Interactions in the Ancient Cognitive Environment." In *Behind the Scenes of the Old Testament: Cultural, Social, and Historical Contexts*, edited by Jonathan S. Greer et al., 333–39. Grand Rapids, MI: Baker Academic, 2018.

Wassell, Blake, and S. R. Llewelyn. "'Fishers of Humans,' the Contemporary Theory of Metaphor, and Conceptual Blending Theory." *Journal of Biblical Literature* 133, no. 3 (2014) 627–46.

Webb, Barry G. *Job*, edited by T. Desmond Alexander et al. Evangelical Biblical Theology Commentary. Bellingham, WA: Lexham Academic, 2023.

Weeks, Stuart. *Instruction and Imagery in Proverbs 1–9*. Oxford, UK: Oxford University Press, 2007.

Weyde, Karl William. "Inner-Biblical Interpretation: Methodological Reflections on the Relationship between Texts in the Hebrew Bible." *Svensk exegetisk a*[set ring over a] *rsbok* 70 (2005) 287–300.

Weymouth, Richard Francis. *The New Testament in Modern Speech: An Idiomatic Translation into Everyday English from the Text of "the Resultant Greek Testament": Commentary*, edited by Ernest Hampden-Cook. London: James Clarke and Co., 1903.

Whybray, Roger N. *The Composition of the Book of Proverbs*. Sheffield, UK: JSOT, 1994.

Williamson, Robert. "'In the Way of Righteousness Is Life': Symbolic Death Transcendence in Proverbs 10–29." *Journal for the Study of the Old Testament* 38, no. 3 (2014) 363–82.

Wilson, Walter T. *Ancient Wisdom: An Introduction to Sayings Collections*. Grand Rapids, MI: Eerdmans, 2022.

———. *The Wisdom of Sirach*. Grand Rapids, MI: Eerdmans, 2023.

Wingren, Gustaf. "'Weg,' 'Wanderung,' Und Verwandte Begriffe." *Studia theologica* 3 (1951) 111–23.

Winston, David. *The Wisdom of Solomon: A New Translation with Introduction and Commentary*. Vol. 43, The Anchor Bible. Garden City, NY: Doubleday & Company, 1979.

Witherington III, Ben. *The Acts of the Apostles: A Socio-Rhetorical Commentary*. Grand Rapids, MI: Eerdmans, 1998.

Wright, N. T. *The New Testament and the People of God*. Vol. 1, Christian Origins and the Question of God. Minneapolis, MN: Fortress, 1992.

Zevit, Ziony. "Echoes of Texts Past." In *Subtle Citation, Allusion, and Translation in the Hebrew Bible*, edited by Ziony Zevit, 1–21. Sheffield, UK: Equinox, 2017.

Scripture Index

OLD TESTAMENT

Genesis
18:19	127
22:18	148
26:4	148

Exodus
21:17	129
22:28	129
31:3	56n128
32:8	127, 128n144
35:31	56n128
36:27	3n8

Numbers
11:31	21

Deuteronomy
5:33	127, 128n144
11:28	96
18:15–20	148
32:21	119n104

Judges
2:22	127

1 Samuel
1:19	120
3:13	129
12:21	119n104

2 Samuel
22:22	37n89, 127

1 Kings
15:34	120
16:19	120
16:26	120

2 Kings
2:11	3n8
21:21	120
21:22	127
22:2	120n110

1 Chronicles
24:10	3n8

2 Chronicles
8	3n8
14	3n8
17:6	127

Psalms
1	83, 84
1:1	84, 86n60, 167
1:6	83, 84, 127, 167
2:2	167
2:12	86n60
5:9	86n60
7:13	86n60
10:5	86n60
11:2	86n60

Scripture Index

Psalms (continued)

Reference	Page
16	101
16:8–11	148
16:9–11	53
18:21	37n89
18:22	86n60
18:31	86n60
18:33	86n60
19	83
19:9	105
24:4	127
24:10	127
25:4	86n60
25:5	86n60
25:8	86n60
25:9	86n60
27:11	86n60
32:8	86n60
35:6	86n60
36:5	86n60
37	83
37:5	86n60
37:7	86n60
37:14	86n60
37:23	86n60
37:34	86n60
39	83
39:2	86n60
49	83
49:14	86n60
50:23	86n60
51	21
51:15	86n60
58:8	86n60
64:4	86n60
67:3	86n60
73	83
77:14	86n60
77:20	86n60
80:13	86n60
81:14	86n60
85:14	86n60
86:11	86n60
89:42	86n60
91:11	86n60
91:13	86n60
95:10	86n60
101:2	86n60
101:6	86n60
102:24	86n60
103:7	86n60
107:4	86n60
107:7	86n60
107:17	86n60
107:40	86n60
110:1	148
110:7	86n60
111:10	111
118:29	167
119	83
119:1	86n60
119:3	86n60
119:5	86n60
119:14	86n60
119:26	86n60
119:27	86n60
119:29	86n60
119:30	86n60
119:32	86n60
119:33	86n60
119:35	86n60
119:37	86n60
119:59	86n60
119:168	86n60
128:1	86n60
137:5	127
138:5	37n89, 86n60
139:3	86n60
139:24	86n60
143:8	86n60
145:17	86n60
146:9	86n60

Job

Reference	Page
1:21	96n157
2:10	96n157
14:2	96n157
14:28	96n157
22:29	96n157
28	80–81
28:12	79
28:28	80, 111
42:10–17	96n157

Scripture Index

Proverbs

Reference	Pages
1:5	47
1:7	59, 72, 105, 111, 112, 121, 124, 132, 142, 144, 152
1:12	48
1:15	42n18, 120
1:29	105, 111
1:31	42n18
2:1–22	59, 72, 121, 124, 132, 142, 144, 152, 153
2:3–6	96n157
2:5	105, 111, 112
2:7	45
2:8	42n18, 52n92
2:12–13	42n18
2:13	42n18, 52n92, 115, 120, 135
2:15	42n18, 52n92, 54, 115
2:16–19	58n138
2:16	115
2:19–20	42n18, 52n92
2:19	115
2:20	42n18
3:5–7	59, 72, 121, 124, 135, 142, 144, 152
3:6	42n18, 115
3:7	45, 64, 112
3:17	42n18
3:23	42n18
3:25	116
3:31	42n18
3:33	116
3:34	96n157
4:10	101
4:11	42n18, 45, 117
4:14–18	59, 72, 121, 124, 142, 144, 153
4:14	42n18, 45, 116
4:18–19	135
4:18	42n18, 132
4:19	42n18, 116
4:25	117
4:26	42n18, 117
4:27	115, 117
5:3–6	58n138
5:4	45
5:6	42n18, 101
5:8	42n18
5:15–20	58n138
5:21	42n18
6:6	42n18
6:12	120
6:20–22	48
6:22	58n138
6:23	42n18, 101, 135
6:24–26	58n138
7:4	58n138
7:5–27	58n138
7:8	42n18
7:19	42n18
7:25	42n18
7:26	45
7:27	42n18
8:2	42n18, 56
8:13	42n18, 111, 115
8:20	42n18
8:22	42n18
8:32	42n18
9	59, 72, 121, 124, 135, 142, 144, 152, 153
9:1–18	57
9:1–2	57
9:3	56
9:6	42n18
9:1–6	58n138
9:10	105, 111
9:13–18	58n138
9:15	42n18
9:18	54, 57
10:1–22:16	60n152
10:1–15:33	60n152
10:8	116
10:9	42n19, 113, 115
10:10	116
10:14	116
10:17	42n19, 101
10:27	111
10:29	37n89, 42n19
10:31	136
11:5	42n19, 115
11:18	136
11:20	42n19, 115
12:1–35	60n151

Proverbs (continued)

12:1–28	60n151
12:15	42n19
12:17	136
12:21	136
12:26	42n19
12:28	42n19, 101
13:1–25	60n151
13:6	4, 42n19
13:15	42n19
13:19	135
13:20	47
14:1–32	70, 72, 121, 124, 135, 142, 144, 152, 153
14:1–18	72, 121
14:1	57
14:2	42n19, 112
14:8	42n19
14:12	42n19, 70n248
14:14	42n19
14:15	70
14:18	135
14:21	96n157
14:26	111
14:27	111
15	70, 72, 121, 124, 142, 144, 153
15:1–33	60n151
15:1	96n157
15:5–19	65
15:9	42n19, 65
15:10	42n19, 65
15:16	111, 112
15:19	42n19, 65
15:24	42n19, 101
15:33–16:9	68
15:33	111
16	68, 70, 72, 121, 124, 135, 142, 144, 152
16:1	68
16:2	42n19, 68, 69
16:6	68, 111, 112
16:7	42n19, 68, 69, 101
16:9	42n19, 68, 69
16:10–15	68
16:17	42n19, 68, 101
16:19	69
16:25	42n19, 68, 70n248
16:27	96n157
16:29	42n19, 68
16:31	42n19, 68
17:23	42n19
18:21	96n157
19:3	42n19
19:16	42n19
19:17	96n157
19:23	105, 111
20:7	47
20:11	115
20:20	129, 135
20:24	42n19
21:2	42n19
21:8	42n19, 115
21:16	42n19, 96
21:21	101
21:29	42n19
22:4	111
22:5–6	42n19
22:5	115
22:14	115
22:25	42n19
23:17	111
23:19	42n19
23:26	42n19
26:13	42n19
27:1	96n157
28:6	42n19
28:10	42n19, 115
28:18	42n19, 115
29:9	47
29:20	96n157
29:27	42n19, 115
30:1–6	64
30:19–20	42n19
31:3	42n19

Ecclesiastes

5:1	96n157
7:9	96n157
7:20	96n157
10:3	79n33
11	79
11:5	79, 79n33

Scripture Index

1:6	83	**Amos**	
11:9	79, 79n33		2
12:5	79n33		

Isaiah

Habakkuk

2

9:15	96
11:1	32n1
11:2	111
11:3	111, 111n60
33:6	111
35:6	117n91
35:10	159
40–55	33, 160
40	168
40:1–11	36
40:3–5	33, 158, 159, 159n81
40:3–4	37
40:3	2, 6, 29, 32, 33, 90, 91, 113, 114, 160, 161, 168, 169
42:16 LXX	114, 114n76
49:11–12	159
52:13	148
53:6	96
60:21	32n42

APOCRYPHA

Wisdom

1:8	87n97
2:5	87n97
2:7	87n97
2:16	87n96, 87n97
5:6	96, 87n96
5:7	87n96
5:14	87n97
6:22	87n97
10:8	87n97
10:17	87n96, 88
11:23	118
12:24	96, 87n96, 88
14:3	88
14:13	87n96
18:23	87n96, 87n98, 88
19:7	87n96, 87n98, 88

Jeremiah

5:4–5	37n89
10:2	120n109
14:22	119n104

Ezekiel

8:1–10	58
11:21	120
34:4	96
36:19	120n109

Hosea

14:9	37n89, 113
LXX 14:10	113

Joel

2, 148

Sirach (Ecclesiasticus; Ben Sira)

1:7	85
1:22	96n157
1:28	96n157
2:1	96n157
2:6	85, 85n76, 85n78
2:15	85, 85n76, 85n78, 86n81
3:1–8	96n157
3:17	96n157
4:10	96n157
5:11	96n157
5:13	96n157
5:26	96n157
6:26	85n76, 86n85
8:15	85n76, 85n78
9:6	105
9:16	105
11:26	85n76, 85n78

Scripture Index

Sirach (continued)

14:20–15:10	86
14:21	85n76, 86, 86n85
14:22	85n76, 86, 86n85
15:11–20	96n157
16:20	85n76, 85n78
17:15	85n76, 85n78
17:19	85n76, 85n78
21:10	85n76, 85n79
21:16	85n76, 85n78
23:1	96n157
23:4	96n157
23:19	85n76, 85n78
25:6	105
28:12	96n157
29:10	96n157
32:20	85n76, 86n82
32:21	85n76, 86n82
32:33	85n78
33:11–13	86n82
33:11	85n76, 86n82
33:13	85n76, 86n82
33:33	85n76
34:25–27	96n157
37:9	85, 85n76, 86, 86n82
37:15	85, 85n76, 86n82
39:24	85n79
47:23	85n76
47:24	85n79
48:22	85n76, 85n78
49:6	85n76, 85n77
49:9	85n76, 85n79

Pseudepigrapha

1 Enoch 42	92

NEW TESTAMENT

Matthew

3:3	32, 155
5	89
9:9	3
24:36	159

Mark

1:3	32
13:32	159

Luke

1:1–4	155
1:3–4	146
1:3	76
1:4	127n140
1:5–2:52	147
1:5	3n8
1:6	3n8
1:7	3n8
1:10	3n8
1:51–52	3n8
1:68	147
1:76–77	160
1:76	113
2:9	108
2:13	108
2:38	147
2:44	100n2
3	114, 159, 160
3:4–6	159
3:4	32, 113, 114
4:14–9:50	34
4:15	127n140
4:31	127n140
5:3	127n140
5:17	127n140
6:6	127n140
7:31–5	3
8:21	170
9:51–19:48	34
9:57	100n2
19:44	3n8
20:21	31, 127n140
21:37	127n140
22:49	5n24
23	134
23:5	127n140
24:21	147
7:27	113
9:39	108

Scripture Index

John

1:23	32, 155
21:24	21

Acts

1–8	99, 100, 101, 106, 107
1:1	76
1:12	101
1:26	3
1:6	3n8
1:8	3n8
1:9	3n8
1:12	103n19
1:16	170
1:24	5n24
2:6	170
2:15	3n8
2:28	101
2:34	5n24
2:37–41	130
2:37–39	130
2:44	170
3	117
3:1–8	117
4:31	5n24
4:32	170
5:5	130
5:11	107, 130, 170
5:14	170
5:17	170
5:21	127n140
5:25	127n140
5:28	127n140
5:42	127n140
6:1	170
6:2	170
6:3	170
6:7	170
7:35	147
7:38	107, 170
7:49	5n24
8:1	107, 170
8:3	107, 170
8:6	139
8:26–40	130
8:26	101, 101n5, 103n19
8:36	101, 103n19
8:39	101, 103n19
9–31	107
9–28	100, 106
9	100, 101, 109, 110, 112, 113, 114, 115, 119, 126, 133, 138, 139
9:1–31	99, 103, 106, 107, 109, 112, 114, 115, 140
9:1–19	103, 108
9:1–2	103, 107, 109, 110, 112
9:1	170
9:2–26:13	100
9:2	ix, 2, 3, 5, 15, 27, 31n31, 37, 100n2, 102, 108, 113, 114, 115, 125, 126, 132, 134, 138, 140, 142, 152
9:3–30	104
9:3	108
9:6	101n5, 104, 106
9:13	170
9:17	102, 139
9:19–30	103
9:25	170
9:26	170
9:27	102
9:31	27, 51, 81, 103, 104, 105, 108, 109, 110, 111, 111n60, 112, 130, 142, 152, 170
9:32	170
9:41	170
10:22	5n24
11:22	170
11:26	127n140, 170
12:1	170
12:5	170
12:7	108
12:19	114
13	112, 113, 116, 119, 120
13:1	170
13:2–14	114
13:4–12	99, 112, 116, 140, 142, 152
13:10	108, 112, 114, 115, 119, 140, 152

Acts (continued)

Reference	Pages
13:11	114
13:16	5n24, 130
13:17–25	150
13:26	5n24, 130
14	116, 118, 119, 120, 122
14:1–20	116
14:1	170
14:3	114
14:4	170
14:7	121
14:8–20	99, 116, 117, 120, 121, 140
14:9–10	122
14:9	121
14:15	121
14:16	116, 120, 121, 122, 140, 149, 152
14:23	170
14:27	170
14:28	114
15:1	127n140
15:3	170
15:4	170
15:5	170
15:10	170
15:22	170
15:35	114, 127n140
16	122, 123, 124
16:5	170
16:7	140
16:11–40	99, 122, 123
16:12	114
16:16–24	122
16:17	15, 27n1, 122, 123, 124, 142, 152
16:18	124, 142, 152
16:25	124, 142, 152
16:26	124, 142, 152
16:29	124, 130, 152
16:30	124, 142, 152
16:31	124, 142, 152
17:31	3n8
18	124, 126, 128
18:5	31n31, 104
18:11	127n140
18:20	129
18:22	170
18:24–28	99, 124, 128
18:24	128, 152
18:25–26	31, 124, 125
18:25	27n1, 124, 125, 127n140, 128, 142, 152
18:26	27n1, 125, 126, 152
18:27	128, 142, 152
18:28	128, 142, 152
19	99, 128, 130, 131, 132
19:1–41	128, 132
19:1–2	94
19:4	142, 152
19:5	142, 152
19:6	152
19:7	129
19:8–12	128
19:8–10	29
19:9	ix, 2, 5, 27, 31, 31n31, 94, 128, 129, 140, 142, 152, 170
19:10	142, 152
19:11–20	131n165
19:11	142, 152
19:13–16	129
19:18	129
19:19	131
19:21	170
19:23–41	128
19:23	ix, 2, 5, 27, 31, 31n31, 112, 128, 130, 140, 142, 152
19:32	131, 170
19:39	131, 170
19:40	131, 170
20:4–5	75
20:6	114
20:16	114
20:17	170
20:20	127n140
20:28	170
21:13	5n24
21:21	127n140
21:28	127n140
21:37–22:29	133
22	133, 135, 136
22:1–22	99, 133, 135, 140

Scripture Index

22:3	133
22:4	ix, 2, 5, 31, 94, 112, 133, 135, 140, 142, 152
22:6	108, 135n179
22:10	135, 142, 152
22:11	133
22:12–16	134
22:13	134, 135, 142, 152
22:14	133, 139
22:16	135, 142, 152
22:21	135, 152
23:12–22	102
24	136, 138
24:1–27	99, 136, 138, 140
24:5	139, 142, 152, 170
24:14	ix, 2, 5, 27, 31, 94, 104, 136, 138, 139, 140, 152, 170
24:15	136
24:16	137
24:17–18	139, 142, 152
24:21	139, 142, 152
24:22–23	136
24:22	ix, 2, 5, 27, 94, 136, 137, 152
24:23	140
25:3	102
25:6	114
25:14	114
25:24	170
26:5	170
26:10	170
26:12–15	102
26:13	102, 108
26:14–28:31	100n3
26:28–32	130
28:22	170
28:31	127n140

Romans

3:17	167
3:25	118
6:4	4
9:26	155
10:13	155
15:27	75

1 Corinthians

8:4	119n104
12:31	167

2 Corinthians

1:22	159
5:7	4
7:1	105
8:23	75

Galatians

1:13	133n171

Ephesians

1:13–14	159
4:13	105
4:30	159
5:21	105

Philippians

2:12	105

1 Thessalonians

1:9	110n104

Hebrews

12:28	105

James

1:2	96n157
1:5	1:8
1:11	96n157
1:13	96n157
1:19	96n157
1:21	96n157
1:22	96n157
1:26	96n157
2:6	96n157
2:13	96n157
2:23	96n157
3:2	96n157
3:3	96n157
3:5	96n157

James (continued)

3:9	96n157
3:10	96n157
3:16	96n157
3:17	81
4:2	96n157
4:6	96n157
4:11	96n157
4:14	96n157
5:2	96n157
5:3	96n157
5:6	96n157
5:11	96n157
5:19–20	96
5:20	96

Jude

11	167

Revelation

15:4	105

DEAD SEA SCROLLS

CD

1:11	90n112
1:13	168, 169
2:6	169

1QH

6:24	90n112
12:4	90n117

1QM

3:10	90n112
11:6	90n112
1QS	29

4:22	90n117
8:13–14	90n117, 91
8:14–16	90
9:6–22	90n117
9:17–18	169
9:17	168
9:18	168
10:21	168, 169
11:13	168
11:17	90n117

4QInstruction

		89
4Q184		91, 92
4Q185		91
4Q434	1 I 3–4	90
4Q434 1 I 4		90
4Q473		90
4Q525		89, 91

GRECO-ROMAN WRITINGS

Hecuba	174
Hippolytus	174
Homer	174
Knights	174
Paremindes	174
Pindar	174
Oedipus at Colonus	174
Oedipus Tyrannus	174

EARLY CHRISTIAN WRITINGS

Canons and Epitome	94
Didache	34, 38, 94, 153
Doctrina	94, 102
The Epistle of Barnabas (Barnabas)	94, 95, 95n148

www.ingramcontent.com/pod-product-compliance
Lightning Source LLC
Chambersburg PA
CBHW062038220426
43662CB00010B/1560